Mexico OtherWise

DIÁLOGOS

A series of course-adoption books on Latin America

Series advisory editor:
Lyman L. Johnson, University of North Carolina at Charlotte

Mexico OtherWise

Modern Mexico in the Eyes of Foreign Observers

Jürgen Buchenau

University of New Mexico Press
Albuquerque

PRINTED IN THE UNITED STATES OF AMERICA

YEAR   PRINTING
10 09 08 07 06 05   1 2 3 4 5 6 7

LIBRARY OF CONGRESS CATALOGING-IN-PUBLICATION DATA

Mexico otherwise : modern Mexico in the eyes of
foreign observers / Jürgen Buchenau [editor].
        p. cm. — (Diálogos)
    Includes bibliographical references and index.
    ISBN 0-8263-2313-8 (pbk. : alk. paper)
    1. Mexico—History—1810—Sources.
    2. Mexico—Social life and customs—19th century—Sources.
    3. Mexico—Social life and customs—20th century—Sources.
    4. Mexico—Description and travel.
    5. Mexico—Foreign public opinion.
    I. Buchenau, Jürgen, 1964–
    II. Diálogos (Albuquerque, N.M.)
        F1231.5.M666 2005
        972—dc22
    2004030819

Book design and composition: Kathleen Sparkes

Text type is Utopia 9/14, 25P6
Display type is Berthold Akzidenz Grotesk and
        Officina Serif

For Ingrid and Alfredo

the travelers

Contents

Part IV

Acknowledgments

The idea of this anthology of foreign writing on Mexico is rooted in personal experience. I was born and raised in Germany, and exposed early on to international travel, thanks to my parent's resolve to let their children see the world. After finishing school, I spent eight months traveling and working in Mexico, where two of my grandparents were born. This first experience observing and living in a different culture led to another such experiment, when I moved to Chapel Hill, North Carolina, for what I believed would be a year of study abroad. That experiment resulted in U.S. citizenship and a career as a historian of Mexico. As both a traveler and an immigrant, I have always been fascinated by the worldview of people on the move, as well as the worlds they describe. For a historian familiar with life in Europe, Mexico, and the United States, the idea of this book is, in many ways, a project about one's own personal and professional trajectory.

This volume is the product of a collaborative effort. I particularly want to thank David Holtby, editor-in-chief of The University of New Mexico Press, and Lyman Johnson, the editor of the Diálogos series and my friend and colleague at the University of North Carolina at Charlotte. This book would not have been possible without their advice and guidance, and an author cannot ask for better editors. I also appreciate the suggestions of Bill French, Tim

Henderson, Michael Scardaville, and Eric Zolov, which pointed me toward sources and secondary literature I might well have otherwise overlooked. I could not have elucidated the background of French traveler Clément Bertie-Marriott without the assistance of Christine Haynes and Paul Worley. The manuscript also benefited from critical readings by Bill Beezley, Carol Hartley, Tim Henderson, and Víctor Macías. Judy Hellman, Isabella Tree, and Sam Quinones—three authors represented in this volume—provided helpful and otherwise elusive information on their personal and professional background for the head notes to their excerpts.

Several staff members and students at the University of North Carolina at Charlotte lent their expertise and assistance to make this a better book. I thank Patrick Jones from the Department of Geography and Earth Science's Cartography Lab for designing the map used in this book, and the Interlibrary Loan staff at the Murrey C. Atkins Library for procuring rare books from research libraries throughout the United States. Two subventions of the Graduate School funded the map as well as several of the permissions to reprint. Tolu Odugbesan helped with the translations from French, and my former graduate students David Johnson and Walter Knox provided important ideas and suggestions.

I also appreciate the following permissions to reprint: B. Traven, *Land des Frühlings* (granted by María Elena Luján); Evelyn Waugh, *Robbery Under Law* (granted by Stirling Literistic Inc.); Irene Nicholson, *The X in Mexico* (granted by Faber and Faber); Judith Hellman, *Mexican Lives* (granted by The New Press); Isabella Tree, *Sliced Iguana* (granted by Gillon, Aitken Associates); and Sam Quinones, *Tales from Another Mexico* (granted by The University of New Mexico Press).

Finally, and most important, I thank my wife, fellow traveler and immigrant Ana-Isabel Aliaga-Buchenau, and my children Nicolas and Julia for their support. They not only gave up too much time that I could have otherwise spent with them, but Anabel, an expert in comparative literature, has also been my best critic throughout this process. Her help in preparing a manuscript on a topic that straddles the disciplinary border between history and literature has been invaluable.

Charlotte, March 2004.

Baja
California
Norte

Sonora

Chihuahua

Coahuila

Baja
California
Sur

Sinaloa

Durango

Zacatecas

Nayarit Aguascalientes
Guan

Jalisco

North
Pacific
Ocean

Colima Michoacá

Morelos

Introduction

The observations of foreigners occupy an important place in what we know about Mexican history today. In the words of historian William Beezley, foreign travelers, sojourners, and immigrants "did not take for granted Mexico's everyday activities, food, clothing, work habits, family arrangements, and housing."[1] What appeared ordinary and less than noteworthy to Mexicans seemed fascinating to foreign observers, who devoted a large part of their accounts to detailed descriptions of Mexican society, culture, politics, and everyday life. For example, nineteenth-century travel accounts, such as Fanny Calderón de la Barca's *Life in Mexico*, still have much to tell us about topics for which few other sources are available, such as dress, feasts and festivals, and patterns of consumption. John Reed's classic *Insurgent Mexico*, an account of Pancho Villa's División del Norte, the largest army of the Mexican Revolution, is important reading for students of the Mexican Revolution. And few analyses of contemporary Mexico are as moving as Judith Adler Hellman's *Mexican Lives*, a collection of essays on the everyday lives of ordinary Mexicans. Whether in 1800 or in 2000, observers found in Mexico a stunning degree of ethnic and regional diversity as well as a dizzying array of apparent contradictions: urban vs. rural, modernity vs. tradition, and rich vs. poor. For that reason, the German hardware merchant Franz Böker, who lived in Mexico from 1899 to 1965, referred to his host country as the "country of unlimited impossibilities," in an obvious allusion to and contrast with the United States.[2]

This anthology presents, in comparative fashion, a broad cross-section of some of the most interesting European and North American writing on Mexico since 1800. During these two hundred years, the end of colonialism in Latin America and the revolution in global transportation gave rise to an unprecedented wave of voyages to—and accounts about—Mexico and the rest of Latin America. The collection is designed primarily for the general reader and student, although specialists in Mexican history will find some previously unavailable sources, as well as a new typology of the writings of foreign observers.

The primary purpose of the collection is to invite the reader to "do history" by examining a set of related primary sources as historical evidence. This exercise not only yields insight into the complexity of Mexican history, but into larger questions of objectivity and subjectivity as well. Like all other historical documents and, indeed, all writing about history, the written observations of foreign observers do not give an accurate portrayal of what they describe. As eyewitness accounts, they are engaging and entertaining, but they also reflect their author's biases, errors, and opinions. Yet their very subjectivity, viewed comparatively across a variety of individual viewpoints, makes them ideal for exposing their readers to working with historical evidence. In addition, these sources present the reader with an international view of Mexican history, an important endeavor in the age of the "global village" in which we live. Just as the United States becomes more international by increasing immigration, so does Mexican history benefit from an international perspective that views a crucial neighbor of the United States as part of a larger global system.

This anthology presents twenty-five excerpts of the writings of foreign observers across each of four periods: the road to independence and the first decades as a sovereign country (1800–1867), the era of Liberal modernization (1867–1910), the Mexican Revolution (1910–1940), and the post–World War II era (since 1945). The first three periods roughly coincide with three predominant means of movement within Mexico—the stagecoach, the train, and the automobile—while the airplane has become the preferred way for foreigners to reach Mexico in the final period. The chronological organization of the book reveals the transformation of both Mexico and the foreign observer writing over time.[3] The selections present a variety of viewpoints in terms of the national origin, gender, and opinion of the writer, and the region of Mexico described. The emphasis is on four major topics important for an understanding of modern Mexico: ethnicity, gender, and race (selections 1–5, 9–10, 16–17, 19, 21, 23–25); cultural differences between Mexicans and foreigners (selections 6–7, 8–9, 13–14, 18–19, 21–22); political stability and instability (selections 2, 5–6, 13–15, 18, 20–22); and the economy and its impact on Mexicans (selections 1, 11–12, 17, 18, 20–21, 23–25). While these topics do not serve as organizing principles of this collection, they facilitate using this work as a supplementary text on Mexican history, and they permit the reader to compare an individual excerpt with others in this volume.

Like all other sources, the excerpts contain biases and distortions that affect a reader's interpretation. In particular, the reader will note the pervasiveness of "Orientalist" concepts in foreign eyewitness writing. As cultural critic Edward Said has pointed out, a variety of nineteenth-century observers from colonial powers such as Britain and France portrayed the Middle East—or the "Orient"—as a single, undifferentiated "other."[4] In other words, Europeans invented the Orient as a category of analysis.[5] As Said argued, "Orientalism can be discussed and analyzed as the corporate institution for dealing with the Orient—dealing with it by making statements about it, authorizing views of it, describing it, by teaching it, settling it, ruling over it: in short, Orientalism as a Western style for dominating, restructuring, and having authority over the Orient."[6] Said's concept applies equally to the writings of European and U.S. observers about Latin America.

Said's famous study is most pertinent for a critical reading of the selections in this volume. Foreign observers did not simply "describe" the cultural, political, and social reality of Mexico, but they also helped invent the categories in which that reality was depicted. Together with the Mexican elite and middle class that served as one of their main sources of information, nineteenth-century observers defined social categories such as ethnicity and race. In doing so, they created an essentialist discourse that subsumed a wealth of cultural difference under single categories such as "Mexican" or "Indian," and they explored the potential and limitations of the country they visited for the benefit of future investors and visitors. In the nineteenth century in particular, they were condescending to Mexicans and often used openly racist and sexist arguments. Even as twentieth-century visitors displayed a greater awareness of and sensitivity to cultural differences, they continued to propagate tropes such as that of Mexico as an "infernal paradise," in which the country became mythologized as a place of paradoxical extremes.[7] Foreign accounts of Mexico thus tell the reader as much about their authors as they do about the society they describe. They are a source for cultural and social history as well as a genre of literature. If historians have generally judged them more kindly than literary critics, it is because of the unique nature of the insight into another culture that they provide.[8]

This brief analysis of the pitfalls of this type of source would not be complete without reference to the significant omissions of fact that characterize eyewitness accounts. Sometimes these omissions represented an important part of the observer's narrative strategy. For example, Fanny Chambers Gooch (selection 9) and Carl Lumholtz (selection 10) construct cultural differences as polar opposites and thus juxtapose images of the supposedly backward, mysterious, and slothful Mexicans and the progressive, honest, and hardworking North Americans. Their narratives neglect to mention the many instances in which they must have witnessed Mexicans behaving in ways that did not conform to their stereotypes. In other cases, the omissions are the result of the author's limited personal experience. Thus Luise Böker (selection 15) portrays life in revolutionary Mexico City as intolerable because she cannot put her own experiences into the context of the rest of Mexico, where conditions were often far worse. Yet another type of omission can occur through memory, for example through the passage of time between the actual experience and the writing of the account. Writing in 1935, Rosa King (selection 13) shows a magnanimous attitude toward Emiliano Zapata's peasant rebels and does not recall feeling personally threatened by their entry into Cuernavaca. Yet in the heat of the conflict in the early 1910s, her missives to British diplomats sounded a very different theme—one in which she expressed outrage at the revolutionaries.

Biases and omissions aside, another important issue for readers to consider is the intertextual nature of this type of source. Foreign visitors did not enter Mexico with a tabula rasa, a blank slate upon which an observing mind could inscribe fresh messages. Not only did they come with preconceived attitudes, prejudices, and opinions, but they were also influenced by the accounts of past observers. For example, as Part I will show, Alexander von Humboldt's seminal *Essai politique du royaume de la Nouvelle Espagne* (selection 1) shaped two generations of travel accounts after its publication in 1811.[9] In the same fashion, Calderón's *Life in Mexico* (selection 3) helped forge the consciousness of subsequent writers. Long after the government of

Porfirio Díaz (1876–1911) had refurbished the port facilities of the city of Veracruz—the point of entry for most visitors—travelers continued to repeat Calderón's harangue about the poor quality of the facilities. Likewise, as Parts II and III reveal, John K. Turner's *Barbarous Mexico* (selection 12) inaugurated three decades of socially conscious journalism, a type of account that sought to redress the imperialist injustices of the past, and applaud Mexico's great revolutionary experiment in social justice and economic progress. In turn, these accounts informed the progressive-minded visitors of the post–World War II era (selections 21 and 23–25)—whether travel writers, academics, or journalists. Talking to one another, quarreling with each other, learning from each other (and often more than from the Mexicans themselves), the authors in the business of describing Mexico were, in the words of one Mexican intellectual, a "traveling theater troupe."[10]

Finally, foreign observers engaged in a complex dialogue with elite and middle-class Mexicans that defies simple analysis and explanation. Humboldt's long essay, for instance, left a huge impact on the Mexican elites, and Conservative and Liberal factions fiercely debated the merits and demerits of his arguments. Yet in part, Humboldt's observations were the product of his conversations with anticlerical, liberal creoles, or whites of Spanish origin. So who influenced whom here? Did Humboldt help *construct* the future political debate of post-independence Mexico, or did his writing *reflect* the antecedents of that debate? While one cannot resolve this particular chicken-and-egg problem, it is clear that the complex symbiosis of foreign visitors and the society they seek to observe often obscures the supposed "authenticity" and "veracity" of their accounts.[11] At the same time, this symbiosis illustrates the value of these sources for studying the complicated interplay between Mexicans and foreign observers.

As a result of these caveats associated with reading the writings of foreign observers, the anthology provides three levels of explanations for the benefit of the reader. Each of the four chronological sections begins with a brief introduction to the respective period in Mexican history, as well as issues affecting the experiences of settlement and travel. Second, a headnote precedes each of the excerpts. This headnote gives background information on the author in order to aid the reader in placing the selection in its proper historical context and in identifying biases and preconceptions that affect the interpretation of the document. Finally, annotations in the text explain Spanish words or obscure terminology; they provide additional historical information whenever necessary; and they also point out some of the more egregious misrepresentations and misleading statements.

An anthology such as this one requires a series of explanations about the editor's approach to and selection of sources. Most importantly, the reader will have noticed the absence of the terms "travel account" or "travel literature" in the foregoing exposition. The act of traveling implies a particular set of circumstances that is often misleading when applied to the narratives of foreign eyewitnesses. It denotes the activity of a stable observer who moves into and out of another country without undergoing processes of adaptation and acculturation during his or her stay. As Mary Louise Pratt has argued in her elaboration of Said's work on European travel writing about Africa and Latin America, this type of observation with "imperial eyes" often subsequently underwrites projects of colonial and imperial expansion.[12] According to Pratt, observers often followed patterns of investment and settlement activity, and contributed significantly to foreign discourses about Mexico, and even to actual efforts at imperial expansion. In particular, the writings of von Humboldt awakened the interests of Europe's great powers, and later contributed to the imperialist projects that culminated in the French Intervention of 1862. Yet one can hardly hold von Humboldt responsible for the appropriation of his ideas. Moreover, as one scholar has pointed out, this enlightened intellectual also provided an anti-colonial discourse that criticized creole brutality toward slaves and peasants in the New World.[13] In the twentieth century, travel accounts continued to be published, including—most recently—the travel book of Isabella Tree, a New Age version of the genre that denounces the negative effects of globalization (selection 24). Like von Humboldt, Tree primarily addresses a foreign audience interested in "ordering" the world according to its cultural precepts.

However, the term "travel" does not capture the diversity of reasons why foreigners came to Mexico, or the variety of motivations behind recording one's experiences (for instance, whether the account was intended for publication), or—most important—the length of stay and the possibility of change in the viewpoint of the observer. Even though few Europeans and North Americans willingly integrated themselves into Mexican society, the process of adopting a hybrid cultural identity was inevitable in the long term.[14] At the very least, the perspective of long-term residents changed as a result of their adaptation to their host society. For example, many immigrants in the United States used to eating food with utensils eventually grab the hamburger or slice of pizza with as much gusto as the native-born population. In addition, these immigrants and long-term sojourners acquired a personal stake in Mexico that forced them to adjust their viewpoint. For example, Carl Christian Sartorius had already spent twenty-five years in coastal Veracruz when he wrote *Mexico: Landscape and Popular Sketches* (selection 5). He would never return to live in his home country. In fact, he wrote as part of an effort to attract German immigration to his "colony" in the tropics. As we have seen, Rosa King (selection 13) lost her hotel during the Revolution, but remained in Mexico and reconciled herself to the new order. Even more muddled are the cases of left-wing "political pilgrims" such as B. Traven (selection 16), who came to observe the Mexican Revolution from up close; Luise Böker, who lived with her husband in revolutionary Mexico City and never expected her private letters to be published (selection 15); and today's scholars and journalists paid to make sense of a society ever more relevant to North Americans in the NAFTA era (selections 23–25). These people do not fit the mold of the classical traveler, and they did not write travel accounts. Thus, the notion of travel literature as a genre creates an "Occidentalist" counterpoint to Pratt's "imperial eyes." This counterpoint posits foreign observers as a monolithic, homogeneous "us" in the service of empire building. As literary critic Lisa Lowe has pointed out, there are many "Orientalisms:" many sets of assumptions, essentialist constructions, and conflicted attempts to understand a different reality.[15]

For lack of a better term, this anthology will therefore refer to "foreign observer accounts" and recognize three distinct categories within the continuum of life experience in Mexico. Depending on the length of stay, degree of adaptation or acculturation, and motivation for writing, it will distinguish between travel accounts, sojourner accounts, and immigrant accounts. The former presupposes a relatively brief trip (one year at most) taken with the objective of exploration and observation, and the latter assumes a long-term emotional and financial engagement with Mexico as a new home. The sojourner category includes the rest: temporary residents, soldiers, Mexico-based journalists, foreign government administrators, and the like.

This approach establishes a framework in which the foreign observer forms part of a continuum bounded by two extremes: the short-term tourist who is interested in a deep tan, and the permanent immigrant whose children have forgotten the language of their foreign-born parent. In turn, this framework helps to understand foreign observer accounts in the context of their above-mentioned limitations as historical sources. Of course, this book does not purport to be a definitive interpretation of foreign observer accounts of Mexico. In presenting and introducing the sources, it leaves the interpretive judgment to the reader, limiting itself to highlighting the complex interplay between the observer and the observed. The work of the editor inevitably adds a second prism through which Mexico is refracted, one evident in the selections I have used and the method of presentation I have employed.

This anthology presents a wide range of viewpoints in terms of national origin, region, and political outlook. In addition to Anglo-American authors who have written the bulk of the foreign literature on Mexico, the book contains excerpts by Germans and Frenchmen, as well as those of one Austrian, Norwegian, and Spaniard, respectively. The focus of the collection is on works from Western Europe and North America—Mexico's major trading partners and, with the exception of refugees from neighboring Central and South America, the origin of more than 90 percent of all immigrants and visitors. Due to the editor's linguistic limitations, only works written in English, French, German, and Spanish have been included. In addition, the anthology seeks to provide a mix of well-known "classics," less famous works, and some altogether new materials (selections 15, 20, and 22) from private and public archives. Several excerpts (6, 10, 15–17, and 20) contain original translations from German, French, or Spanish narratives. While the anthology follows the prominence of Mexico City in both foreign accounts and national cultural, economic, and political life, it also covers most of the major Mexican regions. It includes authors with widely divergent political outlook; from the conservatism of Emmanuel Domenech (selection 6) and Evelyn Waugh (selection 18) to the Marxism of John Reed (selection 14) or Verna Millán (selection 19). It contains excerpts from participants at the highest level of power (selection 6), as well as observers with only a cursory knowledge of Mexico (selection 22). Finally, it includes texts with intended audiences that ranged from one individual in an unpublished letter (selections 15 and 22) to a mass readership.

I have made it a particular point of emphasis to include numerous writings of women. Whether in Europe, Mexico, or the United States, men and women lived in gendered worlds, producing divergent perspectives on Mexico. It is not possible, however, to generalize on this point. For example, although literary critic Sara Mills has pointed out that "women writers tended to concentrate on descriptions of people as individuals, rather than on statements about the race as a whole,"[16] Fanny Chambers Gooch (selection 9), Luise Böker (selection 15), and Verna Millán (selection 19) used anecdotal evidence to make sweeping generalizations about Mexicans. Nonetheless, Mills has a point: at least in the nineteenth century, the majority of women "travelers" went to Latin America to follow their spouses, and therefore described more personal spheres and matters than the male writers.[17] Women described worlds closed to men, such as the convent (selection 3), mistress-servant relationships (selection 9), and the household (selections 9 and 15). Even though women wrote no more than 10 percent of the nineteenth-century travel accounts,[18] their writing represents nine out of the twenty-five excerpts (3, 7, 11, 13, 15, 19, 21, 23–25), including three from the nineteenth century. These selections complement the sources written by men, and they counterbalance some of those written from egregiously macho standpoints (for example, selections 2 and 14).

Despite this diversity of foreign observer accounts, their authors have several characteristics in common. They were all educated and came from a middle- or upper-class background, and many of them (but not all!) had a good command of Spanish and other foreign languages. With few exceptions, they shared a sense of racial and/or cultural superiority over Mexico. This collection contains only non-fiction accounts—an anthology based on literary sources would be a worthwhile, but distinct undertaking.[19] Although it includes illustrations from two accounts that rely heavily on visual representations to express their point of view, it does not purport to duplicate the sampling of the visual and pictorial record of foreign observers provided by another publication.[20]

An anthology such as this one requires substantial editorial work. All translations have sought to capture the tone of the original document. Among the English writings, I have preserved the original grammar and punctuation but corrected misspellings, including that of Spanish words and Mexican names. It has also been necessary to shorten most of the selections in this anthology, an effort that required the use of ellipses (. . .) to substitute for the missing text. Unless otherwise noted, all ellipses and translations in this text are mine. Finally, when possible, I have standardized references to currencies and measurements.

Notes

1. William Beezley, *Judas at the Jockey Club and Other Episodes of Porfirian Mexico* (Lincoln: University of Nebraska Press, 1987), 7.
2. Interview with Gabriele Buchenau, Warleberg, Germany, June 5, 1992.
3. Denoting, of course, the travel of the observers, not that of most Mexicans.
4. The concept of "other" comes from Edward Said, *Orientalism* (New York: Random House, 1979).
5. I use the word "hegemony" in the Gramscian sense, signifying a shared system of meaning that consolidates and justifies the existing class structure and politico-economic system.
6. Said, *Orientalism*, 3.
7. Daniel Cooper Alarcón, *The Aztec Palimpsest: Mexico in the Modern Imagination* (Tucson: University of Arizona Press, 1997), 39–94; Ronald G. Walker, *Infernal Paradise: Mexico and the Modern English Novel* (Berkeley: University of California Press, 1978).
8. June Hahner, *Women in Women's Eyes: Latin American Women in Nineteenth-Century Travel Accounts* (Wilmington, DE: Scholarly Resources, 1998), xi.
9. Walther L. Bernecker, "Reiseberichte als historische Quellengattung im 19. Jahrhundert," in *Die Wiederentdeckung Lateinamerikas: Die Erfahrung des Subkontinents in Reiseberichten des 19. Jahrhunderts,* eds. Walther L. Bernecker and Gertrut Krömer (Frankfurt: Vervuert, 1997), 332–34.
10. Juan Antonio Ortega y Medina, *México en la conciencia anglosajona* (Mexico City: Gráfica Panamericana, 1955), 19.
11. Alfred H. Siemens, *Between the Summit and the Sea: Central Veracruz in the Nineteenth Century* (Vancouver: University of British Columbia Press, 1990), xvii.
12. Mary Louise Pratt, *Imperial Eyes: Travel Writing and Transculturation* (Routledge: London, 1992).
13. Eoin Bourke, "'Der zweite Kolumbus?' Überlegungen zu Alexander von Humboldts Eurozentrismusvorwurf," in *Reisen im Diskurs: Modelle der literarischen Fremderfahrung von den Pilgerberichten bis zur Postmoderne,* eds. Anne Fuchs and Theo Harden (Heidelberg: Universitätsverlag C. Winter, 1995), 137–51.

14. Jürgen Buchenau, "Small Number, Great Impact: Mexico and Its Immigrants, 1821–1973," *Journal of American Ethnic History* 20.3 (2001): 23–49; Buchenau, *Tools of Progress: A German Merchant Family in Mexico City, 1865–Present* (Albuquerque: University of New Mexico Press, 2004).

15. Lisa Lowe, *Critical Terrains: French and British Orientalisms* (Ithaca, NY: Cornell University Press, 1991), 6–7.

16. Sara Mills, *Discourses of Difference: An Analysis of Women's Travel Writing and Colonialism* (London: Routledge, 1991).

17. Hahner, *Women in Women's Eyes*, xvi.

18. Harvey C. Gardiner, "Foreign Travelers' Accounts of Mexico, 1810–1910," *The Americas* 8.3 (Jan. 1952): 321–51.

19. As an example of such an anthology in the Spanish language, see Héctor Sánchez, ed., *Mexico nueve veces contado* (Mexico City: Secretaría de Educación Pública, 1974).

20. Carole Naggar and Fred Ritchin, *México Through Foreign Eyes, 1850–1900: visto por ojos extranjeros* (New York: Norton, 1996).

PART I

Whither the
New Nation?

Mexico experienced a traumatic half-century following its independence from Spain in 1821. Although Baron von Humboldt's famous *Political Essay* had predicted great potential for the colony called "New Spain," the Wars of Independence (1810–1821) presaged a different trajectory. The decade of war claimed tens of thousands of lives, devastated the lucrative silver mines, interrupted transportation and trade routes, and left rag tag armies that answered to caudillo leaders such as Antonio López de Santa Anna. The new nation therefore came into being without de facto government authority over most of its territory, and with nary a penny in the national treasury. During the years 1821–1854, Mexico changed presidents on average more than once a year; loosely organized Conservative and Liberal parties jockeyed for power over the enormous wealth of the Catholic Church and the political organization of the republic, and the United States annexed half of Mexico's territory.

Then, just when many Mexicans might have convinced themselves that things could not get any worse, they did. In the mid-1850s, the Liberal Party came to power with a program of economic modernization. In order to connect their country more effectively to the expanding North Atlantic industrial economies, the Liberals, led by Benito Juárez, attempted to nationalize church wealth and to put public lands into the hands of private investors. In 1858, this effort led to a bloody civil war between Liberals and Conservatives, and after Juárez had triumphed in 1861, French troops landed in Mexico the following year to aid the Conservatives and collect overdue payments on the country's foreign debt. What followed was what historian Jan Bazant has called a "tragi-comedy of errors."[1] Supported by the French invasion forces, the Conservatives nominated the Habsburg Prince Maximilian as Emperor of Mexico. Finally, Juárez had the patriotic cause he needed to crush the Conservatives. With U.S. support after the Union victory in the Civil War, his forces defeated the imperial army. In June 1867, a firing squad executed Maximilian, and the restoration of the republic finally paved the way for political stability, a necessary prerequisite for the era of Liberal modernization.

Despite the chaos of these years, post-independence Mexico remained as alluring to foreign visitors as it had to von Humboldt, one of the first foreigners to be granted almost unlimited travel rights in New Spain. The country still resembled the one that the conquistador Hernán Cortés had described to the Spanish King Charles I after the conquest of the Aztec empire in 1521. When the king inquired about his new realm, Cortés reportedly took a sheet of paper, crumpled it up into a ball, and flattened it to reveal a rugged, virtually impassable mountain landscape. This landscape had produced a rich ethnic diversity in Mexico, and Spanish colonial domination had not eradicated it. In the misty rainforests of Chiapas, on the semiarid plains of Yucatán, in the remote canyons of Chihuahua, in the expansive deserts of Sonora, in the steaming swamps of Tabasco, and in the pine-covered hills of Michoacán, indigenous peoples existed with limited or no contact with colonial authorities. The rich tapestry that was Mexico was home to at least sixty-two indigenous languages in addition to Spanish, the language of the conquistadors and their creole descendants, as well as that of a small African slave population and the mestizos, a growing group of mixed indigenous and European descent.

It is not surprising that this period gave rise to some of the most important foreign observer accounts of Mexico. The travelers during this time were overwhelmingly male, adventurous, and sure of the superiority of Western ways. They competed for explanations of what they saw as the "backwardness" of Mexico: some blamed biological (racial) factors; others the environment; and yet others the legacy of Spanish colonial rule. Most of the visitors, especially those from English-speaking countries, sympathized with the Liberal creoles, who sought to limit the influence of the Catholic Church, open up Mexico to foreign trade, and establish a federal republic. But a few observers, including those Austrian and French nationals who propped up Maximilian's short-lived Empire, naturally favored the Conservatives and their pro-clerical, pro-monarchical program.

This was an era in which one traveled slowly: either, if one was lucky, by the horse-powered stagecoach, or, off the beaten path, astride a *burro*, the Mexican donkey that had long served as the Mexicans' preeminent mode of transportation. Thus visitors acclimated themselves slowly to their new surroundings in a country then populated by only ten to fifteen million people. On the oft-traveled 250-mile trek from the port town of Veracruz to the capital, visitors traveled from the tropical *tierra caliente* (hot country) upwards through the subtropical *tierra templada* (temperate country) into the *tierra fría* (cold country) of the Valleys of Puebla and Anáhuac, with the heart of Mexico at more than seven thousand feet elevation. Along the way, luxuriant, tropical foliage gave way first to rain-soaked forests, then to savannas, and finally to the pine forests and dry plains of the Mexican highlands. Lasting several days, this trip—and the emotions experienced during the journey—cannot be fathomed by the modern traveler who arrives in Concourse F·of the Benito Juárez International Airport after a two-hour flight from Houston.[2]

The seven foreigners whose writings are excerpted in this section described a society that was thoroughly alien to them. Writing from a great diversity of perspectives, these authors shared an ethnocentric belief that Mexicans should learn from European ways. The section begins with two early writings that sought to describe the ethnic and social makeup of Mexico: Alexander von Humboldt's *Political Essay* and Joel R. Poinsett's *Notes on Mexico*. It then moves on to Fanny Calderón de la Barca's observations of life in a Mexico City convent in her *Life in Mexico*, an excerpt that discusses the Catholic Church, as well as the lives of elite women in the nineteenth century. Four selections informed by a variety of imperial and colonizing schemes by the United States and the European powers make up the balance of this section. William S. Henry's *Campaign Sketches* yield insights into the views of an officer in the U.S. Army in the Mexican-American War of 1846–1847. Carl C. Sartorius's *Mexico* was part of an effort to encourage German farmers to settle in Mexico. Emmanuel Domenech's *Le Mexique tel qu'il est* constituted a justification of the French Intervention from a Conservative, pro-monarchy perspective. Finally, Paula von Kollonitz's *The Court of Mexico* comments on the life of the Mexico City elite during the reign of Emperor Maximilian from the perspective of one of the ladies-in-waiting to Maximilian's wife, Empress Carlota (Charlotte).

Notes

1. Jan Bazant, "Mexico from Independence to 1867," in Leslie Bethell, ed., *Cambridge History of Latin America* (Cambridge: Cambridge University Press, 1985), 3:449.

2. A pioneering study of travel and tourism in the nineteenth century is Aida Mostkoff Linares, "Foreign Visions and Images of Mexico: One Hundred Years of International Tourism, 1821–1921," Ph.D. dissertation, University of California, Los Angeles, 1999.

1 A Land of Contrasts

Alexander von Humboldt[1]

Baron Alexander von Humboldt's Political Essay on the Kingdom of New Spain *is the most influential book on Mexico ever penned by a foreign observer. It changed future perceptions of what was then a Spanish colony in three important ways. Most important, its "myth of the wealth of Mexico"[2] awakened the interest of European governments and entrepreneurs. Second, the* Political Essay *elicited fierce debate among the Mexican elite, with an anti-Humboldt discourse framing what after 1821 became the Conservative program, and a Humboldtian discourse shaping the future Liberal platform. Finally, most subsequent travelers to Mexico were familiar with von Humboldt's thought. At the same time ethnocentric, enlightened, racist, and optimistic, the* Political Essay—*only one of a total of sixty-nine works by the author—provides the ideal starting point for the diversity of accounts that follow. The following descriptions of Mexico's indigenous populations and the country's economic potential are deeply influenced by the attitudes of the wealthy creoles with whom von Humboldt associated during his 1803–1804 visits to Mexico City and the central silver mining districts.*

The scion of landed nobility from the vicinity of Berlin, Alexander von Humboldt (1769–1859) was the younger brother of famed linguist and philologist Wilhelm von Humboldt, after whom Berlin's oldest university is named. Alexander was homeschooled and grew up amidst the tight social circle typical of the Prussian aristocracy. After university studies, he joined Prussia's Department of Mines before serving in several other capacities in the government. Bored with this career, von Humboldt studied botany in Vienna, followed by years of independent readings in astronomy, chemistry, and mineralogy. In June 1799, this itinerant aristocrat-scholar set sail for the New World in the company of the French botanist Aimé Bonpland. Influenced by Enlightenment rationalism, von Humboldt sought to understand the world from a global perspective—yet he was also a product of the Romantic era in his fascination with nature and adventure. He remained in Latin America for five years, traveling to present-day Brazil, Colombia, Cuba, Mexico, and Venezuela.[3]

I could not fail to interest the reader by a minute description of the manners, character and physical and intellectual state of those indigenous inhabitants of Mexico. The general interest displayed in Europe for the remains of the primitive population of the new continent has its origin in a moral cause which does honor to humanity. The history of the conquest of America presents the picture of an unequal struggle between nations far advanced in arts and others in the very lowest degree of civilization. The unfortunate race of Aztecs, escaped from the carnage, appeared destined to annihilation under an oppression of several centuries. We have difficulty in believing that nearly two millions and a half of aborigines could survive such lengthened calamities. Such is the interest which the misfortune of a vanquished people inspires, that it renders us frequently unjust towards the descendants of the conquerors. . . .

The Indians of New Spain bear a general resemblance to those who inhabit Canada, Florida, Peru and Brazil. They have the same swarthy and copper color, flat and smooth hair, small beard, squat body, long eye with the corner directed upwards towards the temples, prominent cheek bones, thick lips, and an expression of gentleness in the mouth strongly contrasted with a gloomy and severe look. A European, when he decides on the great resemblance among the copper-colored races, is subject to a particular illusion.

He is struck with a complexion so different from our own, and the uniformity of this complexion conceals for a long time the diversity of individual features. The new colonist can hardly at first distinguish the indigenous, because his eyes are less fixed on the gentle, melancholic or ferocious expression of the countenance than on the red coppery color and dark, luminous and coarse and glossy hair. . . .

The Indians of New Spain generally attain a pretty advanced age. Peaceable cultivators, and collected these six hundred years in villages, they are not exposed to the accidents of the wandering life of the hunters and warriors of the Mississippi and the savannas of the Rio Gila. Accustomed to uniform nourishment of an almost entirely vegetable nature, . . . the Indians would undoubtedly attain a very great longevity if their constitution were not weakened by drunkenness. Their intoxicating liquors are rum, . . . and especially *pulque*,[4] the wine of the country. . . .

The vice of drunkenness is, however, less general among the Indians than is generally believed. . . . In the forests of Guiana and on the banks of the Orinoco we saw Indians who showed an aversion for the brandy which we made them taste. There are several Indian tribes, very sober, whose fermented beverages are too weak to intoxicate. In New Spain drunkenness is most common among the Indians who inhabit the valley of Mexico and the environs of Puebla and Tlaxcala, wherever the maguey or agave are cultivated on a great scale. The police in the city of Mexico . . . collect the drunkards to be found stretched out in the streets. These Indians, who are treated like dead bodies, are carried to the principal guard house. In the morning an iron ring is put round their ankles and they are made to clear the streets for three days. On letting them go on the fourth day, they are sure to find several of them in the course of the week. The excess of liquors is also very injurious to the health of the lower people in the warm countries on the coast which grow sugar cane. It is to be hoped that this evil will diminish as civilization makes more progress among a caste of men whose bestiality is not much different from that of the brutes.[5]

Travelers who merely judge from the physiognomy of the Indians are tempted to believe that it is rare to see old men among them. In fact, without consulting parish registers which in warm regions are devoured by the termites every twenty or thirty years, it is very difficult to form any idea of the age of Indians. They themselves (I allude to the poor laboring Indian) are completely ignorant of it. Their heads never become grey. It is infinitely more rare to find an Indian than a Negro with grey hairs, and the want of beard gives the former a continual air of youth. The skin of the Indians is also less subject to wrinkles. It is by no means uncommon to see in Mexico, in the temperate zone half way up the Cordillera, natives, and especially women, reach a hundred years of age. This old age is generally comfortable, for the Mexican and Peruvian Indians preserve their muscular strength to the last. . . .

The copper-colored Indians enjoy one great physical advantage which is undoubtedly owing to the great simplicity in which their ancestors lived for thousands of years. They are subject to almost no deformity. I never saw a hunchbacked Indian, and it is extremely rare to see any of them who squint or are lame in the arm or leg. . . .

As to the moral faculties of the Indians, it is difficult to appreciate them with justice if we only consider this long oppressed caste in their present state of degradation. The better sort of Indians, among whom a certain degree of intellectual culture might be supposed, perished in great part at the commencement of the Spanish conquest, the victims of European ferocity. The Christian fanaticism broke out in a particular manner against the Aztec priests; . . . all those who inhabited the *teocalli*, or houses of God, who might be considered the depositories of the historical, mythological and astronomical knowledge of the country, were exterminated, for the priests observed the meridian shade . . . and regulated the calendar. The monks burned the hieroglyphic paintings, by which every kind of knowledge was transmitted from generation to generation. The people, deprived of these means of instruction, were plunged in ignorance so much the deeper as the missionaries were unskilled in the Mexican languages and could substitute few new ideas in place of the old. The Indian women who had preserved any share of fortune chose rather to ally with the conquerors than to share the contempt in which the Indians were held. The Spanish soldiers were so much the more eager for these alliances as very few European women had followed the army. The remaining natives then consisted only of the most indigent race, poor cultivators, artisans, among whom were a great number of weavers, porters who were used like beasts of burden, and especially of those dregs of the people, those crowds of beggars, who bore witness to the imperfection of the social institutions and the existence of feudal oppression, and who filled, in the time of Cortés, the streets of all the great cities of the Mexican empire. How shall we judge, from these miserable remains of a powerful people, of the degree of cultivation to which it had risen from the twelfth to the sixteenth century and of the intellectual development of which it is susceptible? If all that remained of the French or German nation were a few poor agriculturists, could we read in their features that they belonged to nations which had produced a Descartes and Clairaut, a Kepler and a Leibnitz?[6]

When we consider attentively what is related in the letters of Cortés, the memoirs of Bernal Díaz written with admirable naiveté, and other contemporary historians as to the state of the inhabitants of Mexico, Texcoco, Cholollan [Cholula] and Tlaxcala in the time of Montezuma II, we think we perceive the portrait of the Indians of our own time. We see the same nudity in the warm regions, the same form of dress in the central table land, and the same habits in domestic life. How can any great change take place in the Indians when they are kept insulated in villages in which the whites dare not settle, when the difference of language places an almost insurmountable barrier between them and the Europeans, when they are oppressed by magistrates chosen through political considerations from their own number, and in short, when they can only expect moral and civil improvement from a man who talks to them of mysteries, dogmas and ceremonies, of the end of which they are ignorant?

I do not mean to discuss here what the Mexicans were before the Spanish conquest; this interesting subject has been already entered upon in the commencement of this chapter. When we consider that they had an almost exact knowledge of the duration of the year, that they intercalated at the end of their great cycle of 104 years with more accuracy than the Greeks, Romans and Egyptians, we are tempted to believe that this progress is not the effect of the intellectual development of the Americans themselves, but that they were indebted for it to their communication with some very cultivated nations of central Asia. The Toltecs appeared in New Spain in the seventh and the Aztecs in the twelfth century; and they immediately drew up the geographical map of the country traversed by them, constructed cities, highways, dikes, canals and immense pyramids very accurately designed.... Their feudal system, their civil and military hierarchy, were already so complicated that we must suppose a long succession of political events before the establishment of the singular concatenation of authorities of the nobility and clergy, and before a small portion of the people, themselves the slaves of the Mexican sultan, could have subjugated the great mass of the nation. We have examples of theocratic forms of government in South America... in which despotism was concealed under the appearance of a gentle and patriarchal government. But in Mexico, small colonies, wearied of tyranny, gave themselves republican constitutions. Now it is only after long popular struggles that these free constitutions can be formed. The existence of republics does not indicate a very recent civilization. How is it possible to doubt that a part of the Mexican nation had arrived at a certain degree of cultivation, when we reflect on the care with which their hieroglyphical books were composed, and when we recollect that a citizen of Tlaxcala, in the midst of the tumults of war, took advantage of the facility offered him by our Roman alphabet to write in his own language five large volumes on the history of a country of which he deplored the subjection? . . .

In the portrait which we draw of the different races of men composing the population of New Spain, we shall merely consider the Mexican Indian in his actual state. . . . The Mexican Indian is grave, melancholic and silent, so long as he is not under the influence of intoxicating liquors. This gravity is particularly remarkable in Indian children, who at the age of four or five display much more intelligence and maturity than white children. The Mexican loves to throw a mysterious air over the most indifferent actions. The most violent passions are never painted in his features; and there is something frightful in seeing him pass all at once from absolute repose to a state of violent and unrestrained agitation. The Peruvian Indian possesses more gentleness of manners; the energy of the Mexican degenerates into harshness. These differences may have their origin in the different religions and different governments of the two countries in former times. This energy is displayed particularly by the inhabitants of Tlaxcala. In the midst of their present degradation, the descendants of those republicans are still to be distinguished by a certain haughtiness of character, inspired by the memory of their former grandeur.

The Americans,[7] . . . like other nations who have long groaned under a civil and military despotism, adhere to their customs, manners and opinions with extraordinary obstinacy. I say opinions, for the introduction of Christianity has produced almost no other effect on the Indians of Mexico than to substitute new ceremonies, the symbols of a gentle and humane religion, to the ceremonies of a sanguinary worship. This change from old to new rites was the effect of constraint and not of persuasion, and was produced by political events alone. In the new continent as well as in the old, half-civilized nations were accustomed to receive from the hands of the conqueror new laws and new divinities; the vanquished Indian gods appeared to them to yield to the gods of the strangers. In such a complicated mythology as that of the Mexicans, it was easy to find an affinity between their divinities and the divinity of the east. Cortés even very artfully took advantage of a popular tradition, according to which the Spaniards were merely the descendants of king Quetzalcóatl, who left Mexico for countries situated in the east, to carry among them civilization and laws.[8] The ritual books composed by the Indians . . . at the beginning of the conquest, of which I possess several fragments, evidently show that at that period Christianity was confounded with the Mexican mythology; the Holy Ghost is identified with the sacred eagle of the Aztecs. The missionaries not only tolerated, they even favored to a certain extent this amalgamation of ideas by means of which the Christian worship was more easily introduced among the natives. They persuaded them that the gospel had, in very remote times, been already preached in America; and they investigated its traces in the Aztec ritual with the same ardor which the learned, who in our days engage in the study of the Sanskrit, display in discussing the analogy between the Greek mythology and that of the Ganges. . . . These circumstances . . . explain why the Mexican Indians, notwithstanding the obstinacy with which they adhere to whatever is derived from their fathers, have so easily forgotten their ancient rites. Dogma has not succeeded to dogma, but ceremony to ceremony. The natives know nothing of religion but the exterior forms of worship. Fond of whatever is connected with a prescribed order of ceremonies, they find in the Christian religion particular enjoyments. The festivals of the church, the fireworks with which they are accompanied, the processions mingled with dances and whimsical disguises, are a most fertile source of amusement for the lower Indians. In these festivals the national character is displayed in all its individuality. Everywhere the Christian rites have assumed the shades of the country where they have been transplanted. . . .

Accustomed to a long slavery, as well under the domination of their own sovereigns as under that of the first conquerors, the natives of Mexico patiently suffer the vexations to which they are frequently exposed from the whites. They oppose to them only a cunning veiled under the deceitful appearances of apathy and stupidity. As the Indian can very rarely revenge himself on the Spaniards, he delights in making a common cause with them for the oppression of his own fellow citizens. Harassed for ages and compelled to a blind obedience, he wishes to tyrannize in his turn. The Indian villages are governed by magistrates of the copper-colored race; and an

Indian *alcalde*[9] exercises his power with so much the greater severity, because he is sure of being supported by the priest or the Spanish *subdelegado*.[10] Oppression produces everywhere the same effects, it everywhere corrupts the morals.

As almost all of the Indians belong to the class of peasantry and low people, it is not so easy to judge of their aptitude for the arts which embellish life. I know no race of men who appear more destitute of imagination. . . .

If, in the present state of things, the caste of whites is the only one in which we find anything like intellectual cultivation, it is also the only one which possesses great wealth. This wealth is unfortunately still more unequally distributed in Mexico than in Caracas, Havana, and especially Peru. At Caracas, the heads of the richest families possess revenue of 200,000 francs.[11] In the island of Cuba we find revenues of more than 6 or 700,000 francs. In these two industrious colonies, agriculture has founded more considerable fortunes than has been accumulated by the working of the mines in Peru. At Lima, an annual revenue of 80,000 francs is very uncommon. I know in reality of no Peruvian family in the possession of fixed and sure revenue of 130,000 francs. But in New Spain, there are individuals who possess no mines, whose revenue amounts to a million francs. The family of the Conde de Valenciana, for example, possesses . . . a property worth more than 25 million francs, without including the mine of Valenciana near Guanajuato which . . . [annually] yields net revenue of a million and a half francs. This family . . . is only divided into three branches; and they possess altogether, even in years when the mine is not very lucrative, more than 2,200,000 francs of revenue. . . . The family of [de] Fagoaga, well known for its beneficence, intelligence, and zeal for the public good, exhibits the example the greatest wealth which was ever derived from a mine. A single seam in the district of Sombrerete gave in five or six months, all charges deducted, a net profit of 20 million francs.

From these data one would suppose capital in the Mexican families infinitely greater than what is really observed. The deceased Count de Valenciana . . . sometimes drew from his mine alone, in one year, a net revenue of no less than six million francs. This annual revenue during the last twenty-five years of his life was never below from two to three million francs; and yet this extraordinary man, who came without any fortune to America, and who continued to live with great simplicity, left behind him at his death, besides his mine, which is the richest in the world, only ten millions in property and capital. This fact, which may be relied on, will not surprise those who are acquainted with the interior management of the great Mexican houses. Money rapidly gained is as rapidly spent. The working of mines becomes a game in which they embark with unbounded passion. The rich proprietors of mines lavish immense sums on quacks who engage them in new undertakings in the most remote provinces. In a country where the works are conducted on such an extravagant scale that the pit of a mine frequently requires two million francs to pierce, the [failure] of a rash project may absorb in a few years all that was gained in working the richest seams. We must add that from the internal disorder which prevails in the greatest part of the great houses of both Old and New Spain, the head of a family is not infrequently straitened with revenue of half a million, though he display no other luxury than that of numerous yokes of mules.

The mines have undoubtedly been the principal sources of the great fortunes of Mexico. Many miners have laid out their wealth in purchasing land and have addicted themselves with great zeal to agriculture. But there is also a considerable number of very powerful families who have never had the working of any lucrative mines. Such are the rich descendants of Cortés. . . . The Duke of Monteleone, a Neapolitan lord who is now the head of the house of Cortés, possesses superb estates in the province of Oaxaca, near Toluca, and at Cuernavaca. The net income from his rents is actually no more than 550,000 francs, the king having deprived the duke of the collection of the *alcabala*[12] and the duties on tobacco. The ordinary expenses of management amount to more than 125,000 francs. However, several governors of the *marquesado*[13] have become singularly wealthy. If the descendants of the great conquistador would only live in Mexico, their revenue would immediately rise to more than a million and a half. . . .

Those who only know the interior of the Spanish colonies from the vague and uncertain notions hitherto published will have some difficulty in believing that the principal sources of the Mexican riches are by no means the mines, but an agriculture which has been gradually ameliorating since the end of the last century. Without reflecting on the immense extent of the country, and especially the great number of provinces which appear totally destitute of precious metals, we generally imagine that all the activity of the Mexican population is directed to the working of mines. Because agriculture has made very considerable progress . . . wherever the mountains are accounted poor in mineral productions, it has been inferred that it is to the working of the mines that we are to attribute the small care bestowed on the cultivation of the soil in other parts of the Spanish colonies.... [But] in Mexico, the best cultivated fields ... surround the richest mines of the known world. Wherever metallic seams have been discovered in the most uncultivated parts of the Cordilleras, on the insulated and desert table lands, the working of mines, far from impeding the cultivation of the soil, has been singularly favorable to it.... Farms are established in the neighborhood of the mine. The high price of provision, from the competition of the purchasers, indemnifies the cultivator for the privations to which he is exposed from the hard life of the mountains. Thus from the hope of gain alone, and the motives of mutual interest which are the most powerful bonds of society, and without any interference on the part of the government, a mine which at first appeared insulated in the midst of wild and, desert mountains becomes in a short time connected with lands under cultivation.... [Agriculture is] the true national wealth of Mexico; for the produce of the earth is in fact the sole basis of permanent opulence.

No doubt the Mexican nation can procure by means of foreign commerce all the articles which are supplied to them by their own country; but in the midst of great wealth in gold and silver, want is severely felt whenever the commerce with the mother country or other parts of Europe or Asia has suffered any interruption, whenever a war throws obstacles in the way of maritime communication. From 25 to 30 million piastres[14] are sometimes heaped up in Mexico [City] while the manufacturers and miners are suffering from the want of steel, iron and mercury. A few years before my arrival in New Spain, the price of iron rose from 20 francs the quintal to 240, and steel from 80 francs to 1,300. In those times when there is a total stagnation of foreign commerce, Mexican industry is awakened for a time, and they then begin to manufacture steel and to make use of the iron and mercury of the mountains of America. The nation is then alive to its true interest, and feels that true wealth consists in the abundance of objects of consumption, in that of things and not in the accumulation of the sign by which they are represented....

In proportion as the Mexican population shall increase and, from being less dependent on Europe, shall begin to turn their attention to the great variety of useful productions contained in the bowels of the earth, the system of mining will undergo a change. An enlightened administration will give encouragement to those labors which are directed to the extraction of mineral substances of an intrinsic value; individuals will no longer sacrifice their own interests and those of the public to inveterate prejudices; and they will feel that the working of a mine of coal, iron or lead may become as profitable as that of a vein of silver. In the present state of Mexico, the precious metals occupy almost exclusively the industry of the colonists. . . .

Notes

1. Alexander von Humboldt, *Political Essay on the Kingdom of New Spain*, trans. John Black (London, Longman, 1811), 1:139–41, 1:148–52, 1:155–70, 1:223–27, 2:404–5, 2:407–8, 3:95, 3:105–7.
2. Bernecker, "Reiseberichte," 332–34.
3. Mary Maples Dunn, "Introduction," in von Humboldt, *Political Essay*, 1–9.
4. Fermented juice of the blue agave plant.
5. Here, von Humboldt's racial stereotyping is especially obvious, particularly as regards character traits.
6. A good example of von Humboldt's racial optimism. Unlike later observers, the author posits that intelligence and civilization are a product of historical circumstance rather than biologically conditioned. He also subsumes the great diversity of Mexico's indigenous cultures under the Aztecs.
7. Here, "Americans" denotes the inhabitants of the Americas without regard to race.
8. This is a popular myth that remains pervasive in the teaching of the Spanish conquest even today. In fact, the Aztecs, though awed by Spanish technology, did not believe Cortés represented Quetzalcóatl. See Camilla Townsend, "Burying the White Gods: New Perspectives on the Conquest of Mexico," *American Historical Review* 108.3 (June 2003), 659–87.
9. Mayor.
10. Local official.
11. Humboldt uses two separate terms—francs and livres—to refer to the French currency. At the time of publication of von Humboldt's book, twenty-four francs or livres equaled one pound, sterling. This section has been edited to refer to francs only in order to avoid confusion.
12. Import tariff.
13. The Marquisate of the Valley of Oaxaca. Originally an entailed estate granted to Hernán Cortés as a reward for his role in the conquest of Mexico.
14. Pesos, the currency of the Spanish empire.

2 A Sketch of Mexican Society

Joel R. Poinsett[1]

Written shortly after the independence of Mexico, Joel Roberts Poinsett's travel account owes much to von Humboldt. As the South Carolina politician and slave owner wrote, "when I turn to the work of this extraordinary man, I am disposed to abandon my journal."[2] Yet Poinsett, who visited Mexico just after eleven years of incessant fighting had led to independence, takes a more somber view of the future than von Humboldt. For instance, he finds the silver mines flooded, and he points out that the cost of transportation in a mountainous landscape imposes limits on the possibilities for U.S.-Mexican trade and the growth of agriculture.[3] The following excerpt is most interesting for its description of urban proletarians, also known as léperos. *In Poinsett's view—no doubt influenced by his origins in a slave state of the U.S. South—racial mixture created the type of moral degradation that would keep Mexico far below the potential identified by von Humboldt. This stereotype of the poor mestizo as a combination of the weaknesses of his Spanish and indigenous ancestors would remain pervasive in nineteenth-century writing about Mexico.*

Born in Charleston as the son of a physician, Poinsett (1779–1854) studied at the University of Edinburgh, where he graduated with a degree of medicine. He spoke several languages, touring Europe and Asia before serving as special U.S. agent in the Southern Cone during the Wars of Independence. Poinsett settled in Charleston, where he bought a plantation and entered into politics. In August 1822, President James Monroe appointed him emissary on a special mission to Mexico, then under the government of Emperor Agustín Iturbide, the winner of the Wars of Independence. The journal of the resulting two-month stay produced the book Notes on Mexico *excerpted below. During his stay, Poinsett founded the Yorkish Masonic lodge, the origin of Mexico's Liberal party. In 1825, Poinsett was appointed the first U.S. minister to Mexico, with a special charge of negotiating the United States' annexation of Texas and other Mexican territory in the north. He left in 1830 having accomplished little except bringing a plant home that still bears his name.[4]*

The gentlemen with whom I have associated are intelligent men; and those who have had it in their power to pursue liberal studies, are fond of literature and science. The Creoles in general possess good natural talents, and great facility of acquiring knowledge. They are extremely mild and courteous in their manners, kind and benevolent towards each other, and hospitable to strangers. Their besetting sin is gambling. The married women are very pleasing in their manners. They are said to be faithful to the favoured lover, and a liaison of that nature does not affect the lady's reputation. The young women are lively and accomplished. They sing and play agreeably, dance well, and know all they have had an opportunity of learning. If they would leave off the detestable practice of smoking, they would be very pleasing and amiable.

This is to be understood as characterizing the society[5] generally. There are certainly some young ladies (very few I am afraid) who do not smoke—some married women (many I hope) who have no lover, or if this would be interpreted to derogate from their charms, who consider him only as a convenient dangler, and are fondly and faithfully attached to their husbands; and there are certainly many gentlemen who are not gamesters.

It is difficult to describe, accurately, a nation composed of such various ranks, and of so many different castes as that of New Spain. The most important distinction, civil and political, was founded on the colour of the skin.

Here, to be white, was to be noble; and the rank of the different castes is determined by their nearer or more distant relation to the whites; the last on the scale being the direct and unmixed descendants of the Africans or Indians.

The character of the Indian population, which exceeds two millions and a half, remains very much the same as that of the lower class of natives is described to have been at the time of the conquest. The same indolence, the same blind submission to their superiors, and the same abject misery are to be remarked. The forms and ceremonies of their religion are changed, and they are perhaps better pleased with the magnificence of the Catholic rites than with their former mode of worship. They take a childish delight in forming processions, in which they dress themselves most fantastically: and the priests in many parts of the country have found it necessary to permit them to mingle their dances and mummeries with the catholic ceremonies. They were oppressed and trodden under foot by their Emperor and *caciques*;[6] and ever since the conquest, they have been oppressed by laws intended to protect them. For the most part, they are distributed in villages, on the most barren and unproductive lands, and are under their own caciques, who are charged with the civil government, and with the collection of the tribute, a tax of about two dollars on each male from ten to fifty years of age.[7]

The castes, that is to say, the mestizos, descendants of whites and Indians; mulattoes, descendants of whites and negroes; *zambos*, descendants of negroes and Indians—are scattered over the country as labourers, or live in the towns as artisans, workmen or beggars. There are some Indians, who have accumulated property, and some few of the castes may be seen living in comfort and respectability, in the cities and in the country; but these instances are rare. From the *cacique*, or Indian magistrate of the village, to the most abject of his fellow-sufferers, they are indolent and poor. The only difference between them is that the *cacique* does not work at all. By a law passed since the revolution they are declared, together with all the castes, to be possessed of the same rights as the whites. The tribute is abolished: but they will be, as a matter of course, subject to the *alcabala*, or tax on the internal commerce, from which they were heretofore exempt. This declaration will produce no alteration in the character of this class of the population. Measures must be taken to educate them, and lands distributed among them, before they can be considered as forming a part of the people of a free government.

The titled nobility are white Creoles, who, satisfied with the enjoyment of large estates, and with the consideration which their rank and wealth confer, seek no other distinction. They are not remarkable for their attainments, or for the strictness of their morals. The lawyers who, in fact, exercise much more influence over the people, rank next to the nobles. They are the younger branches of noble houses, or the sons of Europeans, and are remarkably shrewd and intelligent. Next in importance are the merchants and shopkeepers; for the former are not sufficiently numerous to form a separate class. They are wealthy, and might possess influence, but have hitherto taken little part in the politics of the country—most probably from the fear of losing their property, which is in a tangible shape. The labouring class in the cities and towns includes all castes and colours; they are industrious and orderly, and view with interest what is passing around them. Most of them read; and, in the large cities, papers and pamphlets are hawked about the street, and sold at a cheap rate to the people. The labouring class in the country is composed, in the same manner, of different castes. They are sober, industrious, docile, ignorant and superstitious; and may be led by their priests, or masters, to good or evil. Their apathy has in some measure been overcome by the long struggle for independence, in which most of them bore a part; but they are still under the influence and direction of the priests. They are merely labourers, without any property in the soil; and cannot be expected to feel much interest in the preservation of civil rights, which so little concern them. The last class, unknown as such in a well-regulated society, consists of beggars and idlers—drones that prey upon the community, and who, having nothing to lose, are always ready to swell the cry of popular ferment, or to lend their aid in favour of imperial tyranny. The influence of this class, where it is numerous, upon the fate of revolutions, has always been destructive to liberty. In France, they were very numerous; and the atrocities which disgraced that revolution, are, in a great measure, to be ascribed to this cause. In Mexico, these people have been kept in subjection by the strong arm of the vice regal government; but it is to be feared, that they will hence-forward be found the ready tool of every faction. The priests exercise unbounded influence over the higher and lower orders in Mexico; and, with a few honourable exceptions, are adverse to civil liberty. . . .

The mass of the people here will not for many years consume foreign manufactures. Their dress is simple and they are accustomed to wear cloth made in the country, and in many instances to manufacture it themselves. The Indians and common people wear leather breeches, loose at the knees, a leather jerkin, which descends to within three or four inches of the waistband of the breeches, no shirt nor stockings, sandals of hide, or shoes wide and open about the ankles. Over this dress they sometimes wear a *manta*, (the Poncho of Peru) a square cloth, having a hole in the centre, through which the head is thrust. Cotton is raised in the country, and their flocks furnish abundance of wool of tolerably good quality. Their cloths are dyed of various colours, which they understand how to fix, and to render bright and durable. Their manufactures are either on a very small scale, in towns, or are domestic as in the country, where families make what little they require. The machinery is very defective and the cotton is all separated from the seed by hand. Everything in this country is done by manual labour, and by dint of main strength. In large farms we have seen labourers carrying the corn and blades from the fields to the barn on their backs; some times asses are used for that purpose, and I have thought they might be made very useful in our southern country in that way, especially in harvesting rice. From habit, the labourers in this country will carry very great burdens. A band is placed across the forehead, and another across the breast, which strap on the load, and the man bends forward and moves at a trot. In the city of Mexico water is distributed by men, who carry a very large jar on their backs, supported by a band across the forehead, and a smaller one suspended from a band round the back of the head, which, as they lean forward, swings clear of the body and legs. They carry two loads in this manner from the fountain, up two pair of stairs, for a *medio*, the sixteenth of a dollar. . . .

Our large cities are many of them neater than Mexico, but there is an appearance of solidity in the houses, and an air of grandeur in the aspect of this place, which are wanting in the cities of the United States. With us, however, a stranger does not see that striking and disgusting contrast between the magnificence of the wealthy and the squalid penury of the poor, which constantly meets his view in Mexico. I have described the palaces of the rich—the abode of poverty does not offend the eye. It is beneath the church porches, in miserable barracks in the suburbs, or under the canopy of heaven. There are at least twenty thousand inhabitants of this capital, the population of which does not exceed one hundred and fifty thousand souls, who have no permanent place of abode, and no ostensible means of gaining a livelihood. After passing the night sometimes under cover, sometimes in the open air, they issue forth in the morning like drones to prey upon the community, to beg, to steal, and in the last resort to work. If they are fortunate enough to gain more than they require to maintain themselves for a day, they go to the *pulquería*, and there dance, carouse, and get drunk on *pulque* and *vino mescal*, a brandy distilled from the fermented juice of the agave. Around and under the *pulquerías* are open sheds covering a space of from fifty to a hundred feet; men and women may be seen in the evening, stretched on the ground, sleeping off the effects of their deep potations. These people, called by Humboldt, *saragates* and *guachinangos*,[8] are more generally known by the name of *léperos*.[9] They are for the most part Indians and Mestizos, lively and extremely civil, asking alms with great humility, and pouring out prayers and blessings with astonishing volubility. They are most dexterous pick-pockets, and I heard of some instances of their sleight of hand, that surpass the happiest efforts of the light-fingered gentry of Paris or London.[10]

From what I have said of the *léperos* of Mexico, you will compare them to the *lazaroni* of Naples.[11] The comparison will be favourable to the latter, who work more readily, steal less frequently, and are sober.

[In Puebla], we met more miserable squalid beings, clothed in rags, and exposing their deformities and diseases, to excite compassion, than I have seen elsewhere. Among the principal causes to which this great and growing evil is to be ascribed, are a mild climate and a fertile soil, yielding abundantly to moderate exertions. In countries like these, the people rarely possess habits of industry. They are accustomed to work only so much as is essentially necessary to support life, and to live from hand to mouth. If they meet with any accident, if they lose a limb, or are wasted by disease, they enter the towns and subsist by charity. This is peculiarly the case here, as this town especially abounds in convents. We counted more than one hundred spires and domes in this city. Each of these institutions supports a certain number of poor, who receive a daily allowance of provisions at the convent door, without prejudice to the sums they pick up by soliciting alms in the street. The custom of begging in the streets existed in Mexico before the conquest, and Cortés speaks of the Indians begging like rational beings, as an instance of their civilization. And in fact it was the greatest he could have given. A people in the hunter state never beg or give in charity. In times of scarcity the old and infirm are sometimes killed from compassion. They are useless, and no one is willing to devote any of his labour to support them. In the shepherd state, want and beggary are unknown. They are found only in agricultural, manufacturing, and mercantile communities, and especially under mild climates and in fertile territories, or where, from excess of civilization, the poor are provided for by law. The reason is the same in both cases; the poor are rendered improvident by the provision made for them by nature, or by the regulations of civilized society. . . .

In front of the churches and in the neighbourhood of them, we saw an unusual number of beggars, and they openly exposed their disgusting sores and deformities to excite our compassion. I observed one among them wrapped in a large white sheet, who, as soon as he perceived that he had attracted my attention, advanced towards me, and, unfolding his covering, disclosed his person perfectly naked and covered from head to heel with ulcers. I am not easily affected, but this disgusting sight thus suddenly presented to my view, turned me sick, and I was glad to be near home. No city in Italy contains so many miserable beggars, and no town in the world so many blind. This is, I think, to be attributed to constant exposure, want, and the excessive use of ardent spirits. . . .

It is Sunday, and the inhabitants of the neighbouring villages have crowded into the town to hear mass. The men are well dressed in leather breeches and jackets, and most of them have shirts and stockings, and a manta thrown over their shoulder.

The women are neatly dressed, and look clean and healthy. Their dress consists of a shift, one or more petticoats of striped cotton stuff, and a shawl, which they throw gracefully over the shoulder, and which they are never without when in company. I have seen them washing and cooking, very much distressed to manage this part of their dress, but persevere in wearing it, notwithstanding the inconvenience it put them to. . . .

Strolling through the village, I stopped to speak to two ladies, who were standing at the door of one of the largest and neatest cottages. They invited me in, and seemed delighted to have an opportunity of asking about the fashions of other countries, and how the ladies dressed in the other America. They had on pearl necklaces, and dark striped calico dresses, which cost, they told me, two dollars and a half a yard, and which was certainly not worth half a dollar.

They rejoiced with exceeding great joy at the independence of the country—"Now, that we are not governed by the *gachupines*,[12] we shall be supplied with handsome stuffs at a cheap rate." From a better motive, no doubt, the ladies of New Spain have always favoured the cause of independence. I have, too, found them every where republicans.[13] . . .

I have found the peasantry of this country, both Indians and castes, an amiable and a kind people, possessing the utmost good nature, and great natural politeness. I have never seen in the country, any one of them make use of a vulgar gesture, nor heard a harsh or even an unkind word pass between them. When drunk, they are ungovernable, and are savage and brutal in the extreme; but their drunken fits are "few, and far between;" and when sober, they are humble to their superiors, submissive and docile; and to each other kind and polite. They are, I think, a virtuous and an orderly people, attentive to all the ceremonies of their religion, and observant of their moral duties. Thefts are so uncommon among them, that our baggage was generally left under a shed; and assassinations are extremely rare, and when they do occur, may always be traced to drunkenness. I was surprised to find this state of morals existing among the peasantry of a country, so lately devastated by civil war, forming a strong contrast with the character of the lower orders of people in the capital, and in other large cities in the kingdom, immoral and vicious in the extreme.

Notes

1. Joel Roberts Poinsett, *Notes on Mexico Made in the Autumn of 1822 Accompanied by an Historical Sketch of the Revolution and Translations of Official Reports on the Present State of That Country with a Map by a Citizen of the United States* (Philadelphia: H. C. Carey and I. Lea, 1824), 40–41, 47–48, 72–73, 118–22, 141, 194, 198, 200–201.

2. Poinsett, *Notes on Mexico*, 43.

3. Ibid., 95–96.

4. On Poinsett's career, see, among others, José Fuentes Mares, *Poinsett: historia de una gran intriga* (Mexico City: Editorial Jus, 1951); Dorothy Martha Parton, *The Diplomatic Career of Joel Roberts Poinsett* (Washington: Catholic University of America, 1934); and J. Fred Rippy, *Joel Poinsett, Versatile American* (Durham, NC: Duke University Press, 1935).

5. The word is used here in the sense of "high society" (*buena sociedad, gente bien*).

6. Local boss.

7. A much less favorable description than von Humboldt's, one that does not credit the indigenous Mexicans with having achieved a high level of civilization before the Conquest.

8. A *huachinango* is a red snapper. In colloquial Spanish, the "g" and "h" in this word are freely substituted. This is also the word Cubans used to refer to Mexicans, and it is the likely origin of the word "chilango," a derogatory term for inhabitants of the capital.

9. Literally, "lepers," meaning "untouchables."

10. How different would Poinsett's judgment be today, when Charleston, just like Mexico City, has a visible population of homeless people?

11. Similar class of urban poor in southern Italy.

12. Spaniards.

13. The word "republican" is used here in the original sense: for popular sovereignty and against monarchy.

3 Life in a Convent

Fanny Calderón de la Barca[1]

Fanny Calderón de la Barca's Life in Mexico *trails only von Humboldt's treatise as the most influential foreign firsthand account on Mexico. The author arrived at a chaotic time: a time when caudillos such as Antonio López de Santa Anna contested for national authority, governments changed every several months, and rural banditry was widespread. Her comments on these problems shaped the perceptions of other visitors long after the publication of her volume. They also led to widespread condemnation of her work among Mexico City's upper crust. Calderón does not mince words as regards the corrupt and selfish elite. Although she deleted the names of most of those individuals she mentions in her book, many influential Mexicans were not pleased about harsh criticism coming from a foreigner, let alone a woman. Thus,* Life in Mexico *did not appear in Spanish until 1920.[2] The following excerpt on life in a Mexican convent is included for its fundamental critique of the Catholic Church and elite social mores. It is also a unique portrayal of the lives of elite women in the mid-nineteenth century.[3]*

The fifth child of a distinguished Scottish lawyer, Frances Erskine Inglis (1804–1882) was born in Edinburgh. After her father declared bankruptcy, he moved his family to Normandy, where he died two years later. In 1831, her mother took what remained of her family to Boston, where the Inglis daughters earned their keep as schoolmistresses. In 1838, Fanny married the Spanish minister to the United States, the native Argentine Angel Calderón de la Barca. The following year, Angel was named minister to Mexico, where the couple lived more than two years. In 1843, Fanny published Life in Mexico *after her return to Madrid. Impressionistic and personal, this book contains edited versions of her private letters—letters that were probably intended for publication from the beginning. Written over two years, her work reveals a deepening engagement with Mexico. Therefore, her book begins as a travel account and ends as a sojourner account, and it reveals the author's incipient acculturation.*

Accordingly, on Sunday afternoon, we drove to the Encarnación, the most splendid and richest convent in Mexico,[4] excepting perhaps La Concepción. If it were in any other country I might mention the surpassing beauty of the evening, but as—except in the rainy season, which has not yet begun—the evenings are always beautiful, the weather leaves no room for description. The sky always blue, the air always soft, the flowers always blossoming, the birds always singing. . . .

We descended at the convent gate, were admitted by the portress, and were received by several nuns, their faces closely covered with a double crape veil. We were then led into a spacious ballroom, hung with handsome lustres, and adorned with various virgins and saints magnificently dressed. Here the eldest, a very dignified old lady. . . proceeded to inform us that the Archbishop had, in person, given orders for our reception and that they were prepared to show us the whole establishment.

The dress is a long robe of very fine white cassimere,[5] a thick black crape veil, and long rosary. The dress of the novices is the same, only that the veil is white. For the first half-hour or so, I fancied that along with their politeness was mingled a good deal of restraint, caused perhaps by the presence of a foreigner, and especially of an Englishwoman. My companions they knew well, the *Señorita* having even passed some months there. However this may have been, the feeling seemed gradually to wear away. Kindness or curiosity triumphed; their questions became unceasing; and before the visit was concluded I was addressed as "*mi vida*," "my life," by the whole establishment. Where was I born? Where had I lived? What convents had I seen? Which did I prefer, the convents in France or those in Mexico? Which were largest? Which had the best garden? &c., &c. Fortunately I could, with truth, give the preference to their convent, as to spaciousness and magnificence, over any I ever saw.

The Mexican style of building is peculiarly advantageous for recluses, the great galleries and courts affording them a constant supply of fresh air—while the fountains sound so cheerfully, and the garden in this climate of perpetual spring affords them such a constant source of enjoyment all the year round, that one pities their secluded state much less here than in any other country.

This convent is in fact a palace. The garden, into which they led us first, is kept in good order, with its stone walks, stone benches, and an ever-playing and sparkling fountain. The trees were bending with fruit, and they pulled quantities of the most beautiful flowers for us: sweet peas and roses, with which all gardens here abound, carnations, jasmine, and heliotrope. It was a pretty picture to see them wandering about, or standing in groups in this high-walled garden, while the sun was setting behind the hills, and the noise of the city was completely excluded, everything breathing repose and contentment. Most of the halls in the convent are noble rooms. We . . . admired the extreme cleanness of everything, especially of the immense kitchen, which seems hallowed from the approach even of a particle of dust. This circumstance is partly accounted for by the fact that each nun has a servant, and some have two; for this is not one of the strictest orders. The convent is rich; each novice at her entrance pays five thousand dollars into the common stock. There are about thirty nuns and ten novices.

The prevailing sin in a convent generally seems to be pride, "The Pride that apes humility;"[6] and it is perhaps nearly inseparable from the conventual state. Set apart from the rest of the world they, from their little world, are too apt to look down with contempt which may be mingled with envy, or modified by pity, but must be unsuited to a true Christian spirit.[7]

The novices were presented to us—poor little entrapped things! Who really believe they will be let out at the end of the year if they should grow tired, as if they would ever be permitted to grow tired! The two eldest and most reverend ladies are sisters—thin, tall, and stately, with high noses, and remains of beauty. They have been in the convent since they were eight years old (which is remarkable, as sisters are rarely allowed to profess in the same establishment), and consider La Encarnación as a small piece of heaven upon earth. There were some handsome faces amongst them, and one whose expression and eyes were singularly lovely, but truth to say these were rather exceptions to the general rule.

Having visited the whole building, and admired one virgin's blue satin and pearls, and another's black velvet and diamonds, sleeping holy infants, saints, paintings, shrines, and confessionals . . . we came at length to a large hall decorated with paintings and furnished with antique high-backed arm-chairs, where a very elegant supper, lighted up and ornamented, greeted our astonished eyes: cakes, chocolate, ices, creams, custards, tarts, jellies, . . . orange and lemonade, and other profane dainties, ornamented with gilt paper cut into little flags, &c. I was placed under a holy family, in a chair that might have served for a pope; the *Señora*—and the *Señorita*—on either side. The elder nuns, in stately array, occupied the other armchairs, and looked like statues carved in stone. A young girl . . . brought in a little harp without pedals and, while we discussed cakes and ices, sung different ballads with a good deal of taste. The elder nuns helped us to everything, but tasted nothing themselves. The younger nuns and the novices were grouped upon a mat *á la Turque,*[8] and a more picturesque scene altogether one could scarcely see: the young novices with their white robes, white veils and black eyes; the severe and dignified *madres* with their long dresses and mournful-looking black veils and rosaries; the veiled figures occasionally flitting along corridors; ourselves in contrast, with our worldly dresses and coloured ribbons; and the great hall lighted by one immense lamp that hung from the ceiling. I felt transported three centuries back, and half afraid that the whole would flit away, and prove a mere vision, a waking dream. . . .

After supper, to try the organ we proceeded upstairs to the choir where the nuns attend public worship, and which looks down upon the handsome convent church. I was set down to a sonata of Mozart's, the servants blowing the bellows. It seems to me that I made more noise than music, for the organ is very old, perhaps as old as the convent, which dates three centuries back. However, the nuns were pleased and, after they had sung a hymn, we returned below. I was rather sorry to leave them, and felt as if I could have passed some time there very contentedly; but it was near nine o'clock, and we were obliged to take our departure; so, having been embraced very cordially by the whole community, we left the hospitable walls of the Encarnación.

[Six weeks later:] Some days ago, having received a message from my nun that a girl was about to take the veil in her convent, I went there about six o'clock. . . . I had been [in the church of the convent] but a little while when . . . I followed my guide back into the sacristy, where the future nun was seated beside her godmother, and in the midst of her friends and relations, about thirty in all. She was arrayed in pale blue satin, with diamonds, pearls, and a crown of flowers. She was literally smothered in . . . jewels; and her face was flushed as well it might be, for she had passed the day in taking leave of her friends at a fête they had given her, and had then, according to custom, been paraded through the town in all her finery. And now her last hour was at hand.[9]

When I came in she rose and embraced me with as much cordiality as if we had known each other for years. Beside her sat the *madrina*,[10] also in white satin and jewels; all the relations being likewise decked out in their finest array. The nun kept laughing every now and then in the most unnatural and hysterical manner, as I thought—apparently to impress us with the conviction of her perfect happiness—for it is a great point of honour amongst girls similarly situated to look as cheerful and gay as possible: the same feeling, though in a different degree, which induces the gallant highwayman to jest in the presence of the multitude when the hangman's cord is within an inch of his neck; the same which makes a gallant general, whose life is forfeited, command his men to fire on him; the same which makes the Hindu widow mount the funeral pile without a tear in her eye, or a sigh on her lips. If the robber were to be strangled in a corner of his dungeon; if the general were to be put to death privately in his own apartment; if the widow were to be burnt quietly on her own hearth; if the nun were to be secretly smuggled in at the convent gate like a bale of contraband goods—we might hear another tale.

This girl was very young, but by no means pretty. . . and perhaps knowledge of her own want of attractions may have caused the world to have few charms for her.

But José María cut short my train of reflections by requesting me to return to my seat before the crowd arrived, which I did forthwith. Shortly after, the church doors were thrown open, and a crowd burst in, everyone struggling to obtain the best seat. Musicians entered, carrying desks and music books, and placed themselves in two rows, on either side of the enclosure where I was. Then the organ struck up its solemn psalmody, and was followed by the gay music of the band. Rockets were let off outside the church, and, at the same time, the *madrina* and all the relations entered and knelt down in front of the grating which looks into the convent, but before which hung a dismal black curtain. I left my chair and knelt down beside the godmother.

Suddenly the curtain was withdrawn, and the picturesque beauty of the scene within baffles all description. Beside the altar, which was in a blaze of light, was a perfect mass of crimson and gold drapery—the walls, the antique chairs, the table before which the priests sat, all hung with the same splendid material. The bishop wore his superb mitre and robes of crimson and gold, the attendant priests also glittering in crimson and gold embroidery.

In contrast to these, five-and-twenty figures, entirely robed in black from head to foot, were ranged on each side of the room prostrate, their faces touching the ground, and in their hands immense lighted tapers. On the foreground was spread a purple carpet bordered round with a garland of freshly gathered flowers, roses and carnations and heliotrope, the only things that looked real and living in the whole scene. In the middle of this knelt the novice, still arrayed in her blue satin, white lace veil and jewels, and also with a great lighted taper in her hand.

The black nuns then rose and sang a hymn, every now and then falling on their faces and touching the floor with their foreheads. The whole looked like an incantation. . . . The novice was then raised from the ground and led to the feet of the bishop, who examined her as to her vocation, and gave her his blessing and once more the black curtain fell between us and them.

In the second act, she was lying prostrate on the floor, disrobed of her profane dress and covered over with a black cloth, while the black figures kneeling round her chanted a hymn. She was now dead to the world. The sunbeams had faded away, as if they would not look upon the scene, and all the light was concentrated in one great mass upon the convent group.

Again she was raised. All the blood had rushed into her face, and her attempt at a smile was truly painful. She then knelt before the bishop and received the benediction, with the sign of the cross, from a white band with the pastoral ring. She then went round alone to embrace all the dark phantoms as they stood motionless, and, as each dark shadow clasped her in its arms, it seemed like the dead welcoming a new arrival to the shades.

But I forget the sermon, which was delivered by a fat priest who elbowed his way with some difficulty through the crowd to the grating, panting and in a prodigious heat, and ensconced himself in a great arm chair close beside us. He assured her that she "had chosen the good part, which could not be taken away from her;" that she was now one of the elect, "chosen from amongst the wickedness and dangers of the world" (picked out like a plum from a pie). He mentioned with pity and contempt those who were "yet struggling in the great Babylon;" and compared their miserable fate with hers, the Bride of Christ, who, after suffering a few privations here during a short term of years, should be received at once into a kingdom of glory. The whole discourse was well calculated to rally her fainting spirits, if fainting they were, and to inspire us with a great disgust for ourselves.

When the sermon was concluded, the music again struck up. The heroine of the day came forward, and stood before the grating to take her last look of this wicked world. Down fell the black curtain. Up rose the relations, and I accompanied them into the sacristy. Here they coolly lighted their cigars, and very philosophically discoursed upon the exceeding good fortune of the new-made nun, and on her evident delight and satisfaction with her own situation. As we did not follow her behind the scenes, I could not give my opinion on this point. Shortly after, one of the gentlemen civilly led me to my carriage, and so it was. . . .

I had almost made up my mind to see no more such scenes—which, unlike *pulque* and bullfights, I dislike more and more upon trial[11]—when we received an invitation which it was not easy to refuse, but was the more painful to accept, being acquainted, though slightly, with the victim. . . .

Having gone out in the carriage to pay some visits, I suddenly recollected that it was the very morning of the day in which this young girl was to take the veil. . . . I accordingly called at the house, was shown upstairs, and to my horror found myself in the midst of . . . the relations of the family to the number of about a hundred persons. The bishop himself in his purple robes and amethysts, a number of priests, the father of the young lady in his general's uniform—she herself in purple velvet, with diamonds and pearls, and a crown of flowers, the corsage of her gown entirely covered with little bows of ribbon of diverse colours, which her friends had given her, each adding one, like stones thrown on a cairn in memory of the departed. She had also short sleeves and white satin shoes.

Being very handsome, with fine black eyes, good teeth, and fresh colour—and above all with the beauty of youth, for she is but eighteen—she was not disfigured even by this overloaded dress. Her mother, on the contrary—who . . . was pale and sad, her eyes almost extinguished with weeping—looked like a picture of misery in a ball dress. In the adjoining room long tables were laid out, on which servants were placing refreshments for the fête about to be given on this joyous occasion. . . .

I arrived at the hour appointed, and . . . found the morning party, with many additions, lingering over the dessert. There was some gaiety, but evidently forced. It reminded me of a marriage feast previous to the departure of the bride, who is about to be separated from her family for the first time. Yet how different in fact this banquet, where the mother and daughter met together for the last time on earth!

At stated periods, indeed, the mother may hear her daughter's voice speaking to her as from the depths of the tomb; but she may never more fold her in her arms, never more share in her joys or in her sorrows, or nurse her in sickness; and when her own last hour arrives, though but a few streets divide them, she may not give her dying blessing to the child who has been for so many years the pride of her eyes and heart.

I have seen no country where families are so knit together as in Mexico, where the affections are so concentrated, or where such devoted respect and obedience are shown by the married sons and daughters to their parents. . . . The greater therefore is the sacrifice which those parents make, who from religious motives devote their daughters to a conventual life.

____, however, was furious at the whole affair, which he said was entirely against the mother's consent, though that of the father had been obtained; and pointed out to me the confessor whose influence had brought it about. The girl herself was now very pale, but evidently resolved to conceal her agitation, and the mother seemed as if she could shed no more tears— quite exhausted with weeping. As the hour for the ceremony drew near, the whole party became more grave and sad, all but the priests who were smiling and talking together in groups. The girl was not still a moment. She kept walking hastily through the house, taking leave of the servants, and naming probably her last wishes about everything. She was followed by her younger sisters, all in tears.

But it struck six, and the priests intimated that it was time to move. She and her mother went downstairs alone, and entered the carriage which was to drive them through all the principal streets, to show the nun to the public according to custom, and to let them take their last look—they of her, and she of them.

As they got in, we all crowded to the balconies to see her take leave of her house, her aunts saying, "Yes, child, . . . take leave of your house, for you will never see it again!" Then came sobs from the sisters, and many of the gentlemen, ashamed of their emotion, hastily quitted the room. I hope, for the sake of humanity, I did not rightly interpret the look of constrained anguish which the poor girl threw from the window of the carriage at the home of her childhood.

They drove off, and the relations prepared to walk in procession to the church. . . . The church was very brilliantly illuminated, and as we entered the band was playing one of Strauss's waltzes! The crowd was so tremendous that we were nearly squeezed to a jelly in getting to our places. I was carried off my feet between two fat *señoras* in *mantillas*[12] and shaking diamond pendants, exactly as if I had been packed between two movable feather beds. They gave me, however, an excellent place, quite close to the grating, . . . that is to say, a place to kneel on. . . .

But at the discharge of fireworks outside the church the curtain was dropped, for this was the signal that the nun and her mother had arrived. An opening was made in the crowd as they passed into the church; and the girl, kneeling down, was questioned by the bishop, but I could not make out the dialogue which was carried on in a low voice. She then passed into the convent by a side door, and her mother, quite exhausted and nearly in hysterics, was supported through the crowd to a place beside us, in front of the grating. The music struck up; the curtain was again drawn aside. The scene was as striking here as in the convent of the Santa Teresa, but not so lugubrious. The nuns, all ranged around and carrying lighted tapers in their hands, were dressed in mantles of bright blue, with a gold plate on the left shoulder. Their faces, however, were covered with deep black veils. The girl, kneeling in front, and also bearing a heavy lighted taper, looked beautiful with her dark hair and rich dress, and the long black lashes resting on her glowing face. The churchmen near the illuminated and magnificently-decked altar formed, as usual, a brilliant background to the picture. The ceremony was the same as on the former occasion, but there was no sermon.

The most terrible thing to witness was the last, straining, anxious look which the mother gave her daughter through the grating. She had seen her child pressed to the arms of strangers, and welcomed to her new home. She was no longer hers. All the sweet ties of nature had been rudely severed, and she had been forced to consign her, in the very bloom of youth and beauty, at the very age in which she most required a mother's care, and when she had but just fulfilled the promise of her childhood, to a living tomb. Still, as long as the curtain had not fallen, she could gaze upon her, as upon one on whom, though dead, the coffin lid is not yet closed.

But while the new-made nun was in a blaze of light—and distinct on the foreground, so that we could mark each varying expression of her face—the crowd in the church, and the comparative faintness of the light probably made it difficult for her to distinguish her mother; for, knowing that the end was at hand, she looked anxiously and hurriedly into the church, without seeming able to fix her eyes on any particular object; while her mother seemed as if her eyes were glazed, so intently were they fixed upon her daughter.

Suddenly, and without any preparation, down fell the black curtain like a pall, and the sobs and tears of the family broke forth. One beautiful little child was carried out almost in fits. Water was brought to the poor mother; and at last, making our way with difficulty through the dense crowd, we got into the sacristy.

"I declare," said the Countess to me, wiping her eyes, "it is worse than a marriage!" I expressed my horror at the sacrifice of a girl so young, that she could not possibly have known her own mind. Almost all the ladies agreed with me, especially all who had daughters, but many of the old gentlemen were of a different opinion. The young men were decidedly of my way of thinking, but many young girls, who were conversing together, seemed rather to envy their friend—who had looked so pretty and graceful, and "so happy," and whose dress "suited her so well—and to have no objection to "go, and do likewise."

I went home, thinking by what law of God a child can thus be dragged from the mother who bore and bred her, and immured in a cloister for life, amongst strangers, to whom she has no tie, and towards whom she owes no duty. That a convent may be a blessed shelter from the calamities of life, a haven for the unprotected, a resting place for the weary, a safe and holy asylum, where a new family and kind friends await those whose natural ties are broken and whose early friends are gone, I am willing to admit; but it is not in the flower of youth that the warm heart should be consigned to the cold cloister. Let the young take their chance of sunshine or storm; the calm and shady retreat is for helpless and unprotected old age.

Notes

1. Fanny Calderón de la Barca, *Life in Mexico During a Residence of Two Years in That Country* (London: Chapman and Hall, 1843), 114–17, 154–62.

2. Howard T. Fisher and Marion Hall Fisher, "Introduction," in Fanny Calderón de la Barca, *Life in Mexico*, eds. Howard T. Fisher and Marion Hall Fisher (Garden City, NY: Doubleday & Co., 1966).

3. Calderón converted to Catholicism later on.

4. Refers here to Mexico City.

5. Cashmere.

6. Quoted from the Coleridge poem "The Devil's Thoughts."

7. An overgeneralization. Not all convents housed wealthy women only.

8. Seated in "Oriental" fashion, on the floor.

9. A dramatization that equates entry into the convent with death.

10. In this case, the sponsor of the taking of the veil.

11. A comment on the author's progressing adaptation to life in Mexico.

12. A variant of the veil, this lace garment in dark colors covered a woman's head and shoulders, and was kept in place by tortoise shell combs called *peinetas*.

4 With the Stars and Stripes in Mexico

William S. Henry[1]

This excerpt from William Seaton Henry's Campaign Sketches of the War with Mexico *contains the perspective of a lower-ranking officer in an invading army; a perspective unique in this volume. Like Calderón de la Barca, Henry did not go to Mexico by choice. Once there, however, he was determined to make his mission a success. In his war memoirs, the captain expresses loyalty to his army unit, criticism of members of Congress who do not share the military's resolve to pursue the war, and unswerving condemnation for the enemy. A Jacksonian Democrat, Henry expresses an abiding faith in the success of U.S. farmers; a success that, as he believes, could be repeated in territories to be annexed by the United States. He thus pairs one of von Humboldt's key themes—the potential of Mexican agriculture—with the Manifest Destiny ideal of extending the borders of the United States. Yet he is also wary of incorporating Mexicans into the Union, as he increasingly perceives that his own way of life is incompatible with that of the Mexicans. This excerpt is also interesting for its views on northeastern Mexico, an area that*

received few travelers in the nineteenth century, and for its comments on the impact of the U.S. invasion on Mexican consumer behavior.

The son of a prominent New York lawyer, Henry (1816–1851) was born in Albany, New York. He attended West Point and thereafter was assigned to the Third Infantry regiment. Beginning in April 1836, this regiment fought for the Texan cause in the war of secession from Mexico that resulted in the independence and subsequent incorporation of that state into the United States. In July 1845, the Third Infantry were the first of General Zachary Taylor's army to arrive at Corpus Christi—the prelude to war a year later, during which Henry participated in the march to the Rio Grande, and inland toward Monterrey. His letters home were published in a New York City newspaper and, in revised form, as Campaign Sketches of the War with Mexico *(1847).[2]*

The Mexicans say there has been a special interposition of Divine Providence in our favor, causing the river to rise so that we can transport our troops and supplies to Camargo without any trouble. If they really think so, the omen must be anything but favorable to their cause. It certainly never was intended this lovely land, rich in every production, with a climate that exceeds anything the imagination can conceive of, should remain in the hands of an ignorant and degenerate race. The finger of Fate points, if not to their eventual extinction, to the time when they will cease to be owners, and when the Anglo-American race will rule with republican simplicity and justice, a land literally "flowing with milk and honey;" who will, by their superior mental, if not physical abilities—by their energy and go-ahead-a-tiveness, which no sufferings or privations can retard, which shines alike in the frozen regions of the North and under the burning sun of the South, render available the surprising fertility of the soil, its immense mineral wealth, and populate the country with a race of men who will prove the infinite goodness of our Maker in creating nothing but what is for use and some good purpose.[3]

No part of Texas surpasses in fertility, or equals in salubrity, the Valley of the Rio Grande. The river courses its way from the mountains through a varied climate, which will produce anything, from wheat to sugar and cotton. Nothing can exceed the rich growth of vines. The melon flourishes, and our camp is daily supplied with fine watermelons. This region of country is bound to be settled very rapidly; if nothing else points it out as a desirable location, the fact of the Rio Grande being really a navigable stream is sufficient. In point of health, few regions can surpass it. There are no causes for disease; there are no swamps which, in the heat of summer, throw out their poisonous miasma; the banks are high, and the country preserves that character to the Colorado. Let this boundary be settled, and there will be a tide of emigration to this favored region rarely equaled. If some of our northern farmers would settle here, they could make one flower garden of the river banks, from its source to its mouth. Cultivation can be carried out by white labor, I think, beyond a doubt. No summer climate can exceed it in loveliness; the everlasting breeze deprives the sun of much of its heat. Such evenings! Such a morn! Young people should come here to make love; the old should emigrate and rejuvenate themselves. To the former I say, the moon shines with such bewitching sweetness, no matter how determined they may be to live and die maids, they will find it impossible to resist "the little god:"[4] to the latter, some of the romance of their early days will be renewed, and their frames invigorated by the ocean breeze, which comes every evening laden with coolness and health. . . .

August 7 [1846]. . . . We marched eighteen miles, and encamped at a ranch called Cayetana. Shortly after we arrived, a number of pack-mules came in, laden with fruit from Saltillo. It was packed in crates, and intended for the Matamoros market. There were apples, pears, pomegranates, quinces, and grapes; the latter good, the rest miserable. Being picked green, and exposed for eleven days to the intense heat, they had lost all their flavor. The men bought them in great quantities, and at exorbitant prices. I had a long conversation with the head man of the train; he appeared quite intelligent, and very frank, answering promptly all my questions. Being direct from Monterrey, he had to answer not a few regarding the defenses of the city, troops, &c. He says there are two thousand men at Monterrey, under General [Ignacio] Mejía, and none at Saltillo or San Luis Potosí; that they are daily looking for our arrival via Camargo, and that there will be no fight.

The water at this camp is miserable—nothing more than a hog-wallow. Water, no doubt, of the kind could be obtained by digging; but these miscreatures are too lazy for that. It is a great drawback to any thing like comfort. The inhabitants of the *ranchos*[5] are particular in their inquiries whether the troops are regulars or volunteers. Some of the disgraceful rows, proceeding from a few disorganizers among the latter, have been "bruited" far and wide, establishing for that arm a reputation certainly not to be envied. The inhabitants of this ranch say the Mexicans in their retreat, took every thing they could lay their hands upon, without paying for it. How different is our course of conduct. Here we are, invading an enemy's country as conquerors, and yet levy not one cent; buy everything; not only buy, but pay the most exorbitant prices. I sometimes doubt the good effects of such liberality. Will it not be their interest to continue a war which deprives them of nothing, but adds to their purses? However, we will always have the consolation of knowing we have brought no distress upon the poor.[6]

On the 28th [of August] we received something tangible from the city of Mexico. The report of the civil revolution is confirmed. [President Mariano] Paredes is a prisoner, [Valentín] Gómez Farías declared provisional president;[7] Santa Anna invited to return, and probably by this time in the country. Santa Anna! Through what a strange, up-hill, down-hill series of events has he not passed? Twice president by means of his military popularity; banished from his country, and every thing connected with his name scorned and trampled upon, he lives to see himself recalled by the same fickle beings, placed at the head of their army, and will no doubt re-ascend the presidential chair! Fate! What hast though yet in store for him who is as faithless to his promises as he is devoid of honor? . . .

[October] The question often arises with us, are we to have peace or war at the end of the armistice? By a great majority it is deemed folly to prosecute it in this quarter. Peace, not territory, is certainly the aim of our government; this cannot be obtained by slightly wounding the extremities of the body; we have not touched the heart, nor can we by this route. Until there is a government established which has the power to treat, I do not see that we are any nearer the settlement of our difficulties than previous to the battles of the 8th and 9th of May. We may go on and expend millions, and sacrifice the lives of thousands, without any good result. It strikes me an advance from this point can have no effect upon the settlement. Our better plan is to take Tampico, fortify and keep possession of the Sierra Madre and the Valley of the Rio Grande, until they come to terms. Let them come take it, if they can. If the war is to be prosecuted, let Veracruz be taken, and march directly upon the capital, batter its walls down, and see if some sense cannot be battered into the people. The victories on this frontier, as honorable and glorious as they have been to our army, are mere flashes in the pan as regards the question of peace. The humane and liberal policy pursued by the government in the prosecution of war has a tendency to prolong it. It is the first war of which I ever heard which was an actual benefit to the enemy. Wherever we go, we pay for what we use at two or three times the usual price of the country, and both their civil and religious rights and property are protected. What more prosperous times can they desire? Their cry is, "Come along, gentlemen! Very glad to see you! Come from city to city; you spend your money freely—put us to very little inconvenience, and, really, times are first rate!" I must confess I am tired of this work, and long to see an honorable peace.

The wounded are doing very well—as well as they can with the few comforts and conveniences our medical department is enabled to supply. Nothing can exceed the devotion of our medical officers; they are literally fatigued to death. There was culpable negligence somewhere in not sending more medical officers into the field, but I presume the government, hugging unto themselves the chance of peace, thought there would be no more necessity for their services. The number was reduced so low immediately after the battle [of Monterrey], that one surgeon attended two regiments, four being the usual number in peace.

The great and valiant General [Pedro] Ampudia,[8] after reaching Saltillo, issued his proclamation explaining the fall of Monterrey. To condense matters, he states, on the 21st he repulsed us with the loss of fifteen hundred; on the 22nd the Bishop's Palace fell, but not without great resistance; that, being scarce of ammunition and provisions, a conference was held on the 24th with the enemy, and such terms were made by which they saved their honor, and marched out with their arms; that General Santa Anna was coming, and then we would see who would be the conquerors. Was there ever such stuff and such lies? Mexican to the last. If you were to exterminate a whole army but the general, he would issue a bulletin claiming a victory. If these bulletins are salve to their wounded feelings, they are welcome to write and publish quires. Our loss of "fifteen hundred" is only magnified ten times our loss in the three days' fight. Their deficiency of ammunition is ridiculous. We found cords of it; but they may have thought a month's supply a deficiency. I hope they will always continue thinking so as long as they have that amount of "materiel" to present us with even at the cannon's mouth.

General Santa Anna arrived at Veracruz on the 16th of August. There cannot be a moment's doubt that our government, in permitting his return to the country, believed that his best exertions would be used to effect a reconciliation. All those hopes were immediately crushed upon the promulgation of his proclamation to the people the same day of his arrival. It spoke

war to the knife. He was immediately placed in command of the army...
while he repaired to the tented field in his dream of winning fresh laurels,
and driving the barbarians beyond the Sabine. He infused fresh energy and
life into the people. With an activity characteristic of the man, he repaired to
San Luis Potosí and strained every nerve for the purpose of collecting and
disciplining a large army. On the 11th of October we heard he had arrived at
San Luis with eight hundred men, and that Ampudia had left Saltillo to join
him. Ampudia was ordered to Mexico to explain the fall of Monterrey. We all
think Saltillo will fall into our hands without a blow. General Ampudia
decided upon fortifying the place, and the citizens would not permit it. They
very justly told him he had spent much time and money in fortifying
Monterrey, a city whose natural defenses were much superior to theirs and
had failed to hold it, and they had no idea of having their property destroyed;
a very just conclusion. Taking Saltillo, we have the key to this whole valley;
we are then over three hundred miles from San Luis Potosí, the march to
which is difficult and part of the way over a desert. Having Saltillo, taking
Monclova and Tampico, we can quietly settle down in as lovely a country as
the sun ever shone upon, and tell Mexico to come on. Tell her we have taken
enough to remunerate us for the expenses of the war, and will keep it if she
does not grant us peace by a certain day; then import your families, give
them the land for a mere song, and before one could realize it this valley
would be teeming with an American population. We do not want the valley,
nor would I, if it can be prevented, keep it; but I certainly would not put our
government to any more expense than simply holding it, which, compared
to an onward movement, would be nothing. From what we have seen, I question the feasibility of "dictating a peace at the cannon's mouth;" they are a
stubborn, stiff-necked race: and I think the appearance of emigrants determined to settle this valuable part of her domain would have more effect
upon her than hard knocks. . . .

The more I ride over this region, the more I am struck with its fertility.
Field after field of the finest . . . sugar cane stretch out for miles and miles. All
this luxuriance is the spontaneous gift of nature; compared with ours, there
is really no cultivation. Their ground is broken up by a primitive wooden
plow, made of the crotched limb of a tree, shod with iron: the seed is barely
stuck in, and if it gets one hoeing, it is about all; and yet, with all this neglect,
they make magnificent crops. What would not the land produce by our
preparation, and our care and attention during the early growth of the plant?

A most interesting incident connected with the fall of Monterrey I have nearly forgotten to record. It is stated, and generally believed, that a company of Lancers was commanded by a woman. Her name was Dos Amades. Seized with a patriotic spirit, she unsexed[9] herself, and dressed in the full suit of a captain of Lancers; she desired to be led against the foe, and swore she would never yield until the "northern barbarians" were driven from her native land, or until she shed her last drop of blood in defense of her native country. Previous to our attack, she was paraded before the troops, and greatly excited and augmented their courage. She harangued them, and desired to be posted at that spot where the first shot would fall and where the thickest of the battle should rage. It is reported that on the 21st she led the charge of Lancers which proved fatal to some of our command. . . . There's an example of heroism worthy the day of old! It has remained for Mexico to produce a second Joan d'Arc, but not, like her, successful. She is reported to have been a daughter of one of the former governors of Nuevo León, and after the battle retired to the walks of private life.

On one of my late visits to [Monterrey] I paid an interesting one to a children's (female) school. The school-mistress was a respectable lady; the children had finished their recitations, and were actively engaged embroidering. There were some beautiful creatures among them, and with one bright-eyed little one I should most certainly have had a frolic had I been master of her language. There are several schools in the city, but education is wholly confined to the children of the higher class. The poor are kept in utter ignorance, and under a blind obedience to their priests. Their whole labor is for the Church; a child cannot be christened, a couple married, the dead buried, without extortionate fees for the Church. The priests are our bitterest enemies and opposers, and are the main-spring of the war.

Notes

1. William S. Henry, *Campaign Sketches of the War with Mexico* (New York: Harper and Brothers, 1847), 120–22, 136–37, 160–61, 225–29, 233–34, 241–42.
2. Thomas O. Munnerlyn, "Henry, William Seaton," *Handbook of Texas Online*, *http://www.tsha.utexas.edu/handbook/online/articles/view/HH/fhe39.html* [accessed June 12, 2003].

3. A concise statement of the ideology of Manifest Destiny that was central to U.S. territorial expansion.

4. Eros, the Greek god of love.

5. Small family farms.

6. A very high-minded statement that belittles the brutality of the occupation.

7. Valentín Gómez Farías was one of the most influential Liberals in early republican Mexico.

8. General in charge of repelling the advance of Taylor's army.

9. Behaving in a way that breaches gender stereotypes.

5 A View of Tropical Veracruz

Carl Christian Sartorius[1]

Mexiko: Landschaftsbilder *(translated as Mexico: Landscape and Popular Sketches) by Carl Christian Sartorius is based on the author's life experience as a German plantation owner in the tropical regions of Veracruz. A permanent immigrant, Sartorius retained prejudices shared by many foreign observers. But he acquired a personal stake in the country that precludes Poinsett or Calderón's pessimistic outlook. Like many Mexican Liberals of his day, Sartorius disdained the moral and intellectual faculties of the indigenous and mestizo population, and desired to "improve" his adopted country by "whitening" it through German immigration. Written in a lively, engaging style, his book reads like an invitation to come to Mexico.[2] The following excerpt recalls Sartorius's immediate reaction to the tropics, where he first came into contact with indigenous Mexicans. It shows the fascination of a Romantic immigrant with a verdant, exotic landscape, and his harsh condemnation of what he thought of as primitive people who made the best use of their environment. The beautiful illustrations by the engraver*

Moritz Rugendas highlight this romanticized image of Mexico. The selection is a good example of the climatic determinism of many nineteenth-century observers. Sartorius concludes that what he sees as the "indolence" of the indigenous population is a product of a paradisiacal environment. In spoiling its inhabitants by its bounty, he believes, the tropics offer scant incentive to the type of work and social organization that has made his native Europe the master of the globe.

Sartorius (1796–1872) was born in Gundernhausen in the state of Hesse. As a university student, he took part in the student movement that had begun during the Napoleonic occupation of 1807–1814. Like many other men who joined this movement, Sartorius joined a Burschenschaft *(fencing fraternity) dedicated to forging a united and democratic Germany out of the patchwork of small states dominated by the authoritarian monarchies of Austria and Prussia. In 1818, he had just started a high school teaching position when he was suspended from his job after a crackdown on democratic societies throughout Germany. Six years later, he decided to accompany a friend and fellow democrat to Veracruz, where the two Germans began a small mining operation. Shortly thereafter, Sartorius acquired a sugar plantation. Successful as a sugar cane grower, he founded a small German "colony" in the tropics. He died on his hacienda, and his descendants still live in Mexico today.[3]*

On a fresh October morning we are roused by an unusual bustle on deck; the cry of "Land" is heard, and our destination is before us. To the left, on the level shore, is the port of Veracruz and its fort San Juan de Ulúa. Dark forests, gradually sloping upwards, enclose the sandy shore to the west; then follow several mountain-terraces, one commanding the other, till at length, towering above all, the magnificent cones and indented summits of the dark blue Andes seem to support the clear vault of heaven. Majestically rearing their heads over their fellows, are the snowy summits of the Peak of Orizaba, glowing with the purple rays of the rising sun, and the wild jagged crater of Perote. From the latter the mountains branch off northwards to the sea, terminating in an abrupt rocky wall on the shores of the Gulf, whilst to the south, the Cordilleras extend in a huge semicircle in the distant horizon.

Regarded as a whole, the coast has the same features, whether we trace it to the south or north. Everywhere we find a narrow level tract of coast, not many miles in width, then a gradual ascent by gently inclining slopes to the spurs of the mountains, and finally to the highlands, which, almost uninterrupted, extend for many hundred miles from north to south, nearly parallel with the coast.

The ship has cast anchor between the fort and the town; a few minutes later we are on the quay. Everything is strange here, the language, dress and complexion of the inhabitants, and the town, with its Andalusian-Moorish trappings. Here we behold a group of negroes and mulattoes gesticulating in the most passionate manner, there the copper-coloured Indian silently offering his fruit for sale; the clearer-skinned Mestins[4] urges forward his horse, or trots on an ass after his well-laden mules, whilst the European or Creole dandy, puffing his cigar, examines the new arrivals. On one side the Paris fashions, on the other the lightest possible clothing, consisting of a broad-brimmed straw-hat, coloured or white shirt and ample trousers. The fair sex exhibits the same contrast: on one hand the greatest luxury, on the other half naked. What Northman can fail to be astonished at sight of the fat negress there, who seated comfortably at the door of her house, with a short clay-pipe in her mouth, caresses her perfectly naked offspring, clinging to and clambering about her like a very ape.[5] Who would not cast a glance after that troop of Mestins girls, all mounted, with fluttering ribands in their straw hats, as smoking their cigarettes, they jest with their brown admirer, who seated on his long-eared steed, thrums his *jarana*,[6] and sings jocular songs. The women and girls of the lower classes wear large four-cornered wrappers, much longer than broad, of striped cotton, which covers the head and is folded across the shoulders.[7]

These clothes are worn throughout the whole country; they are becoming, and the brown beauties know well how to coquet with them. No gown . . . covers the upper part of the body; nothing is worn save the fine chemise often embroidered and trimmed with lace, but scarcely sufficing to conceal the shape. From the hips to the feet however they wear a wide petticoat of bright calico or muslin, sometimes with a white under-petticoat, whilst the feet, innocent of stockings, are encased in light silk shoes. The Mexican women have a pretty foot; they are aware of it, and do not disfigure it with wooden shoes or similar elephantine pedestals, like the peasant-women of continental Europe. The dress of the wealthy Creole ladies is pretty, much the same as with Europeans, being regulated by the newest Paris fashions. For church-going, nevertheless, they adhere to the ancient Spanish black *mantilla*, falling from the head over the shoulders, and half way down the arms.

In all the originally Spanish colonies, the towns resemble those of the mother country. Straight streets with raised foot-pavements, massive stone houses with flat roofs, churches in the Italian architectural style of the seventeenth century, with low towers and high cupolas, covered for the most part with parti-coloured shining tiles, meet the eye. The interior of the houses is decidedly Moorish. You enter through an arched gateway into the first court, surrounded by a colonnade, which is repeated in the upper stories. The doors and windows of the apartments all open on this court. In some districts there is a pretty fountain in the centre, round which flowering plants are grouped in large vases. A second court is usually surrounded by the servants' offices, kitchen, stables etc. In Veracruz there are no fountains, the flat sandy soil rendering it impossible; good water for drinking is not even to be had (that from a pond near the town is bad), except that which the tropical storms afford, and which is collected in large stone cisterns.

A strange impression is made by the numerous black vultures, seated in long rows on the buildings, or disputing in the streets with the lean dogs for the refuse of the kitchens. Their exterior is not precisely attractive, but these harmless animals, unwearied in performing the duty of scavengers, prevent the noxious effects that must otherwise arise from the exhalations of so much putrefying animal and vegetable matter, which the people are too idle to remove. From the Mississippi to the La Plata Stream these *zopilotes* or *gallinazos*[8] are of incalculable benefit in the warm countries they frequent; they cannot fail to strike the European immediately.

Among the first impressions made by Veracruz may also be mentioned the shrub-less downs, which environ the town and give it a very dull appearance from the land side. The Gulf Stream coming from Yucatán, proceeds along the whole coast, and conveys the sand towards the shore; the waves wash it on to the flat beach, where the sun quickly dries it, enabling the impetuous north-wind in winter to waft it up to the dreary hills, as we now see them. Nature's indefatigable laboratory must however not be misappreciated. In the rainy season the moistened sand receives so much consistency, that the floating seeds of many a plant can germinate. The dense shade of the climbing plants renders the ground firm, the falling leaves form a thin layer of virgin mould, enabling shrubs to take root, and subsequently affording sufficient nourishment for trees.

On the Mexican shore of the Gulf it is not difficult to observe, that the land constantly receives accessions; the succession of downs and the increase of vegetation may be easily distinguished, accordingly as they recede from the sea. The incessant action of the Gulf Stream maintains the supply of sand, the mouths of the brooks and rivers are raised by it, and the overflowing waters convey the rich soil of the mountains to the lowlands. Although this only takes place occasionally, at the period of the heaviest equinoctial rains, it may nevertheless easily be comprehended why the plains are inexhaustibly fertile, and equally so, why the beds of the rivers gradually rise and produce a corresponding general rise in the lowlands. This creative agency of nature is carried on with infinite slowness, but still so that the result of the labour of three centuries can be distinctly proved; for, to adduce an example, ranges of hills now lie round Veracruz, where in the sixteenth century was a tolerably extensive plain.

Whoever is not detained on the coast by commercial interests, leaves it as soon as possible; for the scorching sun, as everywhere in the tropics calls forth treacherous miasma and relaxes the whole system. The fever season is properly speaking only in the summer months, when heat and moisture operate conjointly. Even at this period, the European paying a short visit to the coast has nothing to fear, provided he diets himself, and keeps in the shade during the midday heat. Altogether indeed the Mexican coast is far less unhealthy than the more northerly situated plains of the Mississippi and Lower Arkansas. One has also the great advantage that higher regions may be arrived at in a few hours, where the tropical atmosphere can be breathed with impunity.

After a ride of three hours we come to the river Antigua, which miserably struggling through layers of sand, reluctantly espouses the ocean. Here the abovementioned appearance is very distinct; we see the bar. . . . which the Gulf Stream deposits along the coast, necessarily sanding up the mouths of all the streams. Ascending the river, we are soon shaded by the densest vegetation, . . . Beware of handling unknown plants! The elegant leaves of [several tropical plants] . . . do not look as if they would burn the incautious hands that approached them; and yet this is often the case. . . .

Let us pause for an instant at a hut and refresh ourselves with some fruit; for the sun is high, and the road hot and dusty. How slight a shelter suffices for these natives of the tropics! A slanting roof covered with palm-leaves rests on piles driven into the ground. Beams, rafters and laths are neither mortised nor nailed, but everything is fastened with bindweed and baste. The walls are bamboo stems bound together, whilst the doors and shutters are of similar materials. The bench, too, is of bamboo staves, also the bedstead, and a sort of repository for a few pots and plates. A fire burns day and night in the middle of the hut, where a pot with beans (*frijoles*) slowly simmers; the stones for crushing the maize stand on one side. The brown inhabitant, of African origin, gladly sells his bananas, pine-apples and oranges, and also brings a draught of water from the river, or perhaps a calabash, with palm-wine, which is admirable for quenching the thirst. . . . A little field of maize near the hut, some dozen of banana stalks, a few fruit trees, . . . constitute all the farming. Hard labour is not approved of by the dweller on the coast, and over-bounteous nature seconds the innate inclination of the *jarocho*.[9] The river supplies him with fish and turtle, the forest with sufficient game ready money is easily obtained by charcoal-burning, which is much in requisition at Veracruz. A few donkeys are included in the family, as without them there would be little comfort. The *jarocho* . . . would be ashamed to carry a *cántaro*[10] of water on his back, although the river is scarcely fifty paces distant from his house; he ties his two large jars together, hangs them across Dapple's back, mounts behind, and steers for the stream. Arrived there, he rides so far in to the water, that the jars are filled of themselves, so that he has not even the trouble of dismounting. If fuel is wanting, the man rides out, to seek for a dry tree, already blown down by the wind, and which is precisely thick enough to be conveyed by his beast. By means of a strap he fastens the end of the wood to the horse's tail, which must now drag the wood, and of course carry his master besides. Arrived at the hut, the log is not cleft, but is passed in at the open door to the fire, and when the end is consumed it is gradually shoved in further, until at the expiration of some days, the house will hold it. This is the tropical *savoir faire*.[11] . . .

An impartial consideration and observation of the Indians during many years forced me to the conclusion that, according to their bodily organization, they are incapable of so high a degree of intellectual development as the Caucasian race. Not that they are deficient in keenness of perception, in distinctness of apprehension, or faculty of combination: but they want the broad and lofty forehead, they are devoid of that ideality which is the inheritance of a higher nervous development, of that subtle element which in Asia and Europe for thousands of years have put forth the finest blossoms of human cultivation. What has the American race done, under the most favourable circumstances of soil and climate in their vast continent? In the north and south, from time immemorial, hunting-tribes wandered hither and thither, like the beasts of prey, through the prairies and forests, opposed to all civilisation, mutually destroying each other, confined to a most narrow circle of the simplest religious ideas, their knowledge of art limited to producing the most indispensable weapons or utensils. On either side of the equator, in Peru and Mexico, where a higher degree of civilisation was developed, where the wandering tribes were rendered stationary by agriculture, and social union had procured a footing for intellectual cultivation: even there the culminating point of civilisation never attained to the practice of humanity. The religious systems of the Incas and Aztecs, their knowledge of astronomy, works of art, and mechanical labours for the purposes of everyday life, are the result of their powers of understanding, of the undeniable imitative talents of the whole race, of their aptitude and artistic skill;[12] but the loftier ideal genius, the speculating Pallas Athene of the Greeks, and the beautifying Charis are wanting. . . .

I shall . . . continue to speak of the Indians as they are now, as they have appeared to me in every-day life. Willingly do I acknowledge their aptitude in learning, and even the children exhibit much handiness, and practical sense. Intellectual creation is not the distinguishing feature of their race; they have little imagination, but diligence and perseverance. The educated Indians, and there are many who devote themselves to jurisprudence and theology, learn their respective sciences, but never get beyond their compendium. We find in them the talent of imitation and comparison, perhaps humour and wit, but no poetry.

The character of the tribes that I had the opportunity of becoming acquainted with, is in general not frank and open, but close, distrustful, and calculating. The Indian does not merely erect this bulwark against the members of another tribe or against the posterity of his oppressors, which would he natural enough; but also against his own people. It lies in his language, his manners, and his history. Thus the salutations of the Indians among themselves, especially of the women, are a long rigmarole of wishes and enquiries after health, which are repeated monotonously and unsympathisingly on both sides, often without looking at each other, or even stopping. The Indian who is desirous of obtaining something of another, never asks for it directly, or without beating about; first he makes a small present, praises this or that, and at last brings forth his wish. If an Indian has a request to make of the judge or burgomaster[13] of his village, who, like himself, is an Indian, and perhaps a relation, even though perfectly justified in making his demand, be first sends an intimate friend with a bottle of brandy or a fat hen . . . in order to ensure the request a good reception. Deputations often came to me from Indian villages, to ask my advice about their local affairs; they always consisted of ten or twelve persons, fearing that one deputy would seek to profit by the matter in some way. The whole train then came into my room, one after the other, a grand dignitary or speaker at the head, each with a present in his hand.

The leader commenced complimenting me with many bows, saying: "Good day, father, how are you? How is our mother, your lady, and the children? See, we come to bring you a trifle, it is little, for we are poor, but you must take the will for the deed." Now the whole troop approach with fowls, eggs, and diverse fruits. It is useless to refuse: "You know my sons, I can't suffer this! If I can be of use to you, I serve you with pleasure. Keep your gifts, and say what you desire."—"Nay, father, we will not speak if you reject these trifles, etc." This ceremony being over, and the right honourable embassy invited to sit, the elders of the community squat on the floor in a semicircle, though there is no lack of chairs; only the spokesman stands erect, and in a carefully digested speech gives utterance to his wishes, the suite gravely nodding their heads from time to time, as if to lay more stress on the words. In their negotiations they are true diplomatists, and are fond of speaking ambiguously, in order to be able subsequently to interpret to their own advantage. In transactions with them, one must be careful to have all the conditions precisely specified.

If after a transaction of the kind, you offer them a glass of rum, every face beams, and significant glances are exchanged; they prefer drinking it outside the door, and he who returns with the empty glass certainly knows how to express his gratitude in such a way as to ensure a further supply of the nectar. If their character be displayed in matters of this kind, it becomes still more evident in numerous little features. The language itself abounds in ambiguous expressions, which they employ in order not to pronounce themselves too definitively. I have heard from priests, who spoke the Aztec tongue with great fluency, that they frequently were incapable of understanding the sense of a confession, as the penitent spoke in riddles and metaphors. An Indian can seldom prevail on himself to tell a stranger his name; and usually gives a false one, lest he should be compromised.[14]. . .

The Indian's dwelling is in keeping with his simple person. In the warmer, well-wooded regions he generally builds his hut of wood. Unhewn logs support the beams and roof, are driven into the ground, and creeping plants which twine around them, supply the place of frame-work. Straw or palm-leaves constitute the roofing; the walls are made of sticks of bamboo, or slender stakes which afford the light free ingress to the interior. The roof on one side is commonly prolonged into a porch, supported upon posts. This main building is ordinarily about twenty five feet long, and fifteen wide, without partitions within. A smaller one is often joined to this to answer the purposes of kitchen. . . .

Inside the hut, upon a floor of earth just as nature formed it, burns day and night the sacred fire of the domestic hearth. Near it, stand . . . a flat and a cylindrical stone for crushing the maize, and the earthen pan *comal* for baking the maize bread. A few unglazed earthen pots and dishes, a large water pitcher, a drinking cup and dipper of gourd-shell constitute the whole wealth of the Indian's cottage, a few rude carvings, representing saints, the decoration. Neither table nor benches cumber the room within, mats of rushes or palm leaves answer both for seat and table. They serve as beds too for their rest at night, and for their final rest in the grave.

The utensils of the man, as a mattock and a hoe, together with a few strings and nets, hang upon the wall, and close by, the weaving apparatus of the women, consisting only of a few simple rods. A number of baskets of woven palm-leaves suspended from the beams above by grass-cordage, contain the scanty provisions of all kinds, salt, beans, rice, eggs, cotton, soap etc. These baskets take the place of chests and cupboards, and are thus hung aloft to protect the contents from the inroads of dogs, ants and children. Upon a longer line hangs a contrivance somewhat larger, perhaps three feet long by two wide, of twigs bound together, in construction similar to the traps in which boys catch titmice. The inside is covered with a piece of matting. Its purpose does not long remain a mystery, for a half naked Indian baby now and then lets his voice be heard; whereupon a push sets the basket in motion like a swing; and the little aeronaut is again brought to a state of slumber.

We entered the hut with the customary salutation. "Ave María!"—"En gracia concebida"[15] was the reply of the man who was sitting upon a log of wood shelling corn. A few chickens are assembled about him and greedily pick up the scattering kernels. These he now and then frightens away with one foot when they come too close. A few children, attired in the simple uniform of Paradise, were playing upon the floor. At our approach they withdrew behind the mother, who was sitting upon the bare ground near the fire, engaged with her spindle, and stirring at intervals the pot over the fire with a stick. A few lean dogs were lying in the ashes. These raised their heads and set up a furious barking, which the master changed to a howl by hurling an ear of corn at their heads; which sent the uncalled-for disturbers into the corner of the hut, where they were so unfortunate as to come into conflict with a setting hen, who defended her nest with the greatest outcry. Hereupon the [baby] in the aerial gondola awoke and brought himself into notice. The mother rose, leaned over the cradle, and quieted the little fellow by offering the breast.

"Could you sell us a little maize for our horses tied under the tree yonder, and provide us something for ourselves to eat?" inquired we of the Indian. A long discussion arose between the man and wife in the Indian language. They were unwilling to render the service, and replied repeatedly that they had nothing. We told them we only wanted a few eggs and beans with tortillas (maize-bread); and promoted our negotiations somewhat by showing our travelling bottle and giving the man a draught from it. The urchin, who will not sleep any more, is bound like a little monkey upon the back of the mother, who with her burden kneels down before the stone, washes it, together with her own hands and arms, and proceeds to crush the half cooked maize and form it into flat cakes. A young stout-built Indian girl who has just arrived from the forest with a heavy load of dry wood assists in preparing the frugal meal, which contains as supplementary ground green Spanish pepper, an infernal dish, which burns the uninitiated to desperation, but by the Indians and Mestizoes is abundantly enjoyed at every meal. We are only able to talk a little with the man in bad Spanish.

The women and children use their Indian language only, which from their mouths sounds soft and pleasant. The people, like all the Indians, are peasants who down in the valley have their little field of maize that is just large enough to produce the year's supply. They also plant beans, pepper, tomatoes, . . . sweet potatoes and cotton, but only enough of each for their own use. Every year a few swine are raised and sold, and also the chickens find their way to market in order to raise ready money for church and parish dues. The Indians in general, with their few wants, have abundance to live upon. In most instances they plant numerous fruit trees around their huts and make a considerable profit by the sale of the fruit. They collect and sell many sorts of raw products from the forest, . . . work as day-labourers, in short have many ways of making their life more comfortable; but they nevertheless adhere to their old mode of living, and the money they earn, the men spend in drink on holidays, or bury it to keep it safe. The lot of the poor woman is much the hardest. She does the greater part of the labour and from the proceeds of it receives nothing.

Notes

1. Carl Christian Sartorius, *Mexico: Landscape and Popular Sketches*, ed. Thomas W. Gaspey (London: Trubner & Co., 1858), 1–6, 64–65, 69–70.

2. For an analysis of Sartorius's writing, see Enrique Covarrubias, *Visión extranjera de México, 1840–1867: el estudio de las costumbres y de la situación social* (Mexico City: Universidad Nacional Autónoma de México, 1998), 55–86.

3. Wilhelm Pferdekamp, *Auf Humboldts Spuren: Deutsche im jungen Mexiko* (Munich: Max Hueber Verlag, 1958), 153–71.

4. Mestizos.

5. Not a coincidental comparison, as the image recurs later in the book.

6. Instrument with four or five strings resembling a guitar.

7. This passage compresses all of Veracruz society into one scene.

8. Two names for the same bird.

9. Native of the state of Veracruz. This paragraph is a good example of climatic determinism.

10. Pot.

11. Know-how.

12. Earlier, Sartorius has explained that these peoples benefited in their development from living in the highlands, a more physically challenging environment. Now he—like Poinsett—gives a pessimistic assessment of the cultural potential of tropical dwellers.

13. Mayor.

14. An overgeneralization based on racial stereotypes.

15. "Conceived in grace."

6 Defending the French Intervention

Emmanuel Domenech[1]

The following selection from Emmanuel Henri Dieudonné Domenech's Le Mexique tel qu'il est *(Mexico as It Is) is unique in that the author occupied a position of power under Emperor Maximilian. In 1862, French invasion forces had helped the Conservative Party, which had just lost a bitter war to their Liberal rivals, topple the government of President Benito Juárez. The grand visions of Emperor Napoleon III combined with the monarchical program of the Conservative Party to produce an invitation to Archduke Ferdinand Maximilian of Habsburg to become Emperor. Domenech, Maximilian's press secretary during the waning days of the Empire, wrote a self-serving sojourner account that defends the French Intervention as a civilizing mission. Like William Henry, he is an invader, a participant in Mexican history who desires to see his role in history vindicated. Unlike Henry, however, he served in the high echelons of power. While Domenech offers many interesting observations about the Mexican economy and society, this excerpt contains comments focused on politics. Written during Maximilian's last days, it illustrates the force of the soon-to-be-triumphant resistance against the foreign invaders, and it provides an ideological justification of the French Intervention. It also displays the*

ideology of a French positivist who equates the national interest of Mexico with blind adherence to European ways.

Born near Lyons as the son of a bottle-top manufacturer, Domenech (1825–1903) became a Catholic missionary, finishing his studies in theology at the Seminary of the Barrens in St. Louis, Missouri. In 1848, Domenech was ordained a priest in San Antonio and subsequently served as the aide of a French missionary in the areas of New Braunfels and Eagle Pass, Texas. After his return to France in 1852, he published three books relating his mission work in the United States. In 1864, Domenech traveled to Mexico to serve as a chaplain to the French invasion troops and became Maximilian's press secretary upon the Emperor's coronation in June of that year. He served in that capacity until Napoleon ordered the French forces out of Mexico in November 1866.[2]

◈

I must now address . . . the intervention candidly. I will reveal why it was unproductive and even deplorable for Mexico and hardly advantageous to France. In addition, I will demonstrate that it would have been one of the most humanitarian, glorious and important interventions of the nineteenth century if Napoleon had found support in Mexico.

Emperor Maximilian's arrival in Mexico pushed aside the French influence, the only one the Mexican government should have relied upon. Here is why. The Emperor, a man of very liberal ideas and not knowledgeable on Mexico, renounced the Conservative Party that had put him in power. He affiliated with the Liberals, handed power to more or less moderate followers of that party, sacrificing his true friends in the process. Thus, a multitude of national nonentities, jealous renegades, . . . in short, all the rejects of the two parties that divide the empire came to gain the people's confidence, honor and social position.[3]

Power thus fell into the hands of people without renown, people with neither convictions nor energy for doing good deeds, with nary a hint of patriotism, and universally disliked; people who betray their country with calculated flattery, blind opposition, notorious inefficiency, and lack of accountability. As a result, [Maximilian's] government fell into absolute disrepute and the intervention that supported it lost its prestige.

Nearly all the government employees, from the ministers to the mayors, belong to the category of men I have just described. A lot of them are public criminals, and if French judges were to try each of them using French laws, the galleys would be busting at the seams.[4] These jealous, envious and stupid men discouraged sincere devotion and the efforts of genuinely honest people. Their narrow ideas and antinational selfishness made them reject all helpful thoughts and constructive advice put forth by patriots and foreigners regarding how to move the country forward for the benefit of social progress, public prosperity and unity. . . . Most of these political eunuchs have such limited intelligence that they occasionally even sacrificed their personal interests to hatred and individual jealousy. They did not want intervention from France or from Emperor Maximilian. They held on to power and honor and would not share it with anyone, much less yield it to foreigners. Their excuse was that—since they knew the country better than we did—they were in a better position to govern it. They forgot all [the damage] that they had done to Mexico since the point in time when they had assumed power. . . . As regards the rebuilding of Mexico, the general consensus had been that the Emperor would restore the country by using the services of all devoted and capable [citizens] . . . without regard to party or nationality.[5]

In addition, the Emperor surprised everyone by his selection of ministers and administrators, and he did not do anything without obtaining prior approval from his advisers beforehand, an . . . approval [that was often] slow in coming. During this time, the government sunk lower in public opinion. Opportunity knocks but once. New, young and active elements are needed to revive [the Mexican] people. Tainted, corrupt and inactive elements have to be eliminated; otherwise, it would be like trying to build a beautiful palace with rotten boards.[6]

Although we were going to give Mexico happiness and existence as a nation, all the government employees that we wanted to install were hostile to us. A conqueror is never loved by the conquered; does national pride not create the most confusing national aversion? I know very well that those who protest the loudest do not represent the people, but one does not know the feelings of those who remain silent, that is, the majority opinion. It is necessary to visit the country in order to discover the truth; from abroad, the truth is never quite clear.[7]

Some people would object by arguing that French intervention is less popular in Mexico than it was three years ago because of the arbitrary acts committed by our officers. That is wrong. These acts were too rare, too unimportant, and sometimes too justified to have thrown our army into the least disrepute.

However often mistreated even by their own regular troops, the Mexicans considered us as an army without discipline, and feared us more than their compatriots. In certain places, they are still so wary of us it is ridiculous; nevertheless, we are generally received with pleasure when we have to stay in a country. We are received reluctantly only when we pass through the districts filled with brigands.

One day, I heard General X to state a truth that all the foreigners repeat among themselves, albeit less emphatically. "What will prevent Mexico from ever making something of itself," said the general, after several years of fighting with the authorities, "are the Mexicans themselves. Their dishonesty, indolence, and incompetence are beyond imagination. When afraid, they ingratiate themselves to us in order to obtain four men and a corporal to defend them. If a bullet to the thigh downs one of these soldiers, they would leave him to die rather than give him a glass of water. While we are traveling, we can scarcely get a piece of meat or whatever it be from them, and even then, they charge us exorbitant prices. If a thief attacks their home with four or five rascals armed with ancient muskets, they hand over their wife, daughters, enough food to feed a hundred people and money rather than defend themselves." This general's judgment was justified everyday in the northern states as evidenced by the occurrences that went on before our eyes.[8]

Another general, leading a small contingent of troops, wrote to the landlord at whose house he and his men were to spend a night, with a request to buy one hundred measures of maize for any price that the landlord might want. The landlord wrote back that he did not have a single grain in his stores. On arriving at the rest stop, the general demanded the keys to the stores, where he found twelve hundred measures of maize that the owner did not want to sell to them because we support the Empire. Irritated, the general asked him to choose between paying a thousand-dollar fine or receiving fifty strokes of the cane. The landlord chose the caning. At once, four men led him to a place where the landlord's rebellious servants and employees had congregated. They were angry at their master and happy to see him being caned. Just before the caning began, the landlord changed his mind and opted to pay the fine. Not all these men are as delicate as this one. I remember an owner who received forty strokes of the cane before wanting to return a pipe, which we all knew he had been instructed by a colonel to steal.

In connection with these acts of justice, I read in the French newspapers a thousand absurd stories on the atrocities [our] forces have allegedly committed in Mexico. On the contrary, I must say that our army is admirable for its patience and level-headedness in the most difficult circumstances. . . . I often saw our soldiers show remarkable stoicism in moments where exasperation and a thirst for vengeance would have been the most natural reaction. When the 62nd regiment left San Luis Potosí, only one or two troops remained in the city. In Mexico [City], the effectiveness of the troops is greatly reduced by the number of the sick and also by. . . unproductiveness. The Liberals resolved to carry out a massacre one Sunday evening, under the impression that they could get the better of the depleted detachments that remained. But the inhabitants were so well informed about the plan that the promenades at the Alameda were unusually empty on the appointed day.

For the next several days, the men ran through certain streets with guns in their hands, trying to stir up the population to commit the massacre and shouting "death to the French!" Several of our soldiers and officers were assaulted and hit by rocks cowardly thrown from behind walls. There were even kidnappings as well as casualties. The political officer preferred to separate himself from the matter rather than warning us against what was being planned against us. The conspiracy went on as planned, but, thanks to the energy of our soldiers, only resulted in the death of Mexicans captured with arms. After this scuffle, they surrendered to us on the sidewalk from twenty steps away, and they saluted us from afar. Fear makes the Mexicans as childish as victory makes them cruel; this became evident by the number of our wounded and the fact that our prisoners were mutilated in the most barbaric ways before being put to death.

In general, the Mexican authorities regard us as enemies. They hinder rather than support our peace mission; they annoy us in a thousand ways, creating a thousand embarrassments that irritate us, discourage us and paralyze our activities. The Mexican authorities neither stopped nor reprimanded the speakers and instigators who insulted and threatened us at the independence celebration and shout out in the streets: Death to Maximilian! Death to Charlotte! Death to the French! Death to the foreigners![9]

Our soldiers were ordinarily received as liberators and acclaimed by the people in all the new places they went. When the insufficient number of the troops or military operations made it necessary for them to leave these places and then to return some time later, their welcome was not as warm the second time around. This is understandable; during the absence of our military, thugs kidnapped, held for ransom, and assassinated those who had expressed their sympathy for the intervention. Seeing these same events repeating themselves, the Mexicans became more careful and more reserved towards us.[10]

The military operations also do not always dovetail with the wishes of the people. The people would like to live with security under French protection; but they do not realize the impossibility of achieving such a desire with the restricted manpower of the occupying army. Our soldiers are not increasing in number,[11] and . . . they could not simultaneously occupy all the corners of a territory as vast as Mexico. Their role restricts them to carrying the flag of the Empire around each region. Having planted the flag there, they can only leave it there under the guard of the Mexican troops and inhabitants themselves, who are encouraged by the fact that out troops are going to continue their peace work somewhere else.

The future of Mexico is a question of money. In order to take political control, money and energy have to become available. The period of . . . weakness has passed; and the Emperor knows it. The money can be produced if His Majesty finds a way to make up for lost time. During the period of Spanish domination, naval customs duties yielded very little for the government. Nevertheless, after covering all of its internal administrative expenses, Mexico still sent shockingly large sums of money to the Spanish Crown, although consumption then was not as it is today. Despite everything, the royal coffers were full of riches. The type of independence that lets a government conform to national wishes is lost not as a result of economic bankruptcy, but rather, as a result of division among the political parties. The federation, in spite of the complete reform to which it subjected the public administration, did not have to submit to pressing needs, even though it was during this period that the scarcity started to become evident. In 1831, the Bustamante administration was still cited as one of those that easily balanced their budget. Thus, the national treasury showed a surplus in revenues.

From the day that Santa Anna, the evil genius of the country, assumed power, however, demoralization took root and a terrible deficit became apparent. Without either fixed principles or convictions, this political Proteus sought to endear himself to the followers who supported him in all his fickleness, and introduced pillage [as government policy. This pillage] was the sole support of his authority; for he toyed with all the parties, who were at the mercy of his whims.[12] That era marked the most extreme shortfall in the history of the treasury, which neither loans from foreign countries, nor the sale of a part of the territory, nor the nationalization of religious funds, nor heavy penalties imposed on private individuals could remedy.

These ever-increasing financial embarrassments caused by Santa Anna will soon disappear. Mr. Langlais and Mr. Friand, bursars with the expenditure task force, gave wise and practical advice which will be followed.

The expense side of the budget, having been significantly reduced this year, will be even lower next year. . . . The national debt, which has risen to millions of dollars, can be recovered under the new administration. The revenue side of the budget will soon reach proportions unknown since independence. Only with time can the work of intervention be successful, and our human and financial sacrifices and future naval power be saved.

The Mexican question lies in this chaotic muddle of domestic, international, political and financial complications. [To] summarize . . .

- Mexico is now a poor country despite its vast natural riches.
- Roads and foreign colonization are needed for it to function.
- Mexicans possess all the vices and qualities of the southern Latin race.
- The Creoles are very intelligent and the most enlightened people in Mexico, while the Indians are the most gentle and hardworking.
- In Mexico, more than anywhere, the political parties are more interested in change than in convictions. . . .
- The monarchical structure, along with a foreign power, is the only form of government possible, and the only type desired by most of the nation.
- The Mexican question is one of honor and influence, which, furthermore, affects our industrial and commercial future, as well as that of all of Europe.
- Our intervention in Mexico was very popular; only the bandits were against us.
- It was good politics to recognize the [U.S.] South in order to aid the intervention.
- When we decided on the expedition into Mexico, it would have made sense to rule for at least five years before relinquishing power. This would have cost us less, and we would have recouped our initial expenses.

- Poorly timed, the political system inaugurated by Emperor Maximilian compromised the Empire, much more so than the opposition against his government.
- Since one cannot form a monarchy with republicans, one must depend on the Conservatives, rather than the Liberals, to rule.
- Because Mexicans demoralized, destabilized, and ruined their country when they were in power, as many foreigners as possible (the French in particular) ought to be in power and installed in the administration.
- The plan by which we will occupy the shipping ports and run the customs services, in collaboration with the Mexican government, could save our work and also save Mexico from republican anarchy or American slavery.
- Emperor Maximilian could save Mexico only by always working in agreement with France. Unfortunately, he nearly never did.
- Without active intervention, acknowledged by the United States, the Mexican empire could have resisted the departure of our troops and could even have consolidated with the new imperial policy; but the United States' attitude, coupled with Empress Charlotte's illness, removed the last human hopes that one could have on this subject.

The only thing left for me to mention are a few words on the abdication of Emperor Maximilian and its consequences. This abdication, reported almost over a year ago by American and German journalists, had not yet been carried out at press time. I even believe that if the Empress's illness does not persuade the Emperor to step down from power, His Majesty will remain on the throne as long as a Mexican will defend him.[13]

Indeed, this is not the time for abdication. . . . On one hand, [Mexicans] see an immense abyss, the horrific past, the destruction of property, and political assassinations reaching proportions of gruesome massacres. On the other hand, they see an active, intelligent, religious and liberal prince, whose only request is to sacrifice himself for the public good. One does not hesitate when choosing between life and death. Today more than ever, the Empire has made property and family available for him. All of Mexico . . . trembles at the thought of power returning to Juárez, . . . Santa Anna, or one of their clones.[14] . . .

Since I do not know the nature of the negotiations supposedly taking place between France and the United States, . . . I do not know what the Americans or Emperor Maximilian will do after the departure of our troops. Feeling more overwhelmed than ever by [his own] radical political party, Mr. Johnson[15] appears to want to distract the attention of the Republicans from his domestic policy, and to flatter them by speeding up the resolution of the Mexican question. Therein lies the most immediate danger, if not the only one. If the U.S. Army or American brigands invade Mexico, it is clear that the Emperor, unable to resist them, will have to leave. One should not assume that [Napoleon's] cabinet will rely on the United States' promise not to intervene in Mexico. . . . If we allow the Americans to destroy our work, on the condition that we will be reimbursed, our retreat will not only be as disastrous as that of Moscow,[16] it will also be just as humiliating.

From another angle, since we do not want Mexico, we cannot remain there forever in order to sustain the throne of a prince who wants the use of our money and army, but who is, essentially, reluctant to submit to our supervision. For Mexico and the Prince, this supervision was both a duty and a necessity. The empire will fall as a result of its refusal to accept this necessity and duty. . . .

Faced with such a situation, France was supposed to become disheartened by its futile efforts to establish our dominance over Mexico and to assert our influence, our industrial, commercial and political future on the new continent. When leaving the Montezuma Empire, France ought to demand, at minimum, that when Emperor Maximilian loses the crown, it be returned to the Parliament of Notables[17] that gave it to him in the first place, so that Mexicans can choose their provisional government themselves. France still holds Mexico's destiny in its flag; if the Yankees take possession of it today, we ought to ask for more than they think it is worth. Let us imitate the English and the Americans, whose political foresight we so admire. The Republican and dynastic opposition could shake the good faith of the masses; but the error could not continue. People like grand ideas, but they also love success. Conceived with genius and pursued with boldness, grand ideas are always crowned with success.

Behind the Mexican expedition, there was more than an empire to start, a nation to serve, markets to create and a billion others to exploit; there was a world dependent on France, happy to submit to our congenial influence, . . . which owes to us the restoration of the political and social life of a civilized people.

Notes

1. Emmanuel Domenech, *Le Mexique tel qu'il est: la verité sur son climat, ses habitants et son gouvernement* (Paris: E. Dentu, 1867), 190–98, 340–48.

2. Ann Lozano, "Domenech, Emmanuel Henri Dieudonné," *Handbook of Texas Online http://www.tsha.utexas.edu/handbook/online/articles /view/DD/fdo9.html* [accessed June 14, 2003].

3. For example, Maximilian reaffirmed Juárez's Reform Laws, and he abolished debt peonage in Mexico.

4. Domenech refers to the problem of corruption in Mexican public offices. Many Mexican politicians, whether Conservative or Liberal, used public office as their best opportunity to line their own pockets. See Barbara Tenenbaum, *The Politics of Penury: Debts and Taxes in Mexico, 1821–1856* (Albuquerque: University of New Mexico Press, 1986).

5. A disingenuous statement. Domenech seems to argue for political inclusiveness here; yet above, he laments that Maximilian has included Liberals in his government.

6. This is a quite apt comment on Maximilian's lack of decisiveness.

7. This statement demonstrates that Domenech underestimates nationalism in Mexico, which will give the Liberals a much-needed boost.

8. Parts of the Mexican north are in the hands of Juárez's army as of the writing of this passage.

9. A variation of Father Miguel Hidalgo's original speech, which included the words *mueran los gachupines* (death to the Spaniards).

10. A familiar, but often-fallacious claim of an occupying power.

11. Napoleon had begun to reduce the number of troops in 1864.

12. A good description of the essence of caudillo politics in Latin America: the exchange of spoils for the political loyalty of a follower.

13. The book went to press about a year before Maximilian's execution in June 1867.

14. An almost humorous juxtaposition of two very different politicians.

15. President Andrew Johnson.

16. Recalls the original Napoleon's disastrous Russian campaign of 1812.

17. An assembly of Mexican notables created by the Conservatives to legalize Maximilian's accession. The Liberal Constitution of 1857 established the authority of Congress, which was dissolved upon the Conservative triumph.

7 Life in Maximilian's Mexico City

Paula von Kollonitz[1]

The following excerpt from Eine Reise nach Mexiko *(translated as* The Court of Mexico*) by Countess Paula von Kollonitz (1830–?) offers a glimpse at gender roles in Mexico City during the 1860s. Although this Austrian lady-in-waiting to Empress Charlotte was confined to the capital for most of her stay and lacked either inclination or opportunity to look beyond her own social set, her book provides an interesting perspective on the lives of elite men and women. In contrast to Calderón, von Kollonitz defends Mexican women against the charges of immorality, and as a Catholic, she welcomes rather than criticizes the Catholic Church. Even more important, she witnessed a capital city at the beginnings of the process of modernization that would spread to the rest of Mexico in the next forty years. Thus, men as well as women begin to conform more strictly to European cultural norms: for example, women no longer smoke as much as they had done in Poinsett's days in the 1820s.*

We do not know much about von Kollonitz's background other than that she was a countess, a member of a noble but poor Viennese family of Croatian origins. In 1864, the thirty-four-year-old was one of two ladies-in-waiting to accompany Charlotte (Carlota), the wife of Emperor Maximilian. At the time of her arrival, Mexico City was teeming with foreigners, particularly Austrian, German, and French citizens (such as Emmanuel Domenech), all seeking to take advantage of a foreign monarch. Von Kollonitz departed the capital after just four months, when the Empress tired of her uppity ways and replaced her with a Mexican. As one chronicler wrote: "Paula von Kollonitz sniffed with a superior air. Her sniffing was fiercely resented."[2]

The whole life of a Mexican bears the impress of a "*dolce far niente*,"[3] he never hastens busily through the streets; his time is never taken up. They rise early, the ladies go in their thick veils to church, the gentlemen begin their morning ride. After the walk upon the Alameda, every one goes home; they generally take a bath; and there are good and cleanly well-arranged public baths in all the streets of the city, as well as bathing-rooms in all the private dwellings. One often sees the Mexican women walking up and down the terraces of the houses to dry their long hair, which falls down like a mantle over their shoulders, and reaches almost to their feet. This daily washing of the hair has one disadvantage: it has a bad effect upon its fine texture and equality of tint. The tails, as thick as one's arm, and originally black, which adorn the little heads of the Mexicans, assume at last a reddish hue.[4]

Time is dawdled away over the completion of the toilet; if there are children in the house, their games are superintended, but they are as gentle and quiet as their parents. I never saw such well brought up children anywhere as in Mexico; no noise, no strife is perceptible. The little beings are prematurely forward, they develop very quickly, and are extremely delicate. It is frightful how many children perish, even in the richest families, where they might have had every luxury. And it is no wonder, when one considers the way in which they are brought up. The women are generally very weak, and there is nothing in their way of life to strengthen and invigorate them. They marry at fourteen or fifteen years of age; they are richly blessed with children; it is not uncommon for one mother to have fifteen or eighteen; the children come very weak into the world, are usually nursed by their extremely delicate mothers, and even from their tenderest age are treated like dolls. Early in the morning, when the sun had just risen, and had in no wise dispersed the coldness of the night, which is very considerable, especially in the shade, I have seen the tiniest creatures smartly dressed and carried with bare neck and arms to the Alameda. They are entirely confided to young Indian girls, and even in the richest houses it is not the custom to give them over to the care of experienced women. In their earliest youth they are taken by their mother to drive in the Paseo,[5] at six o'clock, when I for my part was never able to dispense with a cloak, on account of the cool atmosphere of sunset; the little things sit half naked at the open carriage-windows, and then and there the irrational love of the parents, thoughtlessly and unconsciously sacrifices the health of the children to vanity.

As they grow up, they go to school for several hours of the day. I visited one establishment, and spoke to the superintendent, a French nun, who conducted the education of the girls with the help of several companions of the same order. She assured me she had never seen such quiet, obedient well-disposed children as here. . . . But even at this early age, they want the candor and thoughtless freedom of childhood.

Their intelligence is very early awakened, and is often quite surprising for children of two and three years old; it quickly reaches a certain point, but after that remains in a state of stagnation.[6] "At twelve years of age, they make no further progress,"[7] said the nun, a fine, active, energetic woman, masculine in manner, and of a warm, sympathetic heart.

At eight or ten years old, the poor children sit at the opera till midnight, struggling against sleep, their little heads adorned with artificial flowers. Many die very young; those who do not, especially the females, lead a hot-house life.

Between twelve and one o'clock a luncheon is eaten, which chiefly consists of national dishes. *Tortillas* and *frijoles* take a prominent place at the tables of rich and poor. The first are pastry, made of ground maize, in the shape of a thin disk, as large as a plate, white and tasteless. Among the lower orders, this takes the place of bread; they use it, too, slightly rolled up, instead of spoons. *Frijoles* are little black beans, which thrive particularly well in the neighbourhood of Veracruz; when they have been cooked for a long time, they take the colour of chocolate, and make a very good and tasty food. A ragout of turkey (*guajolote*) prepared with chilis, a kind of pepper, and tomatoes, or apples of paradise, is a favourite dish. Mixed with maize flour, wrapped up in maize leaves, and steamed, it makes the best national dish— the *tamales*. On the whole, the cookery of Mexico is not very enticing to

European palates and stomachs. Lard is used in great quantities in all the dishes, even in the sweet ones. A good soup is almost an unknown thing. Coffee, which grows here of the best kind, is so badly prepared that it is almost impossible to drink it. Chocolate, highly spiced with cinnamon, is, on the contrary, very good, and much drunk.

The afternoon hours are spent in receiving and returning visits. I never saw any book in the hand of a lady, except her prayer-book, nor any work. They write letters, for the most part, with an unpractised hand. Their ignorance is complete: they have not the smallest idea of geography and history. Europe to them consists of Spain, from whence they sprang; Rome, where the Pope rules; and Paris, from whence come their clothes. They have no conception of other countries or other nations, and they could not comprehend that French was not our native tongue. They have themselves but very faint notions of this language, but have made a little progress in it since the invasion of the French.

In many houses there is no regular midday meal, a little chocolate or some dish is prepared; they lead a very moderate life. Wine or beer is rarely drunk, but there is no want of *pulque* at the tables of the rich. When guests are invited there is no end to the number of dishes. In families where regular meal times are observed, places are always laid for more than the members of the house, as some relation or friend is sure to drop in who partakes of the meal uninvited, and is received at it with the greatest goodwill. After the hour at the Paseo, they drive to the theatre, if there happens to be an opera. They usually remain there *en famille*; and joined by a few confidential friends, they play cards, enjoy music, or chatter. The ladies take great delight in music and have great talent for it; they play often very well on the piano, and have harmonious voices. When the young people assemble together, they dance, and these informal enjoyments are called *tertulias*.

The Mexicans delight in the family circle, and the relations between parents and children and brothers and sisters are very tender.

There is one curious habit nearly universal in Mexico. A girl after her marriage does not follow her husband to his home, but he very often becomes a member of his wife's family. In this way a large circle is formed around the elders; daughters, sons-in-law, grandchildren, brothers and sisters-in-law, and cousins of all sorts, inhabit a house too small for their numbers, live upon the generosity of the head of the family, and pay him great respect.

They seldom leave this family circle, or only do so to enter a similar one; their ideas remain very confined, and their interests turn almost exclusively upon their domestic concerns. In one point, however, we are very apt to do Mexican wives a great wrong, that is in respect to their morality. Indeed, the bulwark of relations by which a young wife is surrounded, acts to a great extent as a protection to her; but independently of that, I found them nearly always retiring; and rigid even to prudishness when strangers were inclined to be presumptuous. Their marriages are really domestic and happy; married people are always seen together; and the husband lavishes gifts on his wife, which is considered a special mark of attachment. There is no proof so striking of the virtue of the Mexican women as the great discontent of the French. Once when I asked a young Parisian, who had been sent to Mexico as a punishment for great extravagance, why it was supposed that gentlemen would spend less money there than in France, I received for reply: "in Paris one only ruins oneself through women, whereas in Mexico, they do not exist for us."[8] That there are exceptions, I should not dispute, but such persons are received with great contempt. On this head there is a widespread mistrust of the French and their bragging when they have but trifling grounds for it, is much dreaded.

The unmarried girls are allowed much more licence; they are far more dressy, vain, and coquettish; and are surrounded by suitors, with whom they associate without any restraint, and weave all sorts of love intrigues, in which rendezvous and a secret correspondence both play their part. If a young man pays attentions to a girl for any length of time, he passes as her *novio*.[9] He is not, however, her betrothed, but only gains the right to accompany her in her rides, or to the Paseo, where the carriages stand often in long rows to enable their inmates to see the great world riding or driving by. He is allowed to take place at her side, to sit in her box at the theatre, to protect her, and to accompany her whenever she has need of an escort. No one has a right to be vexed, if she shares her little favours amongst several *novios*, if at one time she attracts them by kindness, at another repels them by her coldness. The Mexican, on his side, exhibits great patience; his wooing, and the indecision of the *novia*,[10] last often for years; but if she at length listens to him, and chooses him for her husband, then he may deem himself fortunate.

The girls also lent a . . . more friendly ear to the homage of the French than was pleasing to their mothers and this led to many disagreeable family scenes, and even to duels between the girls' brothers and the shameless intruders. The French have turned the Spanish substantive *novio*, into a verb *novioter*, to express this sort of intercourse with girls of respectable families; a phase of life quite unknown in their own home. . . .

I heard many disputes about the beauty of Mexican women; on the whole, they enjoy a great reputation for it, and at any rate deserve admiration for the splendour of their hair and teeth, for the deep expression of their black, melancholy eyes, and for their tiny hands and feet. I saw some ladies whose features were so refined, their forms so gracious and charming, and their manners so noble, simple, and unrestrained, that I was filled with admiration whenever I met them.

Fausta Aregunaga, of the rich family of Gutiérrez [Estrada],[11] in Yucatán, was especially one of those whose fairy-like appearance fascinated me. Never have I met with more perfect beauty united to such grace, and whenever I think over all the delightful foreign scenes, after which my soul sometimes longs, then that form of loveliness darts up in my memory, and with the moist glance of that eye, and the smile on those tender lips, gives life to the picture, and breathes over it the deepest enchantment. The bloom of youth lasts but a short time, and in middle life the women become generally very stout. A dark down often shadows the upper lip, and sometimes a lady can boast of a very respectable moustache.

The men are small, delicate, and well formed; so, too, are their hands and feet; and when we wanted to buy some sombreros we perceived that we European ladies had too large heads to wear the hats of the Mexican gentlemen.

I have already spoken of their soft, refined, and retiring manners. Their character is mistrustful and cautious, but for my part I have met with nothing but friendship from the inhabitants of Mexico; and have made their acquaintance in their family circle, and as a guest, and, therefore, on their best side. It is, consequently, very difficult to me to join in any sweeping condemnation of them. But so much is certain, that they themselves, in judging their countrymen, use the bitterest accusations. Not one of them trusts his neighbour; and both are characterized by a third as thieves and traitors.

"Here nothing is organized except theft,"[12] an excessively worthy Mexican said to me. . . . His words were unfortunately, at that time, but too true; for stealing was universal, and not merely the trade of highway robbers, who plundered the [stagecoaches] or attacked haciendas. The example was usually set by the President of the Republic. As he was only elected for three years, generally driven out much sooner by the *pronunciamiento*[13] of a rival, he made use of the short period of his power to feather his own nest, to help his relations into high official positions, and thus to give them the opportunity of imitating his proceedings. The same course was carried out even to the lowest appointments. Men of business made use of the perplexities of the Government to gain concessions for all sorts of undertakings on most favourable conditions, and under pretence of the public prosperity. In this way many a man became, in a very short time, as rich as Croesus. Avarice is a universal failing among the Mexicans; and, even though they may be in some ways extremely generous, even lavish, yet they do not show any great scruples as to the manner in which they earn their money. They are indolent by nature and from long indulgence. When Emperor Maximilian first took in hand the giant work of the reorganization of the State, and looked around the country for men on whose strength he could rely to aid him in his ceaseless activity, none of those who answered his call had any idea of true self-sacrificing exertion.[14]

There was no lack of profession. The Mexican always promises; but the necessity of keeping his word is not at all apparent to him. Negligence in things, both great and small, is a chief feature of his character; he is easily led, and has lost all rigid notions of honour.[15] When I used to hear Mexicans passing judgment upon their own country, my cheeks would blush for shame; this self-aspersion was particularly painful to me.

Moderation is one of the chief virtues of Mexicans. They generally lead very regular lives; and the love of gambling alone entices them into great excesses. There have been some fathers of families who, in a few days, have played away millions, house and home. Of late, games of chance had been strictly forbidden; and I do not think the Emperor Maximilian had any desire to remove the prohibition. Gambling is, therefore, not carried on so large a scale as formerly, nor in public places; but the passion is still indulged in private circles. The game *boliche* is a favourite Mexican amusement.[16] On Sundays, [boliche players] meet at country houses, where there are skittle-alleys; heavy wagers are laid, and large sums frequently lost and won.

The indoor architecture and arrangements of Mexican houses are very pretty and convenient. An extraordinarily steep staircase usually leads into a broad passage which surrounds the court, upon which all the doors open. This is generally covered with nicely woven mats, adorned with standard plants and flowers, and provided with benches. From thence you enter the reception rooms, which, among rich families, are carpeted, and filled with splendid furniture. In many houses it was curious to see, a white marble spit-toon on a wooden base placed, for the benefit of the most distinguished guest, on either side, of the sofa, where it could not fail to catch the eye, far from the modest corner in which, amongst us, such an article is barely tol-erated. Perhaps it had its origin in the times when no lady could live without a paper cigar in her mouth. This fashion has much decreased. Cigarette-smoking by ladies is no longer considered *bon ton*.[17]

The family sleeping- and dwelling-rooms are often wanting in neat-ness and cleanliness; and they use too few rooms for the number of people. The mother and five or six daughters will all sleep in one small apartment. The bedsteads are almost always of iron, large and broad. The dining room is near the kitchen and by means of machinery the dishes and plates are con-veyed in and out by invisible hands through an opening in the wall. The lux-ury of linen material is almost unknown. The wealthy Mexicans get their under-clothing from Paris. Sheets and table-cloths are almost always made of cotton; and I saw the last-named articles in a pitiful condition, even on the tables of the richest people.

The servants are chiefly Indian girls, who do the housework, and are often very clever in needlework and embroidery. They are treated in a very friendly, almost familiar way. Men-servants are not at all common; one foot-man, at most, superintends the waiting at table. The cooks live out of the house, and provide the meals of several families. All the domestic servants call the children of the house, even when grown up and married, *niña* or *niño* (lit-tle one,) and passers-by are frequently accosted by beggars with this title. The custom of shaking hands is widely spread, and adopted towards strangers high and low, and even to servants. Our gentlemen were not a little astonished when the owner of a hairdressing and shaving-saloon came forward to receive them with this friendly greeting. Ladies always embrace on meeting, and tap each other gently with the hand on the shoulder while at the same time questions are put and answers given with great volubility, about their parents, brothers and sisters, children etc. Even when a gentleman and lady meet in the street they exchange such speeches as they pass. The rules of politeness are observed with extreme conscientiousness; the Mexican ladies especially are very dependent upon strict forms of propriety. No lady goes on foot, except in the morning to Mass; it is thought highly incorrect to make purchases or to go into the shops oneself. The most unimportant actions are under strict regulation. It excited positive horror among our new friends when they saw us walking through the streets at all hours of the day with looped-up dresses, examining the regular shops, or, worse still, the Indian booths, and often going on further with our purchases in our hands, or allowing an Indian to carry the larger ones.

And yet nothing in the city of Mexico can be more interesting to Europeans than its street life, especially in the morning, when there is a great deal of business and movement. The Mexican gentlemen ride in troops to their morning airing; to us their riding has something mysterious about it, the horses' step being almost noiseless, as they are not generally shod. The ladies go to church dressed in black and closely veiled. Indians crowd about half-naked, holding long poles, on which six or eight parrots sit side by side, others carry quince preserve, pastry, preserved fruits, candied chestnuts, wax figures, gold and silver ornaments, tortoise-shell combs, *sarapes*,[18] *rebozos*. . . . [19] pots, baskets, and wooden vessels; often too there are poor little humming-birds in cages, which after a few days fall victims to their imprisonment; all those are offered for sale with loud cries, with which mingles the voice of the *aguador*.[20] These objects are very striking, but the Indians themselves are the most striking of all, with their thin figures and primitive attire. Their legs are enveloped in a piece of leather; a cotton cape through which they push their heads, forms the covering for breast and back; their arms and legs are quite free, on their feet they wear sandals, on their heads a thick straw hat. The women are not select in their dress. A piece of cotton stuff wound about them serves as a petticoat, the upper part of the body is but poorly protected, and their charming black-eyed, intelligent children, forego entirely the luxury of clothing. In this guise they sit at the corners of the streets, on the pavements, with a cigarette in their mouths, kneading and baking tortillas, or tying up bunches of flowers in a most artistic manner; they also dress baskets of flowers, in which they offer for sale the fragrant strawberries, which ripen here all the year round. I had a most beautiful bouquet of white roses and violets every day upon my table. By the side of the flowers stand great baskets full of all kinds of rare fruits, which are also sometimes heaped up in pyramids.

Notes

1. Paula von Kollonitz, *The Court of Mexico*, 2nd ed., trans. J. E. Ollivant (London: Saunders, Otley, and Co., 1868), 156–75.

2. Bertita Harding, *Phantom Crown: The Story of Maximilian and Carlota of Mexico* (Mexico City: Ediciones Tolteca, 1960), 173–74.

3. Italian for "sweet do-nothing."

4. More likely, the result of the bleaching effect of the powerful rays of the sun.

5. The Paseo de Bucareli.

6. A sweeping statement that illustrates the author's prejudice.

7. In the original: "A douze ans, ils n'avancent plus."

8. In the original: "A Paris on ne se ruine que pour les femmes, tandis qu'à Mexico elles n'existent pas pour nous."

9. Boyfriend.

10. Girlfriend.

11. Revised to give complete name.

12. In the original: "Chez nous rien n'est organisé que le vol."

13. Coup d'état against the government.

14. Reflects assertions from other travel accounts, which—as this paragraph reveals—many Mexicans have internalized.

15. An oft-repeated stereotype.

16. Bowling played with heavy balls the size of an orange upon sand or grass; also common in Mediterranean countries.

17. Elegant or having good taste. Compare this statement with Poinsett's more than forty years earlier.

18. Hand-woven blankets.

19. Shawls.

20. Water carrier.

PART II

The Modernization
of Mexico

After the restoration of Liberal rule in 1867, Mexico gradually emerged out of the chaos of the previous fifty-seven years. Under Presidents Benito Juárez and Sebastián Lerdo de Tejada, the Restored Republic incrementally strengthened central authority over the next nine years. At the same time, the economy of the United States began to recover after the Civil War, and large-scale U.S. industrialization soon created demand for Mexican tropical commodities. After General Porfirio Díaz seized power in 1876, the Mexican government committed itself to aggressively wooing foreign investments. Díaz invited foreign capital to build up the country's infrastructure, particularly the railroads. In turn, the construction of this infrastructure facilitated the further development of export economies in Mexico's agricultural and mining areas, the modernization of the cities, the emergence of a sizable (if dependent on the state) urban middle class, the beginnings of a steel industry in the northern city of Monterrey, the creation of a sense of nationalism among a broad sector of the literate Mexican population, and the assertion of government control over all states of the republic. Gone were the days when recalcitrant governors and local *jefes políticos* could defy central authority. Following Juárez's efforts at reining in banditry, Díaz built a rural police force, the *rurales*, to help him enforce order in the countryside. He rewarded his loyal supporters but ruthlessly crushed those who opposed him, whether political rivals among the elite or striking workers. In the brutal massacres that ended labor strikes in Cananea, Sonora (1906), and Río Blanco, Veracruz (1908), the internal contradictions of modernization revealed themselves: far from bringing prosperity to a majority of Mexicans, it enriched wealthy landowners and foreign investors while visiting misery upon peasants and workers. These contradictions contributed to the collapse of the Díaz regime in the Mexican Revolution only a few years later.

Perhaps the greatest of these contradictions was the effort to graft a modern, European image on "traditional" Mexico. The elite considered traditional Mexican culture déclassé, and French and U.S. influence, manifested by the arrival of expensive French-made clothes and the bicycle, became the rage. In many ways, Europeanization was no more than skin deep, as the majority of the Mexican population remained unaffected by the cultural trappings of modernization. Even the Porfirians partially retreated from emulating "modern" values: they recognized the value of "traditional" practices such as bullfights for promoting a national culture, and they began to celebrate Mexico's indigenous heritage at the World Fairs.[1] Amidst this tug-of-war between modernity and tradition, many Mexicans ultimately realized that their lives were changing for the worse, especially after the world economic crisis of 1907. Indigenous communities lost their land to private investors favored by the Mexican government; northern peasants saw their independence encroached upon by the *rurales* and other agents of the central state; and industrial workers noticed that many foreign-born employees were treated better than they were.

Porfirian modernization led to a greater influx of foreigners. Entrepreneurs and professionals flocked to Mexico from Britain, France, Germany, Spain, and the United States, forming sizable foreign-born communities in the larger cities. These newcomers contributed to the modernization project in a variety of ways: some became landowners, others invested in mining or railroad construction, and yet others became promoters for the Díaz regime in the United States. Not surprisingly, the foreign observer accounts of this period are less concerned with grand syntheses of Mexican society than their predecessors from the early and mid-nineteenth century. Deeply steeped in imperialist and social Darwinist thought, foreign observers during the Porfiriato rationalized the project of modernization by pointing to Europe and the

United States as the standards of civilization and material progress. Only after the turn of the century did a few observers become appalled enough by the conditions they saw to advertise the cause of the regime's opponents. When they did, however, they brought about a sea change in writing about Mexico, away from imperial justification and toward critique of colonialism and imperialism. Paradoxically, then, the period of high imperialism inaugurated a critical countercurrent that would become an important strain in foreign writing about Mexico in the revolutionary and postrevolutionary periods.

These foreigners traveled far more quickly and comfortably than those only a few decades before. In 1872, the Mexico City-Veracruz railroad was inaugurated, a line that allowed passengers to traverse the distance between the capital and the coast in a mere eight hours. As the scenery rushed by outside the windows of the railroad car, the romance of travel receded into the background. Yet visitors such as the ethnologist Carl Lumholtz still found such romance in the *México desconocido* (unknown Mexico) off the beaten track. Far away from the string of railroad lines that connected Mexico City to the U.S. border and the principal cities of the republic, the unknown Mexico continued to resist the encroachment of the central government upon local autonomy.

The five excerpts in this section comment on the dichotomy between modernity and tradition, and between city and countryside. Written at the beginning of the Porfiriato, the first two selections, from Clément Bertie-Marriott's *Un Parisien au Mexique* and Fanny Chambers Gooch's *Face to Face with the Mexicans*, seek to explain "backward" Mexico to French and U.S. audiences in order to promote foreign investment in and awareness of Mexico. The third piece, from Carl Lumholtz's *Unknown Mexico*, traces the contrast between city and countryside in the 1890s. The last two excerpts, from Charles Flandrau's *Viva Mexico!* and John K. Turner's *Barbarous Mexico*, constitute divergent assessments of the Porfiriato shortly before its fall.

!!i

Notes

1. Beezley, *Judas at the Jockey Club*; and Mauricio Tenorio Trillo, *Mexico at the World's Fairs: Crafting a Modern Nation* (Berkeley: University of California Press, 1996).

8 Three Days of Fiesta in Mexico City

Clément Bertie-Marriott[1]

The following excerpt by French journalist Clément Bertie-Marriott's Un Parisien au Mexique *(A Parisian in Mexico)* reflects on a brief visit to Mexico City in 1884. During this visit, the author witnessed the festivities surrounding three consecutive national holidays: Don Porfirio's birthday on September 14, and the Independence Day celebrations on September 15 and 16. The excerpt is included in this collection for its early judgment on modernization, which, as the author believed, amounted to the consumption of French goods and French cultural influence. Indeed, the French played a key role in the modernization of Mexico undertaken by President Díaz and his allies. In the 1880s, French economic influence reached its zenith. French banks controlled most of the international loans, merchants from the Alpine town of Barcelonnette enjoyed a virtual monopoly on imported garment sales, and a French consortium owned the largest textile plant in the nation.[2] Yet French culture, of global reach during that era, had yet to reach its maximum impact. As readers learn in Bertie-Marriott's account, Mexico City was still *rustic. Many Mexicans, even among the elite, viewed foreign (that is, non-Spanish) cultural influence—associated with Liberal political thought, anti-clericalism, and U.S. expansion—with suspicion.*

As the title of the book implies, its main purpose is to explain Mexico to a Parisian audience. Hence Bertie-Marriott, a traveler without any long-term ties, does not attempt to understand Mexicans on their own terms. Instead, his travel account is laced with unflattering comparisons to Paris. The author complains about the early hours and the constant partying, and he scoffs at the bull tailing and the overt enthusiasm of the audience. The effect of these views on a smart set that eagerly consumed all foreign writing about itself was immediate: the Jockey Club, an association that included Mexico's foremost families, never again hosted a charreada, *or bull-wrestling competition, in Díaz's honor.[3]*

The son of an English father and a French mother, Bertie-Marriott was born in 1848 in Nundersly, England, but was raised in Paris. As a young journalist, he wrote for Le Voltaire, *an anticlerical publication. In satirical style, he poked fun at the world around him, including his own social circle, in* Parisiens et Parisiennes: mes entretiens *(1883). He traveled to Mexico in April 1884 as special correspondent of the daily newspaper* Le Figaro, *just as President Porfirio Díaz was preparing to return to office after a four-year hiatus. Bertie-Marriott remained interested in world affairs after this trip, publishing short works based on interviews with two-time Argentine President Julio Roca (1885) and the Maharajah Duleep-Singh, the last Sikh ruler of Punjab, India (1889). The circumstances of his death are unknown.*

On September 14, 1884, the entire city was geared up to celebrate the birthday of [Porfirio Díaz], the man Mexicans esteem the most. No good fiesta takes place without some horse racing. Like Paris and London, Mexico City has a top-notch jockey club. This club invited General Díaz and his wife, along with four thousand friends—the *crème* of the country—to the racecourse in Peralvillo. A large throng of people presses itself against the sunny track. A squadron of *rurales*,[4] perched proudly on their horses, faces the platform of honor. The platforms are dressed up with swabs of cloth in light shades. It is a superb morning. The imposing silhouettes of the Popocatépetl and Ixtaccíhuatl [volcanoes] loom on the horizon.[5]

Nine o'clock in the morning! This is the first and probably the last time that I go to the tracks at this time—to be sure, it is already three thirty in the afternoon in Paris. The sound of drums rings throughout the field, the wonderful ensemble of the *rurales* intones the national anthem, and soldiers from the military academy present their weapons.

Here comes General Díaz. He steps out of the car and lends his hand to the ever-gracious Doña Carmen—and the excitement erupts. From all sides, the crowd cheers the president-elect, who will not take office until the end of November.[6] Such deafening cheers! In the blink of an eye, the platform is empty. Men, women and children rush towards the general, trying to hold or kiss his hand.

After cadets have staged a march past the tribune, the races begin. The jockeys are dressed in *ranchero*[7] outfits; very short coats, silvered breeches and a folded colored scarf around their neck; quite peculiarly, they mount their horses "saddle-free." In place of horsewhips, these jockeys, up to date with the fads of the times, carry long switches with which to stir up their beasts. The horses bound off as if possessed; only slowing to a gallop every 200 or 300 meters.

Between each race, the ensemble plays exquisite *habaneras*.[8] There are no booking offices to be seen, in fact, there is almost no betting to speak of. I have to say that the absence of bookmakers did not seem to diminish the spectators' interest in the races. Quite the contrary: instead of displaying their joy at the end of the race as we do back home, the crowd follows the horses with shouts throughout the entire race and greets the end of the race with thunderous hand clapping that sounds like a tenor. But it is time for a favorite Mexican pastime, the *coleadero*.[9]

Some thirty bulls have been waiting in an improvised corral. Here come the horse riders who are to take part in this fight of skill versus force. They wear little black coats, tight pants ornamented with silver buttons and a large black felt sombrero. The rich saddle, the harness . . . and the heavy stirrups are marvelously supported by superb beasts with flowing tails. These riders come from the best and richest families in Mexico, and it is not surprising that they look so good on horseback.

Fans of the [*charrería*, the] national sport, spread out all over the arena in order to ambush the bull in its mad dash from one end of the track to the other facing the platforms. The fans chase the bull at full speed, make it change direction and with a powerful cuff, lift it by its tail. The first bull has just been released, and two horsemen charge after it. One of them grabs the animal, but the bull breaks free with a bound, leaving its hunter empty-handed.

Ah! Here comes another one—frenzied cries of "bravo!" erupt. Wenceslao Rubio, from the Jockey Club, has just knocked an enormous bull off its feet, leaving it sprawled on the grass with its four legs up in the air. For an hour, I take part in the changing fortunes of these handsome riders who are fighting in front of their girlfriends and wives in order to confuse these horned beasts to the greatest extent possible. . . .

The following day, September 15, the day before the big national holiday, we dressed even better than the day before. The two main roads, which, to say the truth, are really one road, were decorated at each intersection with commemorative arcs made of flowers and foliage; products of a country where flowers and foliage are marvels that constantly regenerate and that cost no more than what it takes to grow them. Between these arcs were massive façades entirely covered with fresh vegetables. Needless to say, this drew the admiration of the Indian onlookers—the French colony had had a monument constructed, with the colors of the French and Mexican flags, veiled in palm fronds, hidden in the *ahuehuetes*[10] of Chapultepec.

Everywhere one could see statues and portraits of Father [Miguel] Hidalgo—liberator and hero of the national independence that we are celebrating. The Jockey Club stood out in particular because a large placard hoisted on its roof displayed the heroic priest unfurling the flag with the national colors. Another house featured an electrically illuminated poster that showed the outlines of Washington and Hidalgo exchanging the flags of their respective countries. Thought up by the practical sense of a Yankee merchant, this image was thought to be a little too contrived, and it offended the susceptibility of the people. . . . If the two big republics get along well, it is certainly from a distance, and it is natural that this alliance, accompanied by a confusion of flags, did not please those who are patriotic and sensitive to such.

At night, we saw a thrilling light show. . . . As soon as the sun had set, thousands of lights appeared in elegant lanterns in vivid colors and of endless varieties. These lanterns were fastened to windows, balconies, trees and shop fronts. The Venetian glass, with its pale flame and its nauseating smell, was conspicuous by its absence; it had fortunately been replaced by electric lights, the white rays of which illuminated every last nook and cranny of the structure.

Chinese firecrackers sparkle in the air. Troops march past forming a guard of honor in front of the glorious relics from the War of 1810. Like holy relics, old flags riddled with bullet holes and blackened with powder are paraded through the city up to the national theater, where the president and an enormous crowd surround them with resonant shouts.

Ever so often, someone shouts a popular name: "*Viva Hidalgo, viva Morelos, viva Porfirio Díaz, viva Francia!*" and the crowd responds, shouting back with one voice: "*Viva!*"

At 10:50 in the evening, the next day's celebration begins. At the . . . Zócalo, a crowd of people swarms and shouts around the bonfire, casting fantastic shadows. A twenty-gun salute volley and a cannon shot shake the ground. As if it remembered the quake two years ago, the old cathedral . . . lets out a metallic clang from its huge bells, which ring with a clashing noise. At this solemn moment, the men throw themselves into the arms of their neighbor, the women embrace each other, and the Indians, dressed in rags, form a group around the fires while reciting Aztec chants, bizarre songs that probably go back in time. At this time, the *ayuntamiento* (the city council) conducts a reading of the Act of Independence edited and drafted in the Congress of Chilpancingo. At precisely 11 o'clock, the president grabs the national standard and approaches the railing lining the balcony of his palace and cries: *Mexicanos! Viva la independencia! Viva la libertad!*

The Zócalo[11] will be full at night—tradition demands that any true patriot worthy of the title stay awake from 11 P.M. until the following midnight. Those who attempt to do otherwise will be punished, I think, with very troubled sleep. That night, I heard more noise in the street than I had ever heard during twenty-five years in France. The best thing to do in the midst of this uproar is to accept the invitation of . . . two pleasant lawyers. One of them . . . studied in Paris, and our conversation about the Boulevard des Italiens reminded me that I had a homeland on the other side of the salty lake.

I will mention the following people among those who joined us: the brilliant [Manuel] Gutiérrez Nájera, who under the synonym of Duc Job, writes such charming chronicles in the Mexican newspapers; Pancho Garay, the son of Francisco Garay, the erudite engineer and eloquent speaker and representative of the Panama parliament held in Paris ...Max Bass, very upright and generous; Francisco Bulnes, the distinguished speaker who speaks of the English debt in a way that makes the hair on the head of all the debtors stand on end, and who empties the pockets of all the taxpayers; Sánchez Facio, always happy like a Portuguese and spiritual like a Parisian; the well-endowed Peruvian Cazeneuve, who has so many love affairs in churches and in balconies. . . .

We are going to the "Concordia," a restaurant run by Omarini, an Italian, who has found a way of combining different methods of cooking in the same dish. He knows how to make a living by serving these dishes under different names to people with tired palates and hollow stomachs from drinking loaded cocktails. We . . . savor Master Omarini's cooking and drink champagne from bottles with genuine labels until the sun comes out to extinguish the electric lights.

One feature of this independence celebration is that all Mexican girls and women come out in full force, and this should not be counted as the slightest of benefits resulting from the expulsion of the Spanish tyrant. Since women— especially the most beautiful ones—never do anything halfway, the Mexicans, all inhibitions set aside for a day, visit the night diners with their relatives and boyfriends and chat in the common rooms as well as in the private rooms. It is a good day for boyfriends, who all have three or four girlfriends each.[12]

At nine o'clock on September 15, no sooner had we freshened up at the Aragón baths . . . than the festival starts again, if one can even say that it stopped at all. The sun, which is never overcast, wraps a population still jittery from its sleepless night with heat rays like a magic blanket. Windows, balconies and roofs are already black with spectators, leaning their curious heads towards the flood of people coming and going in the narrow streets. From my balcony, our eyes take in the sea of hats, large shields from the sun. The Indian, wrapped up in his brightly colored wool shawl, smokes a cigarette while thanking his lucky stars and the president from the bottom of his heart for offering such a beautiful spectacle to him for free. Independence does not mean much to someone who has always been independent, because he has never needed anything. It is not his business whether the rich throw parties, pay taxes and fight among themselves for the right to govern the country.[13] He only asks that they treat him well—but enough of the political philosophy. This must be the effect of the Italian champagne, the vapors of which have not completely dissipated.

Make way for the march past! For a full five hours, symbolic floats representing all the arts, trades and industries known to man, pass by our windows. Next come twenty thousand armed soldiers. This branch of the military is commanded by General [Sóstenes] Rocha, whom the Parisian boulevard regulars know well, a brave man who has had his own share of adventures, the good and the bad.[14] These tough soldiers, hued black by the reflection of steel, all different sizes, walking with a resolved and resigned air and not the least bit concerned about all the eyes on them, present an extraordinary picture. And how admirable is the group of jockeys, smartly seated on their horses with flowing hair. They resemble art pieces escaped from the Barbedienne![15]

At the head of the troops comes the battalion of students from the military academy—the youngest ones from Chapultepec—a kind of Saint Cyrien of Mexico. They are followed by the *zapadores*, or policemen. Next come the drummers of the mountain artillery who are well respected in this country, followed by a multitude of infantry regiments whose bands play lively tunes. Four regiments of *rurales* . . . who have achieved well-deserved success bring up the rear. This arm of the military is one of the most visibly stunning, full of pomp and pageantry. The uniform of the National Guard is elegant and original. Gray sombreros worn in combat, double-twisted, thick silver neck cords, pants made of yellow chamois leather, buttoned down to the ankle, musketeer gloves, red Windsor ties streaming down their necks, and scarlet coverings rolled behind the silver saddle. These men have a commanding presence, a resolute gait, a distinguished appearance and the ease of troops from the middle ages. They could have rivaled the appearance and brilliance of Cromwell's horsemen.[16] Individually brave and well versed in all the horse drills, these *rurales* form a formidable corps of warriors.

The procession ended at four o'clock in the afternoon. The rest of the day was devoted to a lottery with a jackpot of 100,000 piastres and with countless rounds, in all the bars and *pulquerías*[17] of the capital. The evening's entertainment consisted of fireworks at the Zócalo and an outdoor concert in the garden surrounding the bandstand. A lot of pretty women were there, well dressed in the latest fashions copied from Paris. By midnight, there were no longer any people in the streets. Well, you see, three days of such partying had tired out even the toughest party animals, and we are now back in a land of an early-rising people who love to rise with the sun—this good, old sun to which the Mexicans appear like spoiled children.[18]

Notes

1. Clément Bertie-Marriott, *Un Parisien au Mexique* (Paris: E. Dentu, 1886), 65–77.

2. Jean Meyer, "Les Français au Mexique au XIXème siècle," *Cahiers des Amériques Latines* 9–10 (1974): 62–64.

3. Beezley, *Judas at the Jockey Club*, 7.

4. The mounted rural police force composed in part of former bandits who knew their terrain very well. The *rurales* enforced order and ended decades of violence in the countryside, but often took advantage of their power to enrich themselves.

5. The statement refers to Mexico City's clear mountain air of those years. Today, air pollution has made such a view a rarity.

6. Díaz had served as president from 1876 to 1880. At the time of Bertie-Marriott's visit, he had just "won" a second term in an office he would not relinquish again until 1911.

7. Rural outfit that became a notional "typically Mexican" garb.

8. Cuban popular music that became popular throughout Spanish America in the late nineteenth century.

9. The forerunner of bulldogging or steer wrestling; a form of *charrería* explained in the following paragraphs.

10. A tree considered sacred during Mexica times.

11. Main square of Mexico City, the largest such square in the Western hemisphere, bordered by the Cathedral, National Palace, and City Hall government.

12. Repeats the stereotype found in Poinsett, but repudiated by von Kollonitz.

13. A misleading statement given the existence of debt peonage and other forms of forced labor in Mexico.

14. Captured in the war against the French, Rocha escaped and distinguished himself in Juárez's army.

15. The famous bronze foundry of Parisian sculptor Ferdinand Barbedienne.

16. The reference is to the "New Model Army" of the English Civil War of 1641–1648—strictly disciplined middle-class soldiers fighting for Parliament leader Oliver Cromwell against the king. The implied comparison is evidence of the author's admiration of Díaz.

17. Establishments that serve *pulque*, the fermented juice of the agave plant.

18. This stereotype of Mexicans as children can also be found in Poinsett and Kollonitz.

9 Culture Shock in Northern Mexico

Fanny Chambers Gooch[1]

Like the preceding selection, the following excerpt from Fanny Chambers Gooch's Face to Face with the Mexicans *was written with the primary goal of fostering a deeper understanding of Mexico as a target of foreign investment. Nevertheless, as the reader will quickly discover, this sojourner account is based on a far more intimate knowledge than that of Bertie-Marriott. Unlike that French journalist, who had interacted almost exclusively with the metropolitan elite during his brief stay, Gooch lived in Mexico a total of six years, much of it in Saltillo, Coahuila, a small town in the rural north of the country. As a woman, she came into contact with servants, street and market vendors, and many other lower- and middle-class Mexicans. Nevertheless, Gooch measures "progress" and "civilization" in similar terms to those of Bertie-Marriott, and she is equally guilty of racial stereotypes. She relates episodes that seek to establish her belief that Mexicans are backward, lazy, and, in their majority, stupid. Yet her long residence also induced a degree*

of sympathy and understanding in judging her host society. Based on her first years in Saltillo, the following selection describes Gooch's early difficulties with housekeeping in a culture very different from her own, as well as the limits of modernization in the Mexican north at a time just before industrialization would transform the Monterrey-Saltillo region forever. Sketches by the New York artist Isabel V. Waldo—a portrait painter who knew Mexico only through a stay in the capital—accompany and reinforce Gooch's observations of life in the Mexican north.[2]

Fanny Chambers was born in Hillsboro, Mississippi, as the eighth of thirteen children, some time between 1842 and 1851. She received her formal schooling in Waco, Texas before marrying the Virginian G. W. Gooch, the first of three husbands. Sometime in the late 1870s, the couple moved to Saltillo. Unlike other foreign housewives sent to Mexico to follow a husband's career, Gooch had studied Spanish before she crossed the border. After the divorce from her husband, Gooch returned to Mexico several times in the 1880s, traveling to the national capital and several states in central and south-central Mexico. Like her date of birth, the circumstances of her death are unknown.[3]

The dearth of household furniture and conveniences already mentioned, put ingenuity and will force to their utmost tension, and I felt as if transported to antediluvian days. I have a candid conviction that Mother Noah never had cooking utensils more crude, or a larder more scant, than were mine. . . . This was before the time of railways in Mexico, the "Nacional Mexicano" having only penetrated a few leagues west of the Rio Grande. With the primitive modes of transportation which served in lieu of the railway it was not advisable to attempt bringing household goods so far over a trackless country. The inconveniences that followed were not peculiar to ourselves, but common to all strangers, who like us could neither anticipate nor realize the scarcity of every household appurtenance. . . .

Fortunately for us, a druggist had two spare, pine single bedsteads, which he kindly sold to us for the sum of forty dollars. At an American factory they would have been worth about four dollars each. One was painted a bright red, the other an uncompromising orange. They were cot-like and had flat wire springs, while Mexican blankets constituted the entire bedding, mattresses and all. Pillows were improvised from bundles of wearing apparel.

Fancy how they looked, the only furniture in a gorgeously frescoed room twenty-five by thirty-five feet, and of proportionate height! . . .

A friend lent us six hair-cloth chairs, and a table which had many years before been the operating table of his brother, a surgeon. It was long, green, and sagged in the middle. A carpenter was employed to make the remaining necessary articles of furniture. He labored on the customary *mañana*[4] system, and while his calculations as to time ranged all the way from eight to fifteen days, I found he actually meant from six weeks to three months. He showed samples of his workmanship, rocking-chairs with and without arms, made of pine, stained or painted or varnished, and upright chairs with cane seats. I ventured to ask when he could complete for us a dozen chairs, four rockers, and some tables. Utterly amazed, he looked at me with a smile of incredulity, as if to say "What can you do with so much furniture?" He disapproved of my wish to have oblong and round tables, so I yielded acquiescence to the customary triangular ones which grace the corners of every parlor of respectability.

It now becomes necessary to introduce what proved to me the most peculiar and interesting feature of home life in Mexico. This is not an article of furniture, a fresco, a pounded earthen floor, or a burro or barred casement, but the indispensable, all-pervading, and incomparable man-servant, known as the *mozo*. . . . Forewarned—forearmed! The respectability of the household depending on his presence; one was engaged, the strongest character in his line—the never-to-be-forgotten Pancho. It was perhaps not a just sentence to pronounce upon this individual, but circumstances seemed to warrant the comparison I involuntarily made between our watchful Pancho and a sleepless bloodhound. At night he curled himself up on a simple *petate*[5] with no pillow and only a blanket, and was as ready to respond to our beck and call as in the day.

In this house were two kitchens, representative of that part of the country. In the center of one was a miniature circus-ring about three feet in circumference, consisting simply of a raised circle of clay about one foot high. This constituted the range. Little fires were built within this ring, one under each of the pottery vessels used in the operations. After this uncomfortable fashion the cooking was done, the smoke circling about at its own sweet will and at length finding vent through a small door at one side, the only opening in the room. The sole piece of furniture was a worm-eaten table supported on two legs, the inner side braced against the wall. Its decayed condition indicated that it was at least a hundred years old. . . .

When I inspected these kitchens, it may be imagined that the sight was rather depressing, coupled with the certainty that I could effect no improvement. But we had the luxury of one tiny fireplace, to which in my despair I fled for refuge. In this little treasure, our scheme of housekeeping was inaugurated with results both brave and gay.

Among the latter experiences I may class my first coffee-roasting, not realizing till then that the essential feature of a mill was lacking, and that I was at least five hundred miles from any possible purchase of one. Pancho, however, was equal to the emergency, and, going off, soon returned with a *metate.* . . . It was a decidedly primitive affair, and, like the mills of the gods, it ground slowly, but like them, it also ground to powder. The *metate* is cut from a porous, volcanic rock, and is about eighteen inches long by a foot in width and eight inches in thickness. The upper surface . . . is roughened with indentures; upon this the article is placed and beaten with another stone . . . resembling a rolling pin. . . . This necessity of everyday life was a revelation to me. The color of an elephant, it was quite as unwieldy and graceless, but its importance . . . was undeniable. It had but two competitors to divide the honors with—the maguey plant and the donkey. . . .

The first meal cooked in that dainty little fireplace was more delicious than any that could be furnished at Delmonico's.[6] In his quaint efforts to assist, Pancho perambulated around with an air as all-important as though he were chef of that famous café. But the climax of all was reached in Pancho's estimation when I put a pure white linen cloth on my green, historic table and arranged for the meal. He said over and over: "*muy bonita cena!*" ("Very pretty supper"). But I discovered it was the attractions of my silver knives and forks and other natty tableware from home that constituted the novelty. In his experience fingers were made before knives and forks.

I found my [*mozo*] knew everything and everybody; the name of every street, the price of every article to be bought or sold. My curiosity, I presume, only stimulated his imagination, and the more pleased I appeared at his recitals, the more marvelous were his tales. He gave the lineage of every family of the *gente decente*,[7] for generations, his unique style adding pith and point to his narrations. He told me the story of [Miguel] Hidalgo and [José María] Morelos and [Agustín] Iturbide; the coming of the Americans, the French Intervention, and all the late revolutions, until my head rang with the boom of cannon and the beat of drum. But invariably these poetic narratives were rudely interrupted by some over-practical intrusion. In the same breath in which he completed the recital of the Emperor Iturbide, he suggested that wood was better and cheaper than charcoal for cooking. . . .

The difficulties of all strangers not familiar with the language and idioms of the country were a part of my daily experience. Pancho was by that time master of the situation, and although evidently often amused, his thoughtfulness in relieving me of all embarrassment never failed. Though grave, he had a sense of humor. This was made evident, on one occasion, when I had been using a hot flat-iron. Having finished, I told Pancho to put it in the *cocinera*, meaning the kitchen. I heard a low chattering and smothered laughter between him and the cook. Pancho then returned to my room and . . . said: "Please come to the kitchen." I went, when he placed himself in front of the cook, with his left hand on her shoulder, waved his right arm around the room and said: "*Señora*, look: this is the *cocinera*"—cook—"and this . . . is the *cocina!* Do you want me to put the . . . hot iron in the cook, or in the kitchen?" Then with the forefinger of his right hand moving hastily before his nose, and a waggish smile on his face, the pantomime closed with, "*No usamos así*" ("We don't use them this way"). . . . Soon after the episode of the flat-iron, I heard the long drawn intonation of a vender and paid little heed to him, supposing he was running off a list of his stock in trade, such as pins, needles, tape, thread and other things too numerous to mention. Wanting none of these, I replied: "*Tenemos bastante adentro*" ("We have plenty in the house"). A roar of laughter nearby, and a familiar voice interpreted the man's question humorously enough; he was only asking if I wanted a *chichi* ("wet nurse").[8] . . .

Pancho had so far held the reins as to all household purchases, but in accordance with my ideas of independence and careful management, I announced that I was going to market. He kindly told me it was not customary for ladies to go to market—"the *mozo* did that"—throwing in so many other arguments, also of a traditional nature, that I was somewhat awed by them, though not deterred. Having been accustomed to superintend personally all domestic duties, to be bolted and barred up in a house, without recreation and outdoor exercise, induced an insupportable sense of oppression.

Walking leisurely along the street, absorbed in thought, with Pancho near at hand carrying a basket, I was attracted by the sound of voices and the tramp of feet. Glancing backward, I saw a motley procession of idlers from the lower classes following, which increased at every corner, reminding me of good old circus days, though without the blare of brass instruments, the small boys bringing up the rear. The very unusual occurrence of a lady going to market had excited their curiosity.

The market was a large, pavilion-like building, occupying the center of a spacious plaza. Little tables and bits of straw matting were distributed on all sides; and upon these the trades-people, chiefly women, displayed their wares, fruits, vegetables, nuts, and other commodities. On seeing me, every vendor began shouting the prices and names of articles, entreating the *señora extranjera*[9] to buy. But the strange medley, together with their earnestness, took my breath away, and I could only stand and watch the crowd. In the fantastic scene before me, it would be impossible to tell which of the many unaccustomed features took precedence of the others in point of novelty.

Notwithstanding the crowd, there was no disorder, no loud laughter or unseemly conduct. The courteous meetings between acquaintances, the quiet hand-shakings, the tender inquiry as to the health of each other, the many forms of polite greeting, were strangely at variance with their dilapidated and tattered condition, their soiled garments, half-faded blankets, and time-stained sombreros.

Whole families seemed to have their abiding places in the market. Babies! babies! everywhere; under the tables, on mats, hanging on their mothers' backs, cuddled up in heaps among the beets, turnips, and lettuces, peeping over pumpkins larger than they; rollicking, crying, crowing, and. laughing, their dancing black eyes the only clean, clear spots about them— with and without clothes . . .

Parrots were there by the dozen. On seeing me, some began screaming and calling in idiomatic Spanish: "Look at the *señora extranjera!* Look! Look! *Señorita*, tell me your name!" The rest joined in chorus, and soon an interested crowd surrounded me. They kept close at my heels, inspecting every article I bought, even commenting on my dress, the women lightly stroking it and asking me a thousand questions as to where I came from, how I liked their country, and if I was not afraid of the Mexicans, and invariably closing by saying, "She is far from her home. It is sad for her here."

Here and there the amusing spectacle presented itself of men intently engaged in the occupation among us assigned to women, that of knitting and crocheting baby hoods and stockings of bright wool, and of the funniest shapes I ever beheld.

Vegetables, fruits, and nuts of all kinds were counted out carefully in little heaps, and could only be bought in that way, by retail, wholesale rates being universally rejected. I could buy as many of these piles as I wanted, but each one was counted separately, and paid for in the same way. I offered to buy out the entire outfit of a woman who had a bushel basket in reserve, even agreeing to pay her for the basket; but she only shook her head, and wagged the forefinger, saying, "*No, señora, no puedo*"—("No, madam, I cannot"). . . .

From Pancho's manner I am sure he felt as if his vocation were gone, by the way I had overleaped the bounds of custom in finding out things for myself. Nevertheless, he managed now and then to give some of the vendors an account of our house, its location, and my singular management. But though looking mystified, he never left me for a moment, no matter how long I talked, or asked explanations. . . .

Every eye was upon me when I had the temerity to ask for twenty pounds of sugar, ten pounds of coffee, and a gallon of vinegar. Sugar and coffee were abundant, but the vinegar was in bottles. He handed me one with a flourish, saying, "*Vinagre de Francia.* We have no other." I began to feel that far-away France had become my ally, having, like me, made an invasion on the "costumbres;" the only difference being, that the vinegar bottles were jolted on the backs of meek *burros*,[10] or in carts, a thousand miles, and I had arrived, safe and sound, by diligence.[11] . . .

Going to market, a matter-of-fact affair in the United States, [had] resolved itself into a novel adventure. The heterogeneous assemblage of goods, and the natural and artificial products of the country, astonished me equally with the strange vendors. There was so much that was at once humorous, pitiable, and grotesque. . . . Every day the strange enigma unfolded itself before me, with accrued interest. My lot had been cast among these people, when in total ignorance of their habits and customs. My aim and purpose, above all things, was to establish a home among them on the basis of the one left behind. . . .

Our Mexican friends made daily visits to the house, and were always ready to enjoy with me the latest humorous episode furnished by the servants. I was often assured by these friends that the oddities of their *mozos* and other servants had not occurred to them, as so striking, until my experiences, together with my enjoyment, had presented them in a new light; and that for them I had held the mirror up to nature. This was only possible by keeping up an establishment, one's self part and parcel of the incidents as they occurred. . . .

Variety of scene and character was never wanting. If the interior of the household failed to interest me, I had only to turn through my barred window upon the curious street scenes. . . . Foremost among the objects that claimed my sympathy were the poor, over-laden, beaten donkeys; they seemed ubiquitous, and the picture my window framed never lacked a meek-eyed *burro*, until I could not separate them from their surroundings. They were typical figures, and at last I came to regard any scene from which they were absent as incomplete. They passed in a never-ending procession, bearing every imaginable commodity. I soon noticed that if the leader or "bellwether" of the gang stopped, the rest did the same. If goaded to desperation by the merciless driver, the only resistance they offered was to quietly but doggedly lie down. Often dozens of them passed, with green corn on the stalks, suspended gracefully about them, and in such quantities that nothing was visible but the donkeys' heads and ears, the corn spread out in fan-shape, reminding me of a lady's train, or a peacock in full plumage. . . . Pancho's knowledge of burros was as profound as of other subjects. As fifty of them were passing one morning, he happened to see me gazing on the strange scene, when the oracle broke silence by saying: "*Allí va el ferrocarril mexicano*" ("There goes the Mexican railroad"). . . . At last I was convinced that *burros* are possessed of an uncommon amount of good sense as well as much patience and meekness. Their shrewdness was intensely amusing to me when I saw how keenly they watched the . . . driver unburden one of their *compañeros*, and how quickly they jumped into the place to be also relieved of their terrible loads.[12]

A man with a crate of eggs hanging from his head went trotting by, advertising his business by screaming, "*Huevos! huevos!*" in deafening tones. Pancho . . . called the vendor with the long tangled hair and swarthy skin. After peeping cautiously around, he entered, when I went at once to make the bargain for myself, and to turn over another leaf in the book of my experiences. I wanted to buy two dozen, and handing him fifty cents, told Pancho to count the eggs. The man turned the half-dollar over and over—looking at me and then at the half-dollar, and at last handed the money back to me, saying: "*No se venden así*" ("They are not sold in this way" . . . "only by *reales*" [a coin worth 12.5 cents]. I said: "You sell six for a *real*, . . . it is the same at twenty-five cents a dozen." The words had hardly passed my lips, when he turned and looked me directly in the eye, with an expression which meant, "Well, now, look here, madam, you'll not take advantage of me in that way; I know the customary manner of doing business in this country, and there will be no change in selling eggs." Pancho put in a plea for him, adding: "*Es costumbre del país,*" ("It is the custom of the country"), which reconciled me. The vendor began counting slowly the fingers of his right hand with his left—"*uno, dos, tres, cuatro, cinco,*"—then holding up the index finger of the left hand—*seis*—and extending the six fingers, palms to the front, waved them back and forth before his determined face, as in low guttural tones that made me shiver, he said: "*No, señorita, so-la-men-te seis por un real!* I will only sell them at six for a real"), by dozens—never! Lifting his hat politely, he took his departure.[13]. . .

Seeing everything and everybody so conservative, running in the groove of centuries, reminded me that I was losing sight of my own "*costumbres.*" The little fireplace in which the cooking had been done became distasteful, and I longed for a cooking-stove. A Mexican gentleman whom I did not know, on hearing of my desire, kindly offered to lend us one that he had bought about twenty years before, but had been unable to have it used to any extent, owing to the prejudices of the servants.

With the utmost delight, I saw the *cargador* (porter) enter the big door with this time-worn rickety desire of my heart. But when he slipped it from his head, the rattle of its dilapidated parts made me quake with anxiety. Both Pancho and the cargador exclaimed in one voice, "*Caramba!*" ("Goodness gracious alive!"), gazing with puzzled expressions on the wreck. The cargador was the first to break the silence that followed this ebullition of astonishment. "*Qué atroz!*" ("How atrocious!") he exclaimed. "*Qué barbaridad!*" ("How barbarous!") echoed Pancho. "*Por supuesto que sí!*" ("Well, I should say so"), quoth the cargador. "*Pos cómo no*" ("Well, I'd like to know why it isn't"), said the disgusted Pancho. "She will never get a cook to use it, never!" The cook came into the patio to inspect the stove, and she too spoke in a low voice to the men, but folding her arms and emphatically raising her tone on the last word "*el hígado,*" which explained itself later.

As there was not a flue in the building, the stove was placed in the little fire-place. It had only two feet, which stood diagonally opposite each other, causing the stove to nod and bend in a grim, diabolic way. Being duly settled on its own responsibility by the aid of bricks, Pancho opened one of the doors, when instantly it lay full length on the floor. He walked away, looking back in disgust on the wreck. I ventured to touch the door on the opposite side, when, as if by magic, it, also, took a position on the floor as vis-à-vis; the servants exclaiming: "*Muy mal hecho!*" ("A very bad make, or job!"). . . . "*Pos cómo no!*" ("Well, I should say so!") they all chimed in, the cook glancing at me suspiciously, and folding her arms as she added: "No, *señora*, I cannot use the *estufa*." "Why not?" I asked. "*Porque me hace daño en el hígado*." ("Because it will give me disease of the liver; Mexican servants dislike stoves, and if you keep this one, no cook will stay here,") she replied.

A blacksmith was called to renovate the treasure, but he also worked on the *mañana* system, taking weeks to do his best, and still leaving the stove dilapidated. The cook took her departure, and on Pancho's solicitation dozens came, but a glance at the stove was enough.

Politeness ruled their lives, and native courtesy was stronger than love of truth. Without saying a word about the stove, they would say, "I would like to work for you—you are *muy amable—muy simpática*—amiable and agreeable; but,"—her voice running up to a piping treble—she would add, "*tengo mi familia*"—I have my family—or, "I am now occupied," meaning employed, by Don or Doña Such-a-one.

Pancho always looked on with keen interest during such conversations, his face saying, without a word: "I told you so; these cooks will never adopt your *costumbres americanos*"

The stove was always falling, or some part dropping off. At last one day I went in and saw it careened to one side—both feet off——and both doors down, suggesting that some canny hand had dismantled it. The wreck presented a picture painfully realistic; but before I had time to inquire as to the perpetrator, the stove addressed me:

"I was once an American citizen, bred and born. My pedigree is equal to any of your boasted latter-day ancestry. A residence of twenty years in Mexico has changed my habitudes and customs. You need not try to mend and fix me up—to erect your American household gods on my inanimate form. I am a naturalized Mexican, with all that is implied. I have had my freedom the greater portion of the time since they bought me from a broken-down gringo; for neither the *señora* nor the cooks would use me. I'll do you no good; if you mend and fix me up in one place, I'll break down in another. Content yourself with our *braseros* (ranges) and pottery. Accept our usages, and you will be happy in our country.

You need not wonder at my rust-eaten and battered condition. I have lain undisturbed in the corral for nearly twenty years. During the rainy season, when the big drops pelted me unmercifully, snakes, lizards, centipedes, and tarantulas came habitually to take refuge inside my iron doors. So many different natures coming in close contact, there were frequently serious collisions. These warlike engagements have crippled and maimed me, more than the weather, or any service I have rendered. You will not find a cook who will even know how to make me hot for your use. Take me back to the corral! Take me back!"[14]

Notes

1. Fanny Chambers Gooch [Iglehart], *Face to Face with the Mexicans: The Domestic Life, Educational, Social, and Business Ways, Statesmanship and Literature, Legendary and General History of the Mexican People as Seen and Studied by an American Woman During Seven Years of Intercourse with Them* (New York: Fords, Howard, and Hulbert, 1887), 60–73, 75–83.
2. Gooch commissioned Waldo to illustrate her book during her stay in Mexico City. Gooch, *Face to Face*, 17.
3. Harvey C. Gardiner, "Introduction," in Fanny Chambers Gooch, *Face to Face with the Mexicans*, ed. Harvey C. Gardiner (Carbondale: Southern Illinois University Press, 1966), vii–xx.
4. Tomorrow, meaning in this case at some undetermined point in the future.
5. Sleeping mat.
6. Swanky restaurant in Mexico City still open today.
7. "Decent people;" people of education and money.
8. This paragraph is an unusual instance of poking fun at oneself and Mexicans at the same time.
9. Foreign woman.
10. Donkeys.
11. Stagecoach.
12. By inference, Gooch judges the donkeys to represent the Mexican national character.
13. A good example of using an isolated example for making a larger point. Not having been told otherwise, the disingenuous reader might assume all Mexicans are stupid.
14. An example of the modern-traditional dichotomy Gooch uses to explain national differences between the United States and Mexico.

10 From the Tarascos to Porfirio Díaz

Carl Lumholtz[1]

Carl Sophus Lumholtz's Unknown Mexico *is the first ethnographic exploration of the indigenous peoples of the northwest. The book is a treasure trove of information on societies that have long since lost their autonomy from central Mexico; a key building block in the image that historian Lesley Byrd Simpson would popularize as "many Mexicos" decades later.[2] The idea of many Mexicos not only highlights the struggle to establish national political authority in a country marked by strong regional and local allegiances, but also the multiethnic makeup of Mexico, and, in particular, the cultural and linguistic diversity of the indigenous population. This travel account is also a prime example of what Mary Louise Pratt views as conquest by scientific exploration. In his quest to explore and promote Mexico's diverse heritage, Lumholtz furthered the interests of both foreign investors and the Díaz regime by presenting his research as part of Mexico's exhibits at the World's Fair in Chicago. The following excerpt narrates the last weeks of his trip from Michoacán to Mexico City. After twenty years of Díaz's rule, Lumholtz praises*

the material improvements that both Bertie-Marriott and Gooch still found lacking in the 1880s. The passage not only reveals the author's racial prejudice—an attitude he shared with his nineteenth-century peers—but also his favorable view of the Porfiriato and his vain hope that the old dictator would not forget his own indigenous roots in his treatment of the "Indians."

Lumholtz was born in 1851 near Lillehammer, Norway, the son of an army captain. After obtaining a degree in theology from the University of Christiania, he became a bird collector, a passion that led him on his first major expedition to Queensland, Australia. That trip produced his first book, Among Cannibals *(1889) and a lecture tour in the United States. During his travels in North America, Lumholtz became drawn to the geology and ethnology of the U.S. Southwest—a region with barren mountains that reminded him of his native country. In 1890, he conducted an ethnographic study of the nomadic tribes of Sonora and Chihuahua. On a second trip, he encountered the Tarahumaras of Chihuahua, a people that had existed without any sustained contact with the rest of Mexico and with whom Lumholtz spent eighteen months alone. In 1894, he traveled to the Huicholes and Coras of Nayarit before heading on to the Tarascos of the western state of Michoacán. He died in 1922.[3]*

Next day I started for Uruapan. . . . A Mexican who appeared to be on good terms with the [locals] offered to show me some ruins close to the road, and I had taken him on, thinking he might become useful also as an interpreter, since he spoke Tarasco very well. When we arrived at a plain not far from the village, which, however, could not be seen from that point, we came upon several men ploughing. To avoid suspicion, the guide deemed it wise to tell them what we were about to do; otherwise, he said, they might run to the village, ring the big bell to bring all the people together, and make it unpleasant for us. As it was, the boy I engaged for three *reales* (thirty-seven centavos) to carry the camera boxes and show us the best track up the hill to the ruins, took fright when arriving at the top, saying that he was afraid his father might see him, and abandoned me in a hurry.

To my disappointment the ruins turned out to be only the four walls of a chapel standing close to what seemed to be an old cemetery. Having gone to the trouble of ascending, I photographed it, as well as the imposing peak of Cuitzeo, which rose directly above us. . . . The place was lovely. We were surrounded by glorious pine forests, which covered most of the mountainside; only around the top had wind and weather left some straggling, gnarled, and twisted veterans scattered here and there. I spent barely half an hour here, and then rapidly descended, to lose no time in reaching Uruapan that evening.

Just as we were emerging from the forest and reached the plain, a dozen Indians from the village came marching toward us. The two leaders were armed with muzzle-loaders, the others with machetes and stones. "What are you doing here?" they demanded angrily. "Who gave you permission to come here?" I told them that there was no law against photographing, and that I could not see any harm in it. They calmed down somewhat, yet could not understand why I had not asked for permission to take pictures. "That is what I should have done," I said, "if I had had the time, and now I am willing to go with you and explain everything." "The mischief is already done," they retorted, "and who knows but that you will come back and take possession of our lands!" I assured them that I had no such intentions, and we went together toward the mule which was carrying the camera and which I had left nearby. Their anger rose again as they caught sight of the boy who had shown us the path uphill.

The men lifted the hammers of their guns full cock, put caps on, and pointed the muzzles disagreeably close to the boy's face, scolding him severely all the time, while the youngster vigorously and valiantly pleaded his case. My interpreter grew pale. "I know these people," he said; "they are devils, and I am going now." "Don't you think you had better stay and help me explain matters?" I asked him. "You know I do not speak Tarasco, and surely you are not afraid of the Indians?" He would not be persuaded, but maintained that it was getting late and that he wanted to return home. With a parting injunction, "Don't forget to speak to the prefect about these people!" he was off. He had hardly courage enough to take the money due him, leaving me to settle the matter as best I could with the fanatical crowd that was gathering in the village.[4]

While the twelve emissaries wended their way back, Angel and I packed the camera on the mule and joined the rest of my party, consisting of two Indians, who had been watching the other mules on the plain farther on. "Anyway," laughed Angel, whose stout heart never failed him, "they have only one shot each." He evidently had full confidence in my modern rifle and revolver. As for himself, he carried only a small knife on the road, objecting to large knives, which he considered good only for "the big balls," where there usually is fighting. My other followers were also unarmed, though I had entrusted one with a pistol just for the respect it commands when dangling from a man's belt; inasmuch as he could not shoot I had deemed it safer to leave it unloaded.

The expedition now set itself in motion, and in a quarter of an hour we reached a thicket where the road was narrow. Here I found over thirty Indians waiting for me, sitting sullenly on each side of the path. None of them looked up while the mules passed between them. I ordered my men to wait for me a little farther on, and asked for the *jefe*.[5] In silent dignity a man with an intelligent and quite sympathetic face arose. I drew from my pocket the letter from President Díaz and another from the Governor of the State of Michoacán, and asked my taciturn official whether he could read. To my surprise he said he could, and then he took the documents and read them slowly aloud. This finished, I addressed the assemblage in Spanish:

"I am glad to see that you are able to defend yourselves so well against the whites; but as regards me, you are mistaken. You are opposed to me because the people in Cherán have told you that I kill and eat people. That is a lie! I am a friend of you Indians, and that is why I have come from a distant country to see how you are. I have travelled for nearly five years among tribes just like you, and none of them has ever done me harm; why should you? You have many friends in Mexico and in the countries on the other side of the big sea, and they want to know how you look and how you are, and to hear about your old customs and your ancient history. That is why I have taken pictures of the people and of the country. Some of you think that I am seeking treasures; but I am not looking for money or silver. I have plenty to eat at home, and need not come here to get tortillas and beans."

The Indians held a little council among themselves, and soon gave in. They even invited me to stop in their village, since it was getting late. But when we arrived the women would not consent to this, and there was nothing for us to do but provide ourselves with fat pine wood and continue the journey by torchlight through the pitch-dark night.

Thus ended my last day among the Tarascos of the Sierra. Having been away from civilisation very long and my time being more than up, I had attempted to get through with this tribe as soon as possible, claiming their confidence before they had become properly acquainted with me. The result was that for the entire four months I stayed among them I had to overcome the antagonism not only of the tribe as a whole, but of every district and every hamlet. Without patience and tact an ethnologist can do nothing with primitive people. I feel confident that if I had had, say, six months more, I should have conquered them all and made them my friends. The same *jefe* afterward twice took the trouble to visit me in Uruapan, and bring me antiquities for sale. The Indians have been so imposed upon that one should not wonder when valiant tribes like the Tarascos defend with all their might the last piece of land left to them. Even if they had killed me no one could have blamed them for doing as they have been done by for centuries past.

We arrived at ten o'clock at night at Uruapan where I was not a little astonished to find the streets lighted by electricity. It was a great contrast to the domain of the wild mountaineers I had just left; and the disparity became still more glaring next day when I took a walk through the town.

Uruapan is a Spanish corruption of Urupan, "Where flowers are blooming"—that is, where there is constant spring. In popular opinion Uruapan is the "Paradise of Michoacán," a name it deserves on account of its charming locality no less than its delightful people and superb climate. The temperature is pleasantly warm in the day and at night a cool breeze springs up to sweep away all microbes. Near the town is a magnificent spring, in which rises a river whose abundance of crystal-clear water adds variety to the singularly picturesque beauty of the landscape. The water is used for irrigating orchards of banana and coffee trees, and the coffee raised here is famous as the best in Mexico. In the *tierra caliente* below rice is cultivated. The river also furnishes the motor power for the electric plant, and the town boasts also two cotton mills and a cigar factory.

Uruapan may be called the capital of the *tierra caliente* of Michoacán, and enjoys a great deal of commerce. Especially on Sundays its streets present a most animated appearance, when the Indians from far and near come to dispose of their products. In the evening a well-trained band discourses beautiful music on the Plaza de los Martirios, which is thronged with quite elegantly dressed people. In the so-called casino I was surprised to find a table equal to the best in Mexico, with a charge of three *reales* a meal. I thought at first I had ventured by mistake into some private club, but luckily for me it was really the *fonda*.[6] What a relief, after all the privations and discomforts and fights against prejudice and fanaticism, to find myself at last safe in this haven! To add to my comfort, the photographer of the town, awake to the rare purity of the water, kept a bathing establishment, and I hugely enjoyed the baths. . . . Think of it! Here were Old World culture, the comfort of well-prepared food, with Spanish wines, courteous, liberal people who never thought of asking you whether you were *protestante* or freemason, and only three leagues away barbarians who wanted to kill you for photographing a landscape, who would not allow you to stop over night in their village, and among whom you had either to die of hunger or be thankful for their condescension in selling you miserable tortillas and beans! With all due appreciation for the Indian's many admirable qualities and an honest sympathy for the wrongs he has suffered, what is bred in the bone of civilised man cannot be eradicated at will. The only sphere in which he really feels at home is the one which offers him the benefits of civilisation.[7]

The Tarascos of Uruapan long ago became Mexicanised; that is, they are now without land, spend all the money they earn by their labour in feasts for the saints, and have acquired quite a taste for the white man's brandy. The women, however, are still very industrious. A nice, hard-working girl of thirty told me that among her compatriots there was no one whom she could marry, for she did not like drunken people. Among the Indians in the population there is much goitre, and accordingly many who are deaf and dumb or imbecile.

I did not lose much time in visiting the *barrio*—that is, "the ward of the Indians"—to make myself acquainted with the manufacture of the beautiful lacquer-ware for which Uruapan is famous. The work is done on table-tops, gourds, or principally on trays. . . . The designs nearly always represent flowers, which the artists draw from models before them. The work is admirable, but there is a monotony of ideas. No doubt it could be developed into an art if the painters were properly educated and had a wider scope. . . . One finds also a good deal of rubbish in the market, manufactured mainly by Mexican women, whose product is inferior to that of the Indians. . . .

As the road to Pátzcuaro . . . had of late been infested with robbers, I for the first time in my experience in Mexico considered it best to get an escort, and started at the end of November in company with a sergeant and two cavalrymen. The road . . . is of great advantage to the robbers, and to judge from the sixteen crosses I saw cut into the bark of one tree, *fusilados* (shot ones—that is, robbers who had been executed) must have been plentiful. . . . The lodging house here was utterly uninhabitable for a civilised being, so I stretched myself out for the night in a sheltered place outside of the kitchen, expecting this to be my last uncomfortable night in Mexico.

From here to Pátzcuaro the road was patrolled by *rurales*, on account of a robbery that had been committed the week before. At dusk we arrived at Pátzcuaro, at an elevation of 7,000 feet, which had been described to me as a dull place, "where there are plenty of masses and the people sleep late in the morning." The town is old and quaint, and has eleven churches and a great many priests—more than I had seen in any other place of similar size. The eight thousand inhabitants came originally, for the most part, from [the Basque country in Spain], and are nice and obliging. From the neighbourhood one gets a fine view over the lake with its dirty, greyish-green water, in which thrives the famous salamander, the *axolotl*, frequently offered for sale in the plaza of the town. It is eaten, and from its skin an extract is made which is used as a remedy for asthma.

The shores and islands of the lake are thickly populated with Tarasco Indians. There are more than twenty towns and villages on its banks. An interesting pre-Columbian instrument is still in use among the natives here, namely, a throwing stick, with which they hurl their long reed spears at aquatic birds. The spear nowadays is provided with a triple-pointed iron tip, and the throwing stick . . . has two holes for the fingers, and a groove in which the spear shaft lies.

At certain fixed seasons of the year, and especially prior to the feast of the tutelary saint, it is customary to arrange a chase of all kinds of fowl, principally ducks, geese, widgeons, and sandpipers. The sport is original and picturesque . . . a fleet of from eighty to a hundred small canoes meet, each of the dug-outs manned by three or four individuals, two of whom propel and steer the little craft while the others are left free for the chase. They start from the shore in orderly array, proceeding toward a prearranged locality known to harbour an abundance of water-birds. On the approach to this spot they form in a half moon. . . . Then each hunter gets on his feet, holding in his right hand the throwing-stick Tarasco and the long spear. He bends his body slightly backward, lifts his right arm high up, and hurls his light and sharp-pointed weapon into the multitude of birds. He is pretty sure to harpoon one or two of them. . . . While the hunt is on the canoes maintain the semi-lunar formation, as anyone pushing ahead would run the risk of being wounded by flying spears; besides, only by remaining together can they keep the birds confined. Such hunting expeditions may last for several days and nights, and altogether a considerable number of birds is bagged. As each spear bears the mark of its owner, there are no disputes about the game.

Before pulling the spear out of the body they kill the bird and throw it into the bottom of the canoe. The rich meat of these birds forms an indispensable part of the savoury tamales served at the public banquet with which the feast of the patron saint is celebrated.

I visited the ancient capital of the Tarascos, Tzintzuntzán, which the Aztecs called Huitzizilan, either name meaning "Where there are hummingbirds." The town lies near the lake and can easily be reached on horseback. It is now insignificant, but . . . it was once six miles long. The inhabitants are civilised[8] and speak Spanish only. An attraction which occasionally brings tourists to the place is a large oil painting, supposed to be a Titian, representing the descent from the cross. The Indians zealously guard it, and it is said that neither the desire of the Church nor an offer of twenty-five thousand dollars from an American has induced them to part with it. . . .

The railway which connects Pátzcuaro with the City of Mexico runs in its western half through fertile open country which once belonged to the Tarascos. The country along the route is by no means level or monotonous; near Toluca, fifty miles this side of Mexico City, the grade rising to some 8,500 feet.

There had been great changes in Mexico City since I was here three years ago. The principal streets now were lighted by electricity and looked straight and clean. The people moved about busily, as in the great capitals of Europe, and law and order prevailed everywhere. Happily the picturesqueness of the city has not been effaced, and everywhere one is reminded that this is a historical place full of archaeological and even ethnological interest. Otomí women bring in live ducks from the lakes in the same way as of old, or a young Indian drives a large flock of turkeys through the Alameda with a whip, or water carriers go about peddling their ware. The flower market near the great cathedral continues another custom of ancient times. . . .

In the wards of the poor and in the suburbs pure-bred Aztecs are yet numerous, leading a hand-to-mouth existence as best they can. . . . In a sense the Aztecs were the Romans of the New World. Theirs was the great language that was revered by many tribes. If you ask one of their descendants in his own tongue for anything you want to buy he may make you a present of it. . . . Much may yet be learned in regard to the ancient habits and customs of the tribes in the more remote villages, where the people still speak their own language, as, for instance, on the slopes of Ixtaccíhuatl. . . . They still sacrifice children to the rain god Tláloc, throwing them into the lagoon of Texcoco.[9]

In the afternoon of December 13th I had an audience with President Porfirio Díaz, my third meeting with him. His hair and moustache had turned grey since I saw him last, but [the septuagenarian] still looked as vigorous as a man in the fifties. I told him of what important service I had found the letter which he had been kind enough to give me, and how even where the Indians could not read they had convinced themselves of its genuineness and of my safe character by feeling the paper and looking at the seal. Of course they had never fully grasped the object of my visit, but the purpose of the document had been attained by the word *importante*, which occurred in one of the sentences; it always attracted their attention and paved the way for me to their confidence.

When I mentioned that the President's name was known among the remote tribes I had explored, he smiled and said: "The Indians are good people, if one explains matters to them, but they have been so cheated and imposed upon that they have become distrustful. During the French Intervention nearly all the soldiers of the Liberal Party were Indians, and they have been of the greatest service in saving the country." I did not forget the message with which the Coras and the Huichols had charged me—namely, that Don Porfirio should issue an order that their land should never be given to the whites. To my surprise he asked: "Are there any among them who can write?" I told him that there were and offered to give him names. "Then I will write to them," he said. I hope that letter reached the Indians. The President himself could hardly realise of what service it would be to them. They would treasure it as a powerful talisman against the neighbours for ages to come.

General Díaz has a strain of Mixtec[10] blood in his veins, a fact suggested in his physique and physiognomy, which shows also great force of character, strong willpower, and at the same time benevolence and kindness of heart. In bearing he is dignified, and in manner courteous and urbane, and his great personal magnetism fascinates everybody with whom he comes in contact. He knows his country and its needs better than any other Mexican living, and for nearly a quarter of a century he has governed it judiciously and with rare sagacity. How he has reconstructed the republic, built up a state, and developed a nation is a matter of history. General Díaz is not only a great man on this continent, but one of the great men of our time.

Notes

1. Carl Lumholtz, *Unknown Mexico: A Record of Five Years' Exploration Among the Tribes of the Western Sierra Madre; in the Tierra Caliente of Tepic and Jalisco; and Among the Tarascos of Michoacán* (London: MacMillan and Co., 1903), 2:435–53.

2. Lesley Byrd Simpson, *Many Mexicos*, 4th rev. ed. (Berkeley: University of California Press, 1967).

3. Evon Z. Vogt, "Introduction," in Carl Lumholtz, *Unknown Mexico: A Record of Five Years' Exploration Among the Tribes of the Western Sierra Madre; in the Tierra Caliente of Tepic and Jalisco; and Among the Tarascos of Michoacán* (repr. New York: AMS Press, 1973), vii–viii.

4. As told by Lumholtz—with no additional explanation or qualification—this episode fuels the reader's expectation that indigenous people are savages.

5. Local boss.

6. Inn.

7. A good example of Lumholtz's racist prejudice.

8. Meaning, of European culture.

9. Lumholtz assumes here a far greater degree of knowledge of indigenous societies than he has actually acquired.

10. Indigenous population in the southeastern state of Oaxaca that produced Mitla and other famous archaeological sites.

11 "Military Diazpotism" in Theory and Practice

Charles Flandrau[1]

$$\text{◈}$$

Published at a time when the Porfirian dictatorship began to show its first cracks, Charles M. Flandrau's Viva Mexico! *is unusually balanced in its interpretation of Mexico in general and the Porfiriato in particular, especially considering that it is the work of a U.S. owner of a coffee plantation. While the book praises the material progress of the Porfiriato, this sojourner account is also critical of the dictatorship. "Mexico," Flandrau wrote, "is not a republic, but a military Diazpotism."[2] To be sure, the author subscribes to the same ethnic and racial stereotypes that one finds in the preceding selections. But like Gooch, Flandrau's work is fundamentally shaped by his interaction with ordinary Mexicans, and it displays the kind of genuine sympathy that only a long period of residence can provide. The following excerpt is particularly noteworthy for its sophisticated understanding of the workings of the Porfirian system, a system that depended on making the crucial distinction between constitutional theory and political practice.*

Flandrau (1871–1938) hailed from St. Paul, Minnesota, the older of two sons of a lawyer and agent for the Sioux. In 1879, the family embarked on a one-year journey through Europe, a trip that forever predisposed both children to travel. In 1903, the lifelong bachelor and Harvard graduate traveled to Mexico to join his brother Blair, the owner of a coffee plantation near the remote town of Misantla, Veracruz.[3] While Viva Mexico! *presumes to deal with Mexico on the whole, the episodes about and around this coffee plantation are the greatest strength of this lively, well-written work.*

❖

At first you are both amazed and annoyed by what seems like not only lack of curiosity but positive ignorance on the part of Americans who live in Mexico. As a new arrival, I had an admirable thirst for information which I endeavored to slake at what I supposed were fountains of knowledge as well as of afternoon tea. The tea was delicious and plentiful; but the knowledge simply did not exist.

"What is the population of Barranca?" you ask of an intelligent compatriot who has lived in Barranca for ten years.

"Why, I don't know exactly," he replies, as if the question were an interesting one that had never before occurred to him.

"Oh, I don't mean exactly—but is it eight thousand, or fourteen, or twenty-five? It's rather difficult for a stranger to form an idea; the towns are built so differently from ours. Although they may not be really large, they are so compact that they look more populous and 'citified' than places of the same size in the United States," you explain.

"Yes, that's very true, and it is difficult," he agrees.

"Do you suppose I could find out anywhere? Do they ever take the census?" you pursue.

"The census? Why, I don't know about that. But there's Smith on the bench over there having his shoes shined. He's been in the country for fifteen years—he'll be able to tell you. Smith, I want to introduce a friend of mine who is very anxious to know the population of Barranca and whether they ever take the census."

"The census?" muses Smith, ignoring the population entirely. "I don't know if they take the census, but they take your taxes with great regularity," he declares with a laugh. Then follows a pleasant ten minutes with Smith, during which the reason of your introduction to him does not recur, and after precisely the same thing has happened several other times with several other persons, you would almost rather start a revolution than an inquiry into the population of Barranca.

The specific instance is perhaps a trivial one, but it is typical, and, as I said, you are for a time amazed and irritated, on asking intelligent questions about the federal and state governments, the judiciary, the army, education, morality, and even so obvious a matter as the climate, to receive from American acquaintances replies that are never accurate and rarely as much as inaccurately definite. Some of them frankly admit that, as they never have had personal relations with the establishments you seek to learn about (barring the climate), they have not taken the trouble to inform themselves. Others appear to experience a belated regret at their long indifference, promise to look the matter up and let you know. But they never do, and it is rather discouraging. You yearn to acquire a respectably comprehensive idea of the conditions in which you are living, yet the only people with whom you can carry on any but a most staccato and indispensable conversation are unable to throw light. So, being the only one really intelligent foreigner in the republic, you resort to the medium of art, and begin to read books.

Everyone you know has at some time or other read and enjoyed Prescott's "Conquest,"[4] but it does not emerge that on the subject of Mexico they have ever read anything else, and for a while you quietly revel in your mental alertness and superior intelligence. You are learning all about the country—its institutions and laws, its products and habits—while your listless friends still sit in darkness. Then one fine morning something happens—something of no especial importance, but something that nevertheless serves to insert the thin edge of suspicion's wedge between you and your learning.

You have, for instance, read that "in virtue of the constitution adopted February 5, 1857, arrest is prohibited, save in the case of crimes meriting corporal punishment," and it has seemed to you a wise and just provision. You have also, let us say, employed two competent stone masons to build a coffee tank, a fireplace, a pigpen, or some such useful accessory of life in the tropics, and you become much disturbed when, after they have worked steadily and well for three or four days, they fail to appear. That afternoon as you stroll through the plaza lamenting their perfidy, you are astonished at receiving two sheepish, friendly stone masons who are engaged in laying municipal cobblestones, together with thirty or forty other prisoners, under the eyes of several heavily armed policemen. Unmistakably they are your masons, and with much bewilderment you demand of Smith—who, no doubt, is strolling with you—just what it means.

"It merely means," Smith explains, "that the town is repairing part of the plaza pavement and needs competent masons. So they arrested yours."

"But on what grounds?"

"Oh, drunkenness probably."

"Do you suppose they were drunk? They seemed like very steady men."

"Why, they may have been a trifle elated," Smith laughs. "The assumption that they were isn't a particularly startling one in this part of the world. But that wasn't why they were arrested. They were arrested because they were good masons and the city happens to need them. If they hadn't been drunk, some one would have been sent out to make them so—never, unfortunately, a very arduous undertaking."

"Oh, indeed; how simple and efficacious!" you murmur, and go home to read some more.[5]

Still other wise and just provisions of the same excellent document are that no person may be obliged to work for another person without freely consenting so to work, nor without receiving just remuneration, and that imprisonment for debts of a purely civil nature is prohibited. But as your Spanish gradually improves and you are able to have more sustained talks with the natives, you learn that the entire lives of a great number of peones working on haciendas contain two alternatives, one of which is practical slavery and the other imprisonment for debt to his employer.

A young man goes to work on, say, a sugar plantation for the magnificent wages of thirty-six Mexican cents a day.[6] In the course of time—usually a very short time—he acquires a family. If he acquires it after certain preliminary formalities, such as a marriage ceremony and its attendant festivities, his employer has loaned him the forty or fifty pesos—unpayable sum—necessary to defray the costs of the priest and the piper, and the young man's eternal indebtedness begins from the beginning. If, however, there are no formalities, the financial burden is not assumed until the birth of the first child.

Mexicans of every station adore their children, and even when, as frequently happens among the lower classes, the parents are neither civilly nor religiously married (in Mexico only the civil ceremony is recognized by the law) nothing is too good or too expensive for the offspring. They are baptized and, if the informal union of the parents lasts long enough, they are confirmed. But in Mexico, as elsewhere, the kingdom of heaven costs money, and this money the young man's employer cheerfully advances. Then in the natural march of events some one dies. Death, of course, all the world over, has become one of our grossest extravagances. Again the employer delightedly pays.

Now he has the young man—no longer so young—exactly where his sugar plantation wants him. On thirty-six cents a day there is no possibility of a laborer's paying a debt of a hundred or more pesos and moving away, and if he attempts to depart without paying it, a word from the hacendado to his friend the *jefe político*[7] would suffice to land him in jail and keep him there. It is impossible to deny that on some haciendas, perhaps on many, this form of slavery is a happier, a more comfortable arrangement than would be the freedom so energetically insisted on in the constitution. Still, slavery is neither a pretty word nor a pretty idea, and yet, in spite of the constitution, the idea obtains in Mexico quite as it obtains in the United States.

Then again you read with satisfaction that among other forms of freedom—"freedom of education, freedom to exercise the liberal professions, freedom of thought," and so on—the freedom of the press is guaranteed; guaranteed, that is to say, with the reservation that "private rights and the public peace shall not be violated." The manner in which this reservation can be construed, however, does not occur to you until you read in *El Imparcial* or in the *Mexican Herald*—the best Spanish and American daily papers— an account of, let us say, a strike of the mill operatives at Orizaba, and then, a week later, chance to learn what actually happened.

"I see by the *Herald* that you had a little strike at Orizaba the other day," you remark to the middle-aged British manager of a large Orizaba jute mill, with whom you find yourself in the same swimming pond at the baths of Tehuacan. "The *Herald* said that in a clash with the troops several strikers were killed and twenty-five were injured."

"Did it indeed?" remarks the manager dryly, and later, when you are sitting together in the sun after your bath, he explains that the strike was an incipient revolution engineered by a junta in St. Louis [Missouri],[8] that the Government sent down a regiment from the City of Mexico, that in an impromptu sort of way six hundred strikers were immediately shot, and that the next morning thirty-four were formally, elaborately, and officially exe- cuted. This prompt and heroic measure, he informs you, ended both the strike and the incipient revolution, and as you compare what you have read in the papers with what is the truth, you can tell yourself that it has also ended your illusions as to the freedom of the Mexican press.

In fact you begin to realize why, when you ask American residents of the country for information, their replies are usually so vague, so contradictory, so uninforming. It is not, as a rule, because they know too little, but because they know too much. Theoretical Mexico—the Mexico of constitutions, reform laws, statutes, and books of travel—has ceased, long since, vitally to concern them. It is Mexico as they day by day find it that interests them and that in the least counts. And practical, every-day Mexico is an entirely different, infinitely more mysterious, fascinating affair.

"Does it rain here in summer as much as it does in winter?" I once asked a Mexican lady in a saturated mountain village in the State of Veracruz.[9]

"*No hay reglas fijas, señor*" (there are no fixed rules), she replied, after a thoughtful silence, with a shrug.

No hay reglas fijas! It is not perhaps a detailed description of the great Don Porfirio's republic, but it is a consummate epitome, and once you have committed it to memory and "taken it to heart," your literary pursuits begin to languish. After traveling for three weeks in Mexico, almost anyone can write an entertaining and oracular volume, but after living there for several years, the oracle—unless subsidized by the Government—has a tendency to become dumb. For, in a country where theory and practice are so at variance, personal experience becomes the chart by which one is accustomed to steer, and although it is a valuable one, it may, for a hundred quaint reasons, be entirely different from that of the man whose ranch, or mine, or coffee place adjoins one's own.

In just this, I feel sure, lies much of the indisputable charm of Mexico. *No hay reglas fijas.* Everyone's experience is different, and everyone, in a sense, is a pioneer groping his way—like Cortés on his prodigious march up from the sea. One never knows, from the largest to the smallest circumstances of life, just what to expect, and Ultimate Truth abideth not. This is not so much because Mexicans are instinctive and facile liars, as because the usual methods of ascertaining and disseminating news are not employed. At home we demand facts and get them. In Mexico one subsists on rumor and never demands anything. A well-regulated, systematic, and precise person always detests Mexico and can rarely bring himself to say a kind word about anything in it, including the scenery. But if one is not inclined to exaggerate the importance of exactitude and is perpetually interested in the casual, the florid, and the problematic, Mexico is one, carelessly written but absorbing romance.[10]

Notes

1. Charles M. Flandrau, *Viva Mexico!* (New York: D. Appleton & Co., 1909), 12–22.

2. Flandrau, *Viva Mexico*, 61.

3. C. Harvey Gardiner, "Introduction," in Charles M. Flandrau, *Viva Mexico!* ed. C. Harvey Gardiner (Urbana: University of Illinois Press, 1964), xi–xxv.

4. William H. Prescott's *The Conquest of Mexico* is a Romantic novel recounting the Spanish conquest of Tenochtitlán, 1519–1521. Appealing to a large audience, it is probably the most widely read book on Mexico published in the nineteenth century. Based on the memoirs of the conquistadors, it is also quite biased toward the perspective of the Spanish invaders.

5. The foregoing exchanges with another U.S. expatriate constitute Flandrau's very clever way of making general statements about Mexico while appearing to criticize his fellow foreigners.

6. Eighteen U.S. cents.

7. Local official, usually with sweeping powers.

8. Flandrau refers to the Partido Liberal Mexicano, an anarcho-syndicalist party headed by the Flores Magón brothers who are still celebrated as precursors of the 1910 revolution.

9. The eastern slope of the Sierra Madre Oriental gets more rain than any other area in Mexico.

10. A stereotypical conclusion, but one that is more fine-grained and sophisticated than, for example, Gooch's cultural dichotomies or Lumholtz's crude racism.

12 The Barbarous Porfiriato

John Kenneth Turner[1]

With reason, John Kenneth Turner's Barbarous Mexico *has been called the* Uncle Tom's Cabin *of Mexico—a stirring cry for justice that helped to overthrow an unjust regime. This travel account is the premier example of muckraking journalism about Latin America, the first book written about Mexico with the express and primary purpose of social criticism. The militant socialist Turner not only attacks the brutality of the landowners in Mexico, but he also exposes the complicity of the U.S. government and foreign investors in maintaining and bankrolling the Porfirian system. He thus targets his native country as much as he criticizes the society that he visits, but he does so for a novel purpose: to demonstrate the negative effects of global capitalism. Dozens of progressives from the United States and Europe followed Turner's lead, including John Reed and B. Traven, whose writings are featured in the following section.*

The following excerpt introduces the reader to the brutal conditions on the henequen plantations of the southeastern state of Yucatán. Impersonating a potential investor, Turner gained access to the casta divina *of that state—the "divine caste" of creole and mestizo landowners that lorded it over the Maya peasantry. The technique of assuming a false identity reveals many shocking facets of life on the henequen plantation in the dying days of the Porfiriato. The reader might wonder whether* hacendados—*pinched by the economic crisis of 1907—would provide entirely truthful information to a prospective buyer of their plantation. Thus Turner was far more of an outsider in Mexico than Harriet Beecher Stowe was in the U.S. South, and there is much about his book that is similar to those of other foreign writers. Like Bertie-Marriott, Turner writes from the perspective of an itinerant traveler, someone who had little interaction with ordinary Mexicans. Nonetheless, the account reveals a story untold by Mexican elite sources.*

Turner (1878–1948) grew up in Stockton, California, and he attended the University of California at Berkeley. After graduation, he worked for a variety of newspapers on the West Coast. In 1908, he interviewed the three Flores Magón brothers who are still celebrated today as precursors of the Mexican Revolution. These leaders of the anarcho-syndicalist Partido Liberal Mexicano (PLM) had plotted against Díaz from the United States until the U.S. government imprisoned them for violating its neutrality laws. Turner's outrage about what he had learned from the Flores Magóns led to two trips to Mexico as a correspondent of the American Magazine, *and, in 1910, to the publication of* Barbarous Mexico, *a book that shattered the favorable U.S. public opinion of Díaz. Turner returned to Mexico several times during the Revolution and wrote two more books that attacked President Woodrow Wilson's interventionist policies in Mexico.*

Slavery in Mexico! Yes, I found it. I found it first in Yucatán. The peninsula of Yucatán is an elbow of Central America, which shoots off in a northeasterly direction almost half way to Florida. It belongs to Mexico, and its area of some 80,000 square miles is almost equally divided among the states of Yucatán and Campeche and the territory of Quintana Roo.

The coast of Yucatán, which comprises the north-central part of the peninsula, is about a thousand miles directly south of New Orleans. The surface of the state is almost solid rock, so nearly solid that it is usually impossible to plant a tree without first blasting a hole to receive the shoot and make a place for the roots. Yet this naturally barren land is more densely populated than is our own United States. More than that, within one-fourth of the territory three-fourths of the people live, and the density of the population runs to nearly seventy-five per square mile.

The secret of these peculiar conditions is that the soil and the climate of northern Yucatán happen to be perfectly adapted to the production of that hardy species of century plant which produces *henequen,* or sisal hemp.[2] Hence we find the city of Mérida, a beautiful modern city claiming a population of 60,000 people, and surrounding it, supporting it, vast henequen plantations on which the rows of gigantic green plants extend for miles and miles. The farms are so large that each has a little city of its own, inhabited by from 500 to 2,500 people, according to the size of the farm. The owners of these great farms are the chief slaveholders of Yucatán; the inhabitants of the little cities are the slaves. The annual export of henequen from Yucatán approximates 250 million pounds. The population of Yucatán is about 300 thousand. The slaveholders' club numbers 250 members, but the vast majority of the lands and the slaves are concentrated in the hands of fifty henequen kings. The slaves number more than 100 thousand.

In order to secure the truth in its greatest purity from the lips of the masters of the slaves I went among them playing a part. Long before I put my feet upon the white sands of Progreso, the port of Yucatán, I had heard how visiting investigators are bought or blinded, how, if they cannot be bought, they are wined and dined and filled with falsehood, then taken over a route previously prepared—fooled, in short, so completely that they go away half believing that the slaves are not slaves, that the hundred thousand half-starving, overworked, degraded bondsmen are perfectly happy and so contented with their lot that it would be a shame indeed to yield to them the freedom and security which, in all humanity, is the rightful share of every human being born upon the earth.

The part I played in Yucatán was that of an investor with much money to sink in henequen properties, and as such I was warmly welcomed by the henequen kings. I was rather fortunate in going to Yucatán when I did. Until the panic of 1907 it was a well-understood and unanimously approved policy of the "Cámara Agrícola," the planters' organization, that foreigners should not be allowed to invade the henequen business. This was partly because the profits of the business were huge and the rich Yucatecos wanted to "hog it all" for themselves, but more especially because they feared that through foreigners the story of their misdeeds might become known to the world.

But the panic of 1907 wiped out the world's henequen market for a time. The planters were a company of little Rockefellers, but they needed ready cash, and they were willing to take it from anyone who came. Hence my imaginary money was the open sesame to their club, and to their farms. I not only discussed every phase of henequen production with the kings themselves, and while they were off their guard, but I observed thousands of slaves under their normal conditions.

Chief among the henequen kings of Yucatán is Olegario Molina, former governor of the state and Secretary of Fomento[3] . . . of Mexico. Molina's holdings of lands in Yucatán and Quintana Roo aggregate 15 million acres, or 23,000 square miles—a small kingdom in itself. The fifty kings live in costly palaces in Mérida and many of them have homes abroad. They travel a great deal, usually they speak several different languages, and they and their families are a most cultivated class of people. All Mérida and all Yucatán, even all the peninsula of Yucatán, are dependent on the fifty henequen kings. Naturally these men are in control of the political machinery of their state, and naturally they operate that machinery for their own benefit. The slaves are 8,000 Yaqui Indians imported from Sonora, 3,000 Chinese (Koreans), and between 100,000 and 125,000 native Mayas, who formerly owned the lands that the henequen kings now own.

The Maya people, indeed, form about 95 per cent of the population of Yucatán. Even the majority of the fifty henequen kings are Mayas crossed with the blood of Spain. The Mayas are Indians—and yet they are not Indians. They are not like the Indians of the United States, and they are called Indians only because their homes were in the western hemisphere when the Europeans came. The Mayas had a civilization of their own when the Europeans "discovered" them, and it was a civilization admittedly as high as that of the most advanced Aztecs or the Incas of Peru.

The Mayas are a peculiar people. They look like no other people on the face of the earth. They are not like other Mexicans; they are not like Americans; they are not like Chinamen; they are not like East Indians; they are not like Turks. Yet one might very easily imagine that fusion of all these five widely different peoples might produce a people much like the Mayas. They are not large in stature, but their features are remarkably finely chiselled and their bodies give a strong impression of elegance and grace. Their skins are olive, their foreheads high, their faces slightly aquiline. The women of all classes in Mérida wear long, flowing white gowns unbound at the waist and embroidered about the hem and perhaps also about the bust in some bright color—green, blue or purple. . . . alluringly attired [they] mingle among the fragrant flowers, the art statues and the tropical greenery of the city plaza.

The planters do not call their chattels slaves. They call them "people," or "laborers," especially when speaking to strangers. But when speaking confidentially they have said to me: "Yes, they are slaves."

But I did not accept the word slavery from the people of Yucatán though they were the holders of the slaves themselves. The proof of a fact is to be found, not in the name, but in the conditions thereof. Slavery is the ownership of the body of a man, an ownership so absolute that the body can be transferred to another, an ownership that gives to the owner a right to take the products of that body, to starve it, to chastise it at will, to kill it with impunity. Such is slavery in the extreme sense. Such is slavery as I found it in Yucatán. The masters of Yucatán do not call their system slavery; they call it enforced service for debt. "We do not consider that we own our laborers; we consider that they are in debt to us. And we do not consider that we buy and sell them; we consider that we transfer the debt, and the man goes with the debt." This is the way Don Enrique Cámara Zavala, president of the "Cámara Agrícola de Yucatán," explained the attitude of the henequen kings in the matter. "Slavery is against the law; we do not call it slavery," various planters assured me again and again.

But the fact that it is not service for debt is proven by the habit of transferring the slaves from one master to another, not on any basis of debt, but on the basis of the market price of a man. In figuring on the purchase of a plantation I always had to figure on paying cash for the slaves, exactly the same as for the land, the machinery and the cattle. Four hundred Mexican dollars apiece was the prevailing price, and that is what the planters usually asked me. "If you buy now you buy at a very good time," I was told again and again. "The panic has put the price down. One year ago the price of each man was $1,000."[4]

The Yaquis[5] are transferred on exactly the same basis as the Mayas— the market price of a slave—and yet all people of Yucatán know that the planters pay only $65 apiece to the government for each Yaqui. I was offered for $400 each Yaquis who had not been in the country a month and consequently had had no opportunity of rolling up a debt that would account for the difference in price. Moreover, one of the planters told me: "We don't allow the Yaquis to get in debt to us."[6]

It would be absurd to suppose that the reason the price was uniform was because all the slaves were equally in debt. I probed this matter a little by inquiring into the details of the selling transaction. "You get the photograph and identification papers with the man," said one, "and that's all." "You get the identification papers and the account of the debt," said another. "We don't keep much account of the debt," said a third, "because it doesn't matter after you've got possession of the man." "The man and the identification papers are enough," said another; "if your man runs away, the papers are all the authorities require for you to get him back again." "Whatever the debt, it takes the market price to get him free again," a fifth told me.

Conflicting as some of these answers are, they all tend to show one thing: that the debt counts for nothing after the debtor passes into the hands of the planter. Whatever the debt, it takes the market price to get the debtor free again! Even then, I thought, it would not be so bad if the servant had an opportunity of working out the price and buying back his freedom. Even some of our negro slaves before the Civil War were permitted—by exceptionally lenient masters—to do that. But I found that such was not the custom. "You need have no fear in purchasing this plantation," said one planter to me, "of the laborers being able to buy their freedom and leave you. They can never do that."

The only man in the country whom I heard of as having ever permitted a slave to buy his freedom was a professional man of Mérida, an architect. "I bought a laborer for $1,000," he explained to me. "He was a good man and helped me a lot about my office. After I got to liking him I credited him with so much wages per week. After eight years I owed him the full $1,000, so I let him go. But they never do that on the plantations—never."

Thus I learned that the debt feature of the enforced service does not alleviate the hardships of the slave by making it easier for him to free himself, neither does it affect the conditions of his sale or his complete subjection to his master. On the other hand, I found that the one particular in which this debt element does play an actual part in the destiny of the unfortunate of Yucatán militates against him instead of operating in his favor. For it is by means of debt that the Yucatán slave-driver gets possession of the free laborers of his realm to replenish the overworked and underfed, the overbeaten, the dying slaves of his plantation.

How are the slaves recruited? Don Joaquín Peón informed me that the Maya slaves die off faster than they are born, and Don Enrique Cámara Zavala told me that two-thirds of the Yaquis die during the first year of their residence in the country.[7] Hence the problem of recruiting the slaves seemed to me a very serious one. Of course, the Yaquis were coming in at the rate of 500 per month, but I hardly thought that influx would be sufficient to equal the tide of life that was going out by death. I was right in that surmise, so I was informed, but I was also informed that the problem of recruits was not so difficult after all.

"It is very easy," one planter told me. "All that is necessary is that you get some free laborer in debt to you, and then you have him. Yes, we are always getting new laborers in that way."

The amount of the debt does not matter, so long as it is a debt, and the little transaction is arranged by men who combine the functions of money lender and slave broker. Some of them have offices in Mérida and they get the free laborers, clerks and the poorer class of people generally into debt just as professional loan sharks of America get clerks, mechanics and office men into debt—by playing on their needs and tempting them. Were these American clerks, mechanics and office men residents of Yucatán, instead of being merely hounded by a loan shark, they would be sold into slavery for all time, they and their children and their children's children, on to the third and fourth generation, and even farther, on to such a time as some political change put stop to the conditions of slavery altogether in Mexico.

These money-lending slave brokers of Mérida do not hang out signs and announce to the world that they have slaves to sell. They do their business quietly, as people who are comparatively safe in their occupation, but as people who do not wish to endanger their business by too great publicity-like police-protected gambling houses in an American city, for example. . . . These men buy and sell slaves. And the planters buy and sell slaves. I was offered slaves in lots of one up by the planters. I was told that I could buy a man or a woman, a boy or a girl, or a thousand of any of them, to do with them exactly as I wished, that the police would protect me in my possession of those, my fellow beings. Slaves are not only used on the henequen plantations, but in the city, as personal servants, as laborers, as household drudges, as prostitutes. How many of these persons there are in the city of Mérida I do not know, though I heard many stories of the absolute power exercised over them. Certainly the number is several thousand.

So we see that the debt element in Yucatán not only does not palliate the condition of the slave, but rather makes it harder. It increases his extremity, for while it does not help him to climb out of his pit, it reaches out its tentacles and drags down his brother, too. The portion of the people of Yucatán who are born free possess no "inalienable right" to their freedom. They are free only by virtue of their being prosperous. Let a family, however virtuous, however worthy, however cultivated, fall into misfortune, let the parents fall to debt and be unable to pay the debt, and the whole family is liable to pass into the hands of a henequen planter. Through debt, the dying slaves of the farms are replaced by the unsuccessful wageworkers of the cities.

Why do the henequen kings call their system enforced service debt instead of by its right name? Probably for two reasons—because the system is the outgrowth of a milder system of actual service for debt, and because of the prejudice against the word slavery, both among Mexicans and foreigners. Service for debt in a milder form than is found in Yucatán exists all over Mexico and is called peonage. Under this system, police authorities everywhere recognize the right of an employer to take the body of a laborer who is in debt to him, and to compel the laborer to work out the debt. Of course, once the employer can compel the laborer to work, he can compel him to work at his own terms, and that means that he can work him on such terms as will never permit the laborer to extricate himself from his debt.

Such is peonage as it exists throughout all Mexico. In the last analysis it is slavery, but the employers control the police, and the fictional distinction is kept up all the same. Slavery is peonage carried to its greatest possible extreme, and the reason we find the extreme in Yucatán is that, while in some other sections of Mexico a fraction of the ruling interests are opposed to peonage and consequently exert a modifying influence upon it, in Yucatán all the ruling interests are in henequen. The cheaper the worker the higher the profits for all. The peon becomes a chattel slave.

The henequen kings of Yucatán seek to excuse their system of slavery by denominating it enforced service for debt. "Slavery is against the law," they say. "It is against the constitution." When a thing is abolished by your constitution it works more smoothly if called by another name, but the fact is, service for debt is just as unconstitutional in Mexico as chattel slavery. . . . On the other hand, if the policy of the present government is to be taken as the law of the land, the slave business of Mexico is legal. In that sense the henequen kings "obey the law." Whether they are righteous in doing so I will leave to hair-splitters in morality. Whatever the decision may be, right or wrong, it does not change, for better or for worse, the pitiful misery in which I found the hemp laborers of Yucatán.

The slaves of Yucatán get no money. They are half starved. They are worked almost to death. They are beaten. A large percentage of them are locked up every night in a house resembling a jail. If they are sick they must still work, and if they are so sick that it is impossible for them to work, they are seldom permitted the services of a physician. The women are compelled to marry, compelled to marry men of their own plantation only, and sometimes are compelled to marry certain men not of their choice. There are no schools for the children. Indeed, the entire lives of these people are ordered at the whim of a master, and if the master wishes to kill them, he may do so with impunity. I heard numerous stories of slaves being beaten to death, but I never heard of an instance in which the murderer was punished, or even arrested. The police, the public prosecutors and the judges know exactly what is expected of them, for the men who appoint them are the planters themselves. The *jefes políticos*, the rulers of the political districts corresponding to our counties who are as truly czars of the districts as Díaz is the Czar of all Mexico, are invariably either henequen planters or employees of henequen planters.[8] . . .

And they say the Mexican is happy! "As happy as a peon," has come to be a common expression. Can a starving man be happy? Is there any people on earth—any beast of the field, even—so peculiar of nature that it loves cold better than warmth, an empty stomach better than a full one? Where is the scientist that has discovered a people who would choose an ever narrowing horizon to an ever widening one? Depraved indeed are the Mexican people if they are happy. But I do not believe they are happy. Some who have said it lied knowingly. Others mistook the dull glaze of settled despair for the signature of contentment.

Most persistent of all derogations of Mexicans is the one that the Spanish-American character is somehow incapable of democracy and therefore needs the strong hand of a dictator. Since the Spanish-Americans of Mexico have never had a fair trial at democracy, and since those who are asserting that they are incapable of democracy are just the ones who are trying hardest to prevent them from having a trial at democracy, the suspicion naturally arises that those persons have an ulterior motive in spreading such an impression. . . .

The truth of the whole malignment of Mexicans as a people seems very plain. It is a defense against indefensible conditions whereby the defenders are profiting. It is an excuse—an excuse for hideous cruelty, a salve to the conscience, an apology to the world, a defense against the vengeance of eternity.

The truth is that the Mexican is a human being and that he is subject to the same evolutionary laws of growth as are potent in the development of any other people. The truth is that, if the Mexican does not fully measure up to the standard of the highest type of European, it is because of his history, a most influential part of which is the grinding exploitation to which he is subjected under the present regime in Mexico.[9]

Notes

1. John Kenneth Turner, *Barbarous Mexico* (New York: Cassell, 1912), 6–15, 286.

2. Before the advent of synthetic fabrics, sisal hemp was used, among other purposes, for making binder twine for harvesting grains. The Yucatecan planters enjoyed a virtual monopoly on this crop.

3. Development.

4. "Panic" refers to the global economic crisis of 1907–1908.

5. Members of an indigenous people from the northwestern state of Sonora. The Yaquis were engaged in a long, losing struggle against landowning families encroaching on their land. The Díaz regime had thousands of Yaquis deported to Yucatán.

6. This statement refers to the fact that the Yaqui is treated as a chattel slave rather than a peasant, who—despite his inferior condition—enjoyed some legal rights.

7. Turner refers to the state of Yucatán.

8. Turner's portrayal of social conditions in this excerpt is a bit simplistic. There were also Maya who were not slaves, and remote areas of Yucatán even featured an indigenous rebel movement, the Chan Santa Cruz, a holdover from the Caste Wars from the 1840s.

9. Illegal even in Porfirian Mexico, the practices Turner describes were proscribed in the 1917 Constitution. Nonetheless, as the reader has learned from Flandrau, theory does not equal practice, and other forms of forced labor have continued to the present day.

Part III
Revolution and Reconstruction

Unlike any other event in modern Mexican history, the Revolution of 1910 captivated foreign observers. On November 20, 1910, a broad coalition of Mexicans led by the wealthy landowner Francisco I. Madero took up arms to drive the old dictator Díaz out of power. Over the following ten years, Mexico was wracked by violence that claimed hundreds of thousands of lives.[1] First, Madero took control, reestablishing the constitutional democracy that Díaz had abolished. But he soon found out that Mexico's economic and social problems could not be solved by democracy alone. For example, in the southern state of Morelos, Emiliano Zapata's peasant army demanded the return of village land usurped by large landowners during the Porfiriato. Disappointed with Madero's slow pace of reform, the villagers rebelled—a rebellion that discredited Madero in the eyes of Mexican army leaders and foreign diplomats, who conspired to overthrow and assassinate the president in February 1913.

During the ensuing dictatorship of General Victoriano Huerta, Zapata joined a diverse array of northern revolutionaries that sought to topple the military regime. In Chihuahua, Pancho Villa's "Dorados" fought for municipal autonomy and freedom from government repression. Just east of that state, in

Coahuila, "First Chief" Venustiano Carranza carried the banner of his slain friend Madero, promising to pair democracy with economic opportunities for all Mexicans. And in the northwestern state of Sonora, Alvaro Obregón and Plutarco Elías Calles led a faction of middle-class revolutionaries committed to public education and the reform of labor laws. In July 1914, the revolutionary armies drove Huerta into exile, only to then fight each other for control over Mexico. Over the next year, Obregón's forces defeated the Dorados, ushering in the Carranza presidency, but the fighting continued until 1920.

After the chaos came reconstruction based on the Constitution of 1917. Authored by the victorious factions, the new constitution incorporated many key popular demands such as land reforms and effective collective bargaining for urban labor. However, many of its clauses would await implementation, as the revolutionary generals who dominated Mexico struggled with continued unrest and the legacy of a decade of destruction. From 1920 to 1928, the Obregón-Calles coalition led the nation into the first phase of reconstruction, a phase marked by the rebuilding of agriculture and financial institutions. In the face of opposition from landowners and foreign investors, the Mexican government made sporadic, half-hearted, and inconsistent attempts to implement the nationalist and pro-labor provisions of the constitution. After Obregón's assassination in July 1928, Calles became the arbiter of Mexican political life as so-called *jefe máximo*, or supreme chief. The Maximato (1928–1935) featured the construction of a ruling party that would dominate Mexican politics under various names until the year 2000. During the Maximato, the economy suffered along with those of the rest of the world in the Great Depression era. In 1935, President Lázaro Cárdenas clipped Calles's power. To the acclaim of peasants and workers, Cárdenas used a more favorable domestic and international climate to implement many of the promises of the Constitution in the third and final phase of reconstruction. By the end of the Cárdenas administration in 1940, peasants had received forty-two million acres of land; workers had unionized to an unprecedented degree; and the Mexican government had expropriated the foreign-owned oil industry.

The cultural, economic, and social life of Mexicans changed dramatically during the 1910–1940 period. The Revolution motivated a rethinking of the Mexican nation among the elite and middle classes—a rethinking that contributed to an officially sponsored effort by mural painters such as Diego Rivera to craft a new, official version of Mexican history inclusive of the indigenous population. Industrialization accelerated in the north and around Mexico City, drawing many rural inhabitants to the urban centers. Public education now reached small towns and villages, as Obregón and Calles launched an ambitious program of bringing the worldview of the revolutionary state to the Mexican peasants.

Even though efforts to limit the predominant economic influence of foreigners constituted one of the key goals of the victorious Carranza-Obregón coalition, foreigners continued to travel to and play a significant role in revolutionary Mexico. The upheaval temporarily weakened but did not interrupt foreign trade, and in 1940, U.S. investments had tripled, in real terms, from their level in 1910. Indeed, these thirty years of revolution and reconstruction are not just the period of what Mexican writer Octavio Paz has labeled the "fiesta of bullets" and its long aftermath, but also the era during which the United States asserted its primacy over European influence in Mexico. Ironically, the very era in which "Mexico for the Mexicans" became a stock phrase witnessed a new surge in travel and immigration to that country. In the wake of increased U.S. influence and improvements in transportation, modern tourism began to play an important role. In addition, during the 1920s and 1930s, the economic dislocations wrought by World War I and the Great Depression brought an unprecedented number of Europeans to live in Mexico.

Significantly, many of those who arrived during this turbulent era came as critics of U.S. influence, as "political pilgrims" who cheered on a Revolution that they thought represented a healthy response of an underdeveloped nation to international capitalism.[2] The writings of many of these followers of John Turner, the muckraking journalist who had pioneered socially conscious writing about Mexico, buttressed the official ideology of the revolutionary government. The political pilgrims included novelists such as B. Traven, Katherine Anne Porter, and John Steinbeck, as well as journalists Ernest Gruening and Carleton Beals, and historian Frank Tannenbaum. Even the more conservative British novelists Graham Greene, Aldous Huxley, D. H. Lawrence, and Evelyn Waugh used their writing as a means of social criticism and hence contributed to the trend toward politically critical writing emblematic of this era.[3]

Tourists, immigrants, and political pilgrims all mostly traveled by automobile—that quintessentially "American," individualist means of transportation. Travel by car dramatically affected the foreign observers' ways of seeing Mexico. Not only did the landscape zoom by an automobile window even faster than by the window of a train compartment, but the driver also determined the direction in which this fast-moving car was going. Even though the quality of Mexican roads left much to be desired in this period, travel by automobile allowed foreign observers to compress their experience into a relatively short time, and to access precisely those places they wished to see. In the process of making spatial movement easier and more efficient, the art of "getting there" disappeared, and it became far less likely for the visitor to stumble upon unexpected surprises. As a result, preconceived notions and agendas became even more important than before in shaping the viewpoint of foreign observers.

The seven readings in this section react to the Mexican Revolution in very different ways. The first three selections span the years 1911 to 1915, and reflect on the period of most intense fighting among the revolutionaries. Rosa King's *Tempest over Mexico* relates the experiences of a British hotel owner in Morelos; John Reed's *Insurgent Mexico* gives a U.S. radical's account of life in Villa's army; and Luise Böker's previously unpublished letters to her mother manifest the anguish of a German housewife in Mexico City. The other four readings, all written by immigrants and visitors during the years 1927 to 1939, critique the process of reconstruction. B. Traven's *Land des Frühlings* shows a German/U.S. novelist's view of the role of the "Indian" in revolutionary Mexico; Luis Araquistáin's *La revolución mejicana* comments on Mexican labor and revolutionary nationalism from the perspective of a socialist journalist from Spain; Evelyn Waugh's *Robbery Under Law* provides a conservative British critique of the Cárdenas regime; and Verna Millán's *Mexico Reborn* narrates the experience of a U.S. woman married to a Mexican physician who played a prominent role in Cardenista Mexico.

⁙

Notes

1. The number of casualties has been estimated between 500,000 and 2,000,000.

2. Helen Delpar, *The Enormous Vogue of Things Mexican* (Tuscaloosa: University of Alabama Press, 1992), 15–53; Drewey Wayne Gunn, *American and British Writers in Mexico, 1556–1973* (Austin: University of Texas Press, 1974), 76–77.

3. Gunn, *American and British Writers in Mexico*, 76–180.

13 With Zapata in Cuernavaca

Rosa E. King[1]

Rosa King's Tempest over Mexico *tells the story of a British woman who owned a hotel in the city of Cuernavaca, Morelos. The following excerpt recounts King's impressions of General Emiliano Zapata, the principal hero of the struggle for the return of village lands to indigenous Mexicans. Zapata's refusal to compromise his principles and this martyr's death in 1919 found him many admirers, including King. At least that is what she tells us with the benefit of hindsight. A staunch opponent of the Revolution during the 1910s, King had mellowed by the time she wrote this book in 1935, no doubt influenced by the passage of more than two decades living in Cuernavaca. Thus, this immigrant account appreciates the reasons why ordinary peasants took up arms and risked their life to fight a Revolution. While not dispensing with most of the standard stereotypes, it goes a long way toward understanding the motivations of the revolutionaries. The following selection reflects on the events of May 1911, when Madero's coalition had just triumphed over Díaz's forces.*

King visited Mexico for the first time in 1905 in the company of her husband, who, like her, was a British subject. The Library of Congress gives the year of her birth as 1865; other than that, historians do not know any details of her upbringing. During her stay in Mexico, she grew to love Cuernavaca, the capital of Morelos, then a quaint, colonial town fifty miles south of Mexico City, in the subtropical climate zone at four thousand feet elevation. After the death of her husband in 1907, she returned to Cuernavaca with her daughter to begin a new life. She opened a tea parlor and shortly thereafter bought the Bella Vista Hotel, located near the town's main square. In part to protect her investment, King remained in Cuernavaca even after the outbreak of the Revolution. Only when she feared for her own and her daughter's life did she seek refuge in Mexico City. When King returned to Cuernavaca, she found her hotel in ruins, but nonetheless remained there until her death.[2]

"Quickly close everything, *Señora* King! The fierce Zapata is coming, killing and destroying everything in his path!" It was one of the leading men of the town who stood panting in my portal. "The rebels met our garrison at Cuautla, and cut it to pieces. Only a handful of troops are left to tell the tale; you will see them limping in." Wounded, on foot, tied up in old rags they came—the remnant of Cuernavaca's invincible garrison. Most of the men would never have made the thirty miles from Cuautla if it had not been for the help of their women, who had pushed them and dragged them along. The doors of the townsfolk were closed to them. With the fierce Zapata coming, the people no longer knew the Federals[3] and the belligerent *soldaderas*[4] who cared for them. In the end we foreign women, who had nothing to fear from either side, sent out coffee and bandages. An American named Robinson, a mining engineer, went out to the crest of a hill at the entrance to the town to await the approach of Zapata, and to assure him and his ally [Manuel] Asúnsolo, both of whom were known to him personally, that no further resistance would be made. I was more interested than alarmed myself, but it occurred to me that the American lady who was running my tearoom for me was alone with two pretty daughters and might be frightened. I sent word for her and her daughters to come over to the Bella Vista and together we stood at the window to watch the Revolution enter Cuernavaca.

No Caesar ever rode more triumphantly into a Roman city than did the chief, Zapata, with Asúnsolo at his side, and after them their troops—a wild-looking body of men, undisciplined, half-clothed, mounted on half-starved, broken-down horses. Grotesque and obsolete weapons, long hidden away or recently seized in the pawnshops, were clasped in their hands, thrust through their belts, or slung across the queer old saddles of shapes never seen before. But they rode in as heroes and conquerors, and the pretty Indian girls met them with armfuls of bougainvillea and thrust the flaming flowers in their hats and belts. There was about them the splendor of devotion to a cause, a look of all the homespun patriots who, from time immemorial, have left the plough in the furrow when there was need to fight. I thrilled with the remembrance that Don Miguel Hidalgo y Costilla, the father of Mexican independence, had led an army equipped with weapons as crude as bars of iron, shovels, and pitchforks.[5]

All afternoon the wild-looking bands rode in. At six o'clock we heard shots and screams and feared that fighting had begun among them. Instead we found that the shots were fired in jubilation: the prison doors in the old palace had been opened and all the prisoners set free; political prisoners, murderers—all free! I shall never forget those men and women as they ran like hunted animals past my house seeking cover. In the old days they would have been shot as they ran, and they still believed they must be targets.

The generals had closed all places of drink, so far as they could, knowing that their men would be unmanageable if permitted to become intoxicated. A pathetic band of eight or ten pieces played that night in the Zócalo[6] to excited throngs—strange music on unheard-of instruments, sometimes wailing, sometimes riotous with a tumultuous sweetness, and again harsh and discordant. They played the wailing of four centuries of wrong that had been done them, and the awakening of justice. It was music to those savage men and to those who loved the cause for which they fought; but as I listened I shivered a little, and I was glad that I was an Englishwoman and this was not my Revolution.

Two days later I was forced into contact with the Revolutionists to protect the little factory I had established at San Anton. Much to my indignation I heard that the men were sacking it. The only way I knew to stop the depredation was to go to see Zapata the chief, and insist on my right as an Englishwoman. I told my manager, Nevin, what I meant to do, and added, "You come with me as interpreter." Willie Nevin was aghast, and at first refused to accompany me; but I insisted. I know now that it was only ignorance that gave me courage. When we reached the military headquarters, the troops pointed their rifles directly at me, and at trembling Willie behind me, and while many of the guns were antiquated there were plenty, taken from the Federals at Cuautla, that looked as if they would shoot—and straight. I knew so little Spanish that I could only make them understand I wished to enter by parting their rifles right and left with my hand and saying firmly "*Jefe*," which I knew meant "Chief." They allowed me to enter, but stared at a woman who dared to face them in this manner. Perhaps it was their very amazement that made them let me pass to Zapata's quarters. But my efforts to see him were in vain; the beloved general was sleeping, and could not be disturbed. By this time the succession of guns and savage looks I had been meeting was having its effect on me and my knees were trembling. I knew, however, that I must hold my own or my prestige was going and without that I could do nothing in Cuernavaca. On I marched, with Willie still behind me, to find the next chief, General Asúnsolo. We climbed upstairs in the old barracks to the room a young Indian pointed out with his rifle. To my surprise the room was perfectly clean, the bed spotless, order and neatness on every hand—something I knew to be unusual with an army on campaign. The man who received me addressed me courteously—in English. It was General Asúnsolo himself.

From the time I met General Asúnsolo I had no more fear. Asúnsolo was different from the grim, determined Indians about him, more like the men to whom I was accustomed. He was, oddly enough, a young man of aristocratic family, educated in the United States of America, and full of life and the love of American "ragtime"—"jazz," they call it now. He had joined the Revolution for the adventure, I think, and because he thought it likely to succeed. His mere presence in the Revolutionary army was reassuring to me. When I told him my trouble he said courteously, "The raids on your factory shall end at once, *Señora* King," and he kept his promise. Nor did his kindness end there, for I could not have wished better care than was taken of me and my property during the six weeks he was in Cuernavaca with his troops.

One little incident occurred about this time which, if I had taken it more seriously, might have suggested to me that the peace and order we were enjoying depended on a very delicate balance between explosive elements. I was sitting on the verandah one evening after dinner with the two pretty American girls, the daughters of the American lady who had taken over the tearoom for me. We were watching the antics of the invaders, who were amusing themselves in the plaza. To our surprise, one of the Indians suddenly came over and sat down next to the elder of the two girls. He was a young fellow, hung with pistols, and with very little clothing on under the three or four cartridge belts that covered his body. The girl was too frightened to say anything. My indignation was tremendous. I went over to the boy and told him to move at once, thinking my size, as I am quite tall, would quell him. To my great wonder he simply turned around and said, "Oh, no, madam, these are different times. The *peón* is now the master." The girl translated for me. My English blood was boiling. It was all I could do to refrain from knocking him off the chair. Instead, however, I went to some Mexicans who were sitting near by and asked their help. One of them, a young doctor, promptly took the Indian by the neck and threw him out of his seat. The boy, on the floor, pulled a pistol. Luckily for us, at this moment two or three other soldiers who had seen the trouble from the plaza across the street, seized their companion-in-arms and held him fast. I do not know which of us the boy meant to shoot, and I do not think he much cared, but it probably would have been me because of my interference.

When the soldiers had been told what happened they carried off the boy as a prisoner to General Asúnsolo, the man I had made my friend. The general sent word at once to ask if I would like to have an example made of him; if so, he would have him shot that night or in the morning. This message alarmed me more than the boy had. I sent word please not to do anything quite so desperate, just keep him locked up for two or three days. I had not been living among and observing these people without learning a little about them, and I realized that what the boy had done had been occasioned simply by his elation over the glory of his troops. Their victories had gone to his head. After he was released he came to me to apologize, and was soon made happy by the present of a little money. From that time on until Asúnsolo's troops left town, he acted as the personal guard for all of us at my house; and very good he was to us.

On the twelfth of June, Mr. Madero, the presidential candidate who had led the movement to overthrow the dictatorship, came to Cuernavaca to confer with General Zapata, who had been fighting in his behalf. Zapata arranged a "review" in his honor, and we all turned out to see the show. We were not disappointed.

Surely, all the strength of the Zapatistas was kept for action, for they wasted none on uniforms or martial drill. Poor fellows, in their huge straw hats and white cotton *calzones*,[7] with cotton socks in purple, pink, or green pulled outside and over the trouser legs. They were equipped with rifles of all sorts, and one little cannon. But even the cannon looked proud of being a follower of the brave leader, Emiliano Zapata. Among the troops were women soldiers, some of them officers. One, wearing a bright pink ribbon around her waist with a nice bow tied in back, was especially conspicuous. She was riding a pony and looked very bright and pretty.

Treacherous little ribbon! It gave the game away, for it was soon seen by that vivid bit of color that the troops were merely marching around a few squares appearing and reappearing before Don Francisco Madero. The pathetic attempt to please Madero by seeming stronger in numbers than they were was funny, but it was sad, too. Behind that sham was indomitable spirit. Mr. Madero's face, far from expressing any consciousness of the amazing reappearance of the same "battalions" in such quick succession, was perfectly impassive. He knew that passing before him was the embryonic power that would win the Revolution.[8] . . .

[After Zapata's death in 1919] I asked the [troops] about Zapata, and then, for the first time, I felt an eagerness, a kind of expectation stirring behind their guarded words. Little by little they brought out the tales of Zapata's prowess in battle, of his terrible just anger, and his goodness to the weak. . . . They used the same words I did—"Revolution, Zapata, government"—but it seemed to me they meant something different by them. I remember old Pepe's wrinkled face, creased with silent laughter, as she spoke of the snares laid by [Carranza's men] to trap the cunning fox, Zapata—"as though the *jefe* were to be caught with snares like a common man, or killed by a bullet like anyone else!" I told them, in my turn, what I had heard in Mexico City, that there was no leader in Mexico so popular as Zapata, since all men knew that he fought not for his own gain, but only "that there might be the same laws for the poor man as for the rich"; and that when he was in the capital the people would have made him president, but he would not let them, saying he was not the man for the place.

"*Cómo no,*" they nodded gravely. Their shrewdness told them that no man could walk wisely among matters he did not understand, and it was for this that they despised the Federal generals sent out to them. It was, I sensed, the essence of their trust in Zapata that he stayed close to the soil of his *tierra*, whose needs were part of him; eschewing honors and wealth, and sleeping always away from the towns, in a hidden place that no man knew; like a holy person dedicated to the service of his people, perhaps.

And then I caught the rhythm of their feeling, and understood that to them *la revolución* was infinitely more than the Revolution of 1910. It was the long continuous movement of resistance, like a rolling wave, that had swelled against Cortés and his conquistadors, and the greedy Aztec war lords before them; that had engulfed the armies of Spain and the armies of France as it now engulfed the hacendados. It was the struggle of these people for a birthright, to develop in their own way, in spite of strangers who came greedily to skim the cream, and, ignorantly, to make the people over. And so silent and vast and unceasing was the struggle that it seemed to me as though the sleeping earth itself had stirred to cast off the artificial things that lay heavy on it.

Notes

1. Rosa E. King, *Tempest over Mexico* (Boston: Little, Brown, and Co., 1935), 62–69 and 293–95.

2. For an analysis of King's work and the scarcity of information on King as an author, see Alicia Diadiuk, *Viajeras anglosajonas en México* (Mexico City: SepSetentas, 1973), 99–118.

3. Díaz's army; the "federal" troops.

4. Women soldiers.

5. This is written with the benefit of hindsight. It is likely that King was quite frightened of the Zapatistas at that time.

6. Just as in Mexico City, the main square of Cuernavaca.

7. Trousers.

8. Another comment made in hindsight.

14 ¡Viva Pancho Villa!

John Reed[1]

The following excerpt from Insurgent Mexico *by John Silas Reed (1887–1920) describes the encounter of a progressive U.S. intellectual with the forces of General Pancho Villa. It is particularly interesting for illustrating the dynamics of Villa's cult of leadership, and particularly the role of machismo. The passage reveals the perspective of someone sympathetic to the plight of Mexico's rural poor, yet accustomed to judging political culture and consciousness by Western models. Among the Villistas, Reed found much courage, machismo, and enthusiasm for fighting, but not the commitment to a revolutionary ideology that he was seeking. He encountered, but could not understand, a peasant political consciousness fundamentally different from his own Harvard education.*

Reed was born in Portland, Oregon. After his graduation from Harvard, he traveled to England and Spain, followed by a trip to Mexico. He crossed the border in the summer of 1913 in search of the forces of General Villa, the head of the famous "División del Norte," the largest of the four revolutionary armies opposing dictator Victoriano Huerta. A journalist with strong socialist and

anarcho-syndicalist tendencies, Reed hoped to find a strong class conscious-
ness among the Mexican rural poor—a class consciousness that, as Reed
hoped, could serve as a base for a socialist revolution in Mexico. What Reed
found, instead, was the magnetic personality of General Villa. This four-month
trip produced Insurgent Mexico *(1914), a book now considered a classic among*
eyewitness accounts of the Revolution. As war correspondent of a U.S. maga-
zine, Reed next journeyed to war-torn Europe and wrote The War in Eastern
Europe *(1916), a testimony of the horrors of World War I. After a short respite*
in the United States occasioned by health problems, Reed traveled to Russia,
where he became an enthusiastic observer and supporter of the 1917 Bolshevik
Revolution. His famous account of these events, Ten Days that Shook the
World, *describes the climactic days leading up to Vladimir I. Lenin's seizure*
of power. A close friend of Lenin's, Reed eventually returned to Moscow to stay.
He was buried with other Bolshevik heroes inside the Kremlin wall.[2]

The Tropa[3] had already ridden on ahead, and I could see them, strung out
for half a mile in the black mesquite brush, the tiny red-white-and-green
flag bobbing at their head. The mountains had withdrawn somewhere
beyond the horizon, and we rode in the midst of a great bowl of desert,
rolling up at the edges to meet the furnace-blue of the Mexican sky. Now
that I was out of the coach, a great silence, and a peace beyond anything I
ever felt, wrapped me around. It is almost impossible to get objective about
the desert; you sink into it—become a part of it. Galloping along, I soon
caught up with the Tropa. . . .

Captain Fernando at the head of the column turned and roared: "Come
here, Meester!" The big man was grinning with delight. "You shall ride with
me," he shouted, clapping me on the back. "Drink, now," and he produced
a bottle of *sotol*[4] about half full. "Drink it all. Show you're a man." "It's too
much," I laughed. "Drink it," yelled the chorus as the Tropa crowded up to
see. I drank it. A howl of laughter and applause went up. Fernando leaned
over and gripped my hand. "Good for you, *compañero!*"[5] he bellowed, rolling
with mirth. The men crowded around, amused and interested. Was I going
to fight with them? Where did I come from? What was I doing? Most of them
had never heard of reporters, and one hazarded the opinion darkly that I was
a gringo and a Porfirista, and ought to be shot.

The rest, however, were entirely opposed to this view. No Porfirista would possibly drink that much *sotol* at a gulp. Isidro Amayo declared that he had been in a brigade in the first Revolution[6] which was accompanied by a reporter, and that he was called *Corresponsal de Guerra.*[7] Did I like Mexico? I said: "I am very fond of Mexico. I like Mexicans too. And I like *sotol, aguardiente, mescal, tequila, pulque,*[8] and other Mexican customs!" They shouted with laughter.

Captain Fernando leaned over and patted my arm. "Now you are with the men (*los hombres*). When we win the *Revolución* it will be a government by the men—not by the rich. We are riding over the lands of the men. They used to belong to the rich, but now they belong to me and to the *compañeros.*"

"And you will be the army?" I asked.

"When the *Revolución* is won," was the astonishing reply, "there will be no more army. The men are sick of armies. It is by armies that Don Porfirio robbed us."

"But if the United States should invade Mexico?"

A perfect storm broke everywhere. "We are more *valiente*[9] than the Americanos—The cursed *gringos* would get no further south than Juárez—Let's see them try it—We'd drive them back over the Border on the run, and burn their capital the next day!"

"No," said Fernando, "you have more money and more soldiers. But the men would protect us. We need no army. The men would be fighting for their houses and their women."

"What are you fighting for," I asked. Juan Sánchez, the color bearer, looked at me curiously. "Why, it is good, fighting. You don't have to work in the mines!". . .

"We are fighting," said Isidro Amayo, "for *Libertad.*"

"What do you mean by *Libertad*?"

"*Libertad* is when I can do what I want!"

"But suppose it hurts someone else?"

He shot back at me Benito Juárez's great sentence: "Peace is the respect for the rights of others!"

I wasn't prepared for that. It startled me, this barefooted mestizo's conception of Liberty. I submit that it is the only correct definition of Liberty—to do what I want to! Americans quote it to me triumphantly as an instance of Mexican irresponsibility. But I think it is a better definition than ours—Liberty is the right to do what the Courts want.[10]. . .

It was while Villa was in Chihuahua . . . that the artillery corps of his army decided to present him with a gold medal for personal heroism on the field.

In the audience hall of the Governor's palace in Chihuahua, a place of ceremonial, great luster chandeliers, heavy crimson portières, and gaudy American wallpaper, there is a throne for the governor. It is a gilded chair, with lion's claws for arms, placed upon a dais under a canopy of crimson velvet, surmounted by a heavy, gilded, wooden cap, which tapers up to a crown.

The officers of artillery, in smart blue uniforms faced with black velvet and gold, were solidly banked across one end of the audience hall, with flashing new swords and their gilt-braided hats stiffly held under their arms. From the door of that chamber, around the gallery, down the state staircase, across the grandiose inner court of the palace, and out through the imposing gates to the street, stood a double line of soldiers, with their rifles at present arms. Four regimental bands grouped in one wedge in the crowd. The people of the capital were massed in solid thousands on the Plaza de Armas before the palace.

"*Ya viene!*" "Here he comes!" "Viva Villa!" "Viva Madero!" "Villa, the friend of the poor!"

The roar began at the back of the crowd and swept like fire in heavy growing crescendo until it seemed to toss thousands of hats above their heads. The band in the courtyard struck up the Mexican national air, and Villa came walking down the street.

He was dressed in an old plain khaki uniform, with several buttons lacking. He hadn't recently shaved, wore no hat, and his hair had not been brushed. He walked a little pigeon-toed, humped over, with his hands in his trousers pockets. As he entered the aisle between the rigid lines of soldiers he seemed slightly embarrassed, and grinned and nodded to a *compadre*[11] here and there in the ranks. At the foot of the grand staircase, Governor [Manuel] Chao and Secretary of State [Silvestre] Terrazas joined him in full-dress uniform. The band threw off all restraint, and, as Villa entered the audience chamber, at a signal from someone in the balcony of the palace, the great throng in the Plaza de Armas uncovered, and all the brilliant crowd of officers in the room saluted stiffly.

It was Napoleonic!

Villa hesitated for a minute, pulling his mustache and looking very uncomfortable, finally gravitated toward the throne, which he tested by shaking the arms, and then sat down, with the Governor on his right and the Secretary of State on his left.

Señor Bauche Alcalde stepped forward, raised his right hand to the exact position which Cicero took when denouncing Catiline,[12] and pronounced a short discourse, indicting Villa for personal bravery on the field on six counts, which he mentioned in florid detail. He was followed by the Chief of Artillery, who said: "The army adores you. We will follow you wherever you lead. You can be what you desire in Mexico." Then three other officers spoke in the high-flung, extravagant periods necessary to Mexican oratory. They called him "The Friend of the Poor," "The Invincible General," "The Inspirer of Courage and Patriotism," "The Hope of the Indian Republic." And through it all Villa slouched on the throne, his mouth hanging open, his little shrewd eyes playing around the room. Once or twice he yawned, but for the most part he seemed to be speculating, with some intense interior amusement, like a small boy in church, what it was all about. He knew, of course, that it was the proper thing, and perhaps felt a slight vanity that all this conventional ceremonial was addressed to him. But it bored him just the same.

Finally, with an impressive gesture, Colonel Servín stepped forward with the small pasteboard box which held the medal. General Chao nudged Villa, who stood up. The officers applauded violently; the crowd outside cheered; the band in the court burst into a triumphant march.

Villa put out both hands eagerly, like a child for a new toy. He could hardly wait to open the box and see what was inside. An expectant hush fell upon everyone, even the crowd in the square. Villa looked at the medal, scratching his head, and, in a reverent silence, said clearly: "This is a hell of a little thing to give a man for all that heroism you are talking about!" And the bubble of Empire was pricked then and there with a great shout of laughter.

They waited for him to speak—to make a conventional address of acceptance. But as he looked around the room at those brilliant, educated men, who said that they would die for Villa, the peon, and meant it, and as he caught sight through the door of the ragged soldiers, who had forgotten their rigidity and were crowding eagerly into the corridor with eyes fixed eagerly on the *compañero* that they loved, he realized something of what the Revolution signified.

Puckering up his face, as he did always when he concentrated intensely, he leaned across the table in front of him and poured out, in a voice so low that people could hardly hear: "There is no word to speak. All I can say is my heart is all to you." Then he nudged Chao and sat down, spitting violently on the floor; and Chao pronounced the classic discourse.[13]

Villa was an outlaw for twenty-two years. When he was only a boy of sixteen, delivering milk in the streets of Chihuahua, he killed a government official and had to take to the mountains. The story is that the official had violated his sister, but it seems probable that Villa killed him on account of his insufferable insolence. That in itself would not have outlawed him long in Mexico, where human life is cheap; but once a refugee he committed the unpardonable crime of stealing cattle from the rich *hacendados*. And from that time to the outbreak of the Madero revolution the Mexican government had a price on his head.

Villa was the son of ignorant peons. He had never been to school. He hadn't the slightest conception of the complexity of civilization, and when he finally came back to it, a mature man of extraordinary native shrewdness, he encountered the twentieth century with the naïve simplicity of a savage.

It is almost impossible to procure accurate information about his career as a bandit. There are accounts of outrages he committed in old files of local newspapers and government reports, but those sources are prejudiced, and his name became so prominent as a bandit that every train robbery and holdup and murder in northern Mexico was attributed to Villa. But an immense body of popular legend grew up among the peons around his name. There are many traditional songs and ballads celebrating his exploits—you can hear the shepherds singing them around their fires in the mountains at night, repeating verses handed down by their fathers or composing others extemporaneously. For instance, they tell the story of how Villa, fired by the story of the misery of the peons on the Hacienda of Los Alamos, gathered a small army and descended upon the Big House, which he looted, and distributed the spoils among the poor people. . . . His reckless and romantic bravery is the subject of countless poems. . . . Everywhere he was known as The Friend of the Poor. He was the Mexican Robin Hood.

Villa has two wives, one a patient, simple woman who was with him during all his years of outlawry, who lives in El Paso, and the other a cat-like, slender young girl, who is the mistress of his house in Chihuahua. He is perfectly open about it, though lately the educated, conventional Mexicans who have been gathering about him in ever-increasing numbers have tried to hush up the fact. Among the peons[14] it is not only not unusual but customary to have more than one mate.[15]

One hears a great many stories of Villa's violating women. I asked him if that were true. He pulled his mustache and stared at me for a minute with an inscrutable expression. "I never take the trouble to deny such stories," he said. "They say I am a bandit, too. Well, you know my history. But tell me; have you ever met a husband, father or brother of any woman that I have violated?" He paused: "Or even a witness?"

It is fascinating to watch him discover new ideas. Remember that he is absolutely ignorant of the troubles and confusions and readjustments of modern civilization. "Socialism," he said once, when I wanted to know what he thought of it: "Socialism—is it a thing? I only see it in books, and I do not read much." Once I asked him if women would vote in the new Republic. He was sprawled out on his bed, with his coat unbuttoned. "Why, I don't think so," he said, startled, suddenly sitting up. "What do you mean—vote? Do you mean elect a government and make laws?" I said I did and that women were already doing it in the United States. "Well," he said, scratching his head, "if they do it up there I don't see that they shouldn't do it down here." The idea seemed to amuse him enormously. He rolled it over and over in his mind, looking at me and away again. "It may be as you say," he said, "but I have never thought about it. Women seem to me to be things to protect, to love. They have no sternness of mind. They can't consider anything for its right or wrong. They are full of pity and softness. Why," he said, "a woman would not give an order to execute a traitor."

"I am not so sure of that, *mi general*," I said. "Women can be crueller and harder than men."

He stared at me, pulling his mustache. And then he began to grin. He looked slowly to where his wife was setting the table for lunch. . . . He said, "come here. Listen. Last night I caught three traitors crossing the river to blow up the railroad. What shall I do with them? Shall I shoot them or not?"

Embarrassed, she seized his hand and kissed it. "Oh, I don't know anything about that," she said. "You know best."

"No," said Villa. "I leave it entirely to you. Those men were going to try to cut our communications between Juárez and Chihuahua. They were traitors—Federals.[16] What shall I do? Shall I shoot them or not?"

"Oh, well, shoot them," said Mrs. Villa.

Villa chuckled delightedly. "There is something in what you say," he remarked, and for days afterward went around asking the cook and the chambermaids whom they would like to have for President of Mexico.

He never missed a bullfight, and every afternoon at four o'clock he was to be found at the cockpit, where he fought his own birds with the happy enthusiasm of a small boy. . . Sometimes in the late morning he would send a fast courier after Luis León, the bullfighter, and telephone personally to the slaughterhouse, asking if they had any fierce bulls in the pen. They almost always did have, and we would all get on horseback and gallop through the streets about a mile to the big adobe corrals. Twenty cowboys cut the bull out of the herd, threw and tied him and cut off his sharp horns, and then Villa and Luis León and anybody else who wanted to would take the professional red capes and go down into the ring; Luis León with professional caution, Villa as stubborn and clumsy as the bull, slow on his feet, but swift as an animal with his body and arms. Villa would walk right up to the pawing, infuriated animal, and, with his double cape, slap him insolently across the face, and, for half an hour, would follow the greatest sport I ever saw. Sometimes the sawed-off horns of the bull would catch Villa in the seat of the trousers and propel him violently across the ring; then he would turn and grab the bull by the head and wrestle with him with the sweat streaming down his face until five or six *compañeros* seized the bull's tail and hauled him plowing and bellowing back.

Villa never drinks nor smokes, but he will outdance the most ardent *novio* in Mexico. When the order was given for the army to advance upon Torreón, Villa stopped off at Camargo to be best man at the wedding of one of his old *compadres*. He danced steadily without stopping, they said, all Monday night, all Tuesday, and all Tuesday night, arriving at the front on Wednesday morning with bloodshot eyes and an air of extreme lassitude.

Notes

1. John S. Reed, *Insurgent Mexico* (New York: D. Appleton & Co., 1914), 35–37, 40, 113–18.
2. Daniel W. Lehman, *John Reed and the Writing of Revolution* (Athens: Ohio University Press, 2002).
3. Group of troops of unspecified number.
4. Strong locally distilled hard liquor, as potent as moonshine in the United States.
5. Comrade.
6. The rebellion against Díaz.

7. War correspondent.

8. An enumeration of several typical Mexican alcoholic beverages.

9. Brave.

10. An eloquent attempt to find common ground with people motivated by very different political objectives.

11. The term *compadre* denotes a man with whom the speaker shares ties as the godfather of one of his children, or vice versa. *Compadrazgo*—the forging of godfather-godchild bonds—was and still is an important strategy in establishing friendship and patron-client relationships in Mexican politics.

12. Classic series of orations in 63 BCE in the Roman Senate by Marcus Tullius Cicero against Lucius Sergius Catiline, who had plotted conspiracy to reach the powerful post of Consul in the Roman Republic. These orations have become the standard of classical Latin. The reference reveals Reed's high degree of formal education.

13. The foregoing episode is a classic example of caudillo political culture, and Reed does not understand that Villa's apparent humility in fact masks his authority over the situation.

14. Peasants.

15. An example of the stereotypes that plague the writings of this Marxist just as they do those of more conservative authors.

16. The government troops of General Huerta.

15 Keeping House in Revolutionary Mexico City

Luise Böker[1]

The following letters written by a German woman to her mother document everyday life in Mexico City during the Revolution. As of the writing of these letters, Mexico City had been spared the worst of the fighting with the exception of the "tragic ten days" of February 1913 that resulted in the coup d'état of Victoriano Huerta and the death of President Madero. In the winter of 1915, however, the inhabitants of the capital got firsthand experience with the consequences of the revolution. General Emiliano Zapata's troops besieged Mexico City—then controlled by General Obregón—cutting it off from its food supply. To the chagrin of the foreign residents, Obregón seized money and arms from the wealthy and issued decrees requiring special payments from foreigners. To illustrate his power, he ordered foreign residents who did not comply to sweep the streets. Böker's letters shed light on the famine in Mexico City and the confrontation between revolutionaries and privileged foreigners.[2] Just like Rosa King's, this account gives the perspective of an immigrant observer with a large stake in the situation. The

*letters represent the viewpoint of a privileged German who feared for her fam-
ily's lives and property, all in the shadow of the war consuming her home continent. However, unlike King's account, which enjoys the benefit of hindsight,
her letters constitute an immediate reaction to the Revolution. Unlike Reed,
Böker loathed the revolutionary leaders, men who ultimately proved to be far
more moderate than she feared at the time.*

*The daughter of a Polish-born father and a German mother, Julia Luise
Pocorny (1882–1977) hailed from the small town of Lennep in western Germany.
In 1904, she married Franz Böker, the director of a hardware store in Mexico City.[3]
She accompanied Böker to Mexico, and the couple raised six children there. After
twenty-two years in Germany to ensure her younger children's upbringing in the
culture of her ancestors, Luise Böker returned to Mexico City in 1948, where she
lived until her death. She was this editor's great-grandmother.[4]*

Dear Mother:

February 26, 1915: I should have kept a diary over the last eight to ten days
so that you can appreciate all the mood swings that we have been through.
Actually, the main emotions were those of depression and anger about our
impotence with respect to the situation and the bandits here. Since today,
the mood has been different, as all foreign merchants unanimously agreed
to close their stores this morning, sealing the doors with the insignia of the
respective consulate. That is our salvation, and come what may: after these
terrible years. . . . we have resolved to let go of our earthly possessions as long
as we can once again live a decent life. We hope for great results from this
manner of proceeding that brought together people from the United States,
Britain, France, Spain, and Germany—in short, all nations in concert.
Something like this has never happened before in Mexican history.[5]

Carranza signed a decree three days ago that demanded five million
pesos from us [bankers and merchants]—half in silver currency, the other half
in paper—by 6 P.M. tonight; and that was only the beginning, as demands for
more millions were in the works. [Obregón] requisitioned this amount under
the pretext of providing bread and corn to the poor, but the money was supposed to go to his government. . . .

Meanwhile, our life here has been going downhill. . . . We have no bread;
vegetables are virtually unavailable; only carrots and cabbage and, every once

in a while, artichokes. The quality of the meat has become so poor that one does better without it, and everything that is still available costs a fortune. Thank God our milkman has supplied us with milk; I also still have been able to obtain beer and butter, although with difficulties. . . . The poor [Mexican] people, whose main staple is maize—tortillas are . . . almost unaffordable when one is lucky enough to find them. According to data gathered by our diplomatic representatives, the government has caused this situation by moving all food . . . away from here to Veracruz to be shipped overseas to France and the United States.[6]

By now we have eaten—very late, because Franz had a meeting [with fellow foreign entrepreneurs] where everyone . . . unanimously agreed to remain firm until Carranza has given in on all points. The negotiations with him only work through diplomats via telegraph. This terrible man, Obregón, who is his representative here in this city, is left out of these discussions.[7] He is possibly even worse than Carranza; he is a dangerous character. None of these men carry a grudge against us; for instance, they have already lifted the tax decree and exempted the foreigners from the special taxation. But that is not sufficient: other decrees will need to be rescinded as well, and, above all, Carranza needs to guarantee that food can enter the city. One gets the impression that this fellow is at the end of his rope: when there is no more [money], the business of the revolution has lost its purpose. By God, we are so angry—how many leaders have exploited Mexico, its people and us, only to funnel the money to a secure place where no one can get it? This is the most astonishing thing that has ever happened on Earth—the people have been sucked dry, and the money has gone into someone else's pocket. We are only still alive because the Mexican people are so obtuse that they tolerate anything.[8] Otherwise, the hungry and needy rabble would have already killed us in their anger. We do not like to leave the house anymore; at each corner one . . . sees throngs of hungry men and women who stare at you with greedy eyes.

After all, boundless indolence and obtuseness lie at the root of Mexico's undoing; otherwise, something like Carranza's rule would not have been possible. Despite all revulsion, one has to admire this leader's skill: he ensconces himself in the harbor [of Veracruz], does business with foreign interests, lets his people starve and cashes in on the process. To be sure, he cannot do this without the help of certain foreigners, and the honorable Mr. Bryan will certainly get his percentage.[9]

March 7: I have let much time elapse before writing again. I had hoped to write something more encouraging, but things have not changed here. . . . The Carrancistas are still wielding the scepter of power, and they continue their theft of people, objects, and food. Our international co-operation of merchants has accomplished quite a bit—we have not made payments to the government; and all of our stores remain closed. Most importantly, the International Committee sent a communiqué to the press in the United States designed to inform the public about the conditions in Mexico and to make them aware of the dirty business in which their government engages here. . . . [10]

What a relief that the riffraff, despite the starvation and deplorable conditions among them, have not harmed us foreigners in any way. . . . The Carrancistas themselves are a much greater threat to us. . . . Today, at gunpoint, they forced a German woman to surrender a cauldron filled with hard-earned milk. Similar events occur on a daily basis. Otherwise they have been busy evacuating all week. Every day, trains filled with troops and objects depart. They sack churches and houses, it is incredible. The trams stopped running a week ago; the government sent the conductors off to Veracruz; and the engines of the cars and the best material away as well. Everything is on hold: most Mexican stores have closed as well, and an assembly of Mexican merchants has been taken hostage . . . just like the priests. . . . Yesterday [Franz] came home so late that I started to get frightened. When I voiced my worries, [my eight-year old daughter] Liesel said: "Mother, he has been arrested;" whereupon my [three-year old] boy became restless and said that he wanted to "phone.". . .

Thank God I am very calm, and I am preparing for worse times, especially in terms of the food shortage. The last eight days have aggravated it considerably. There is hardly any diversity in our diet anymore: rice, beans, lentils, everything we have at home.[11] Vegetables and milk are enormously expensive and almost unavailable; I bake bread myself . . . one can learn anything under these circumstances. I will strike meat from the menu; one cannot trust the slaughterhouse anymore, and it is of bad quality. As long as they leave us the five liters of milk a day [for a family of five] I will be content. But keeping house is difficult; you have no idea. Since our plight has persisted for a long time, we have to ensure a halfway proper diet for our children. And who will come in after these robbers [Obregón and Carranza] leave? All outlying areas of town are in the hands of the Zapatistas, and they also plunder without inhibition. And Villa is committing unspeakable crimes in the North as well, as we have heard. In general, however, conditions are better wherever Carranza is not; the question of food does not exist, and stores remain open in the [areas controlled by the Villa/Zapata alliance]. The situation here is too wild. . . . The day before yesterday, someone stole from our warehouse two of our mules bearing the German imperial seal. That is fortunate, because in light of the high price of animal feed, these animals would have eaten us out of house and home very soon. And we do not need the mules anyway. An Englishman wants to shoot his two trusted horses because he has nothing left to eat. I had to kill our chickens for lack of feed; the ducks are still alive, and our big dog needs feeding because we desperately need him for our protection. Now we make breakfast rolls[12] with bean meal—a pig bean bread in the literal sense of the term. . . . Today we hear a concert of gunshots around us. . . . Hopefully you do not learn too much about the conditions here so that you do not worry. The war[13] and worry about our dear relatives at the front do enough of that. That must drive you crazy. We think of that many times each day, and it gives us some consolation amidst our awful situation. . . .

March 8: The shootings around our house last night scared us and made all of us nervous. The children woke up, and we put our boy's bed into a corner where it could not be hit by a stray bullet; we closed the windows and turned off the light, and then we all slept well despite the gunshots in the distance, albeit with wild dreams, at least in my case. Today our children have school, despite everything, after eight days of vacations.[14] Not a single Mexican school remains open, and only very few of those of other nations. . . . The children just got back, disappointed that they did not "experience" anything such as a shooting. . . . I can imagine that all the difficulties that the world is going through today will make each of us much more mature and tranquil; more modest and content with their lot in life. You are experiencing a grand, uplifting time that does not bear comparison with our experience: we are gazing at dirty, low politics.[15] . . .

March 9: It is a crazy country—peace by day, war by night. One cannot go out after dark, *i.e.*, seven P.M., then the shooting begins. We rarely hear about the deaths that must result from the gunfire. Yesterday, there were casualties on the Paseo [de la Reforma]. The rabble killed a Swedish gardener who used to work for us just outside the city. People in the outlying districts of the city suffer terribly; they get robbed by both sides. Mexico has never seen such anarchy. Today, an angry Carrancista riding in our street right in front of us shot at a dog, but fortunately did not kill it. . . . Good night.

March 11: We have fortunately got rid of Carranza's gang.[16] We heard the good news this morning, whereupon everyone looked forward to fresh breakfast rolls. That might take a while: this execrable gang left just last night; at eight o'clock, all church bells began to ring and continued to ring all morning. Many Zapatistas came by here, greeted by the people as the saviors from our famine. So yet another act is upon us. What had begun as a comedy at the outset of the Revolution . . . has turned into a tragedy. This last period of six weeks was particularly awful, and the last few days were scary. Always gunshots in our immediate neighborhood; one never knew whether one could go out or not; a stray bullet could cause disaster. We sent the children to school with much trepidation. . . .

What will happen now? Will Carranza be back in six weeks? In light of the fiasco his gang has just orchestrated, a fiasco that included [new] taxes, blackmail, and demagoguery, his rule could not end well. . . . The only thing the [Carrancistas] have accomplished glamorously is the famine. We are all waiting for maize, flour, vegetables, and, above all, water . . . what a relief that will be! I am quite aware that everything will take a long time to return to normal; who knows how much these fellows have ruined forever. . .

Notes

1. From Luise Böker to Marie Pocorny, Archivo Boker, S.A. de C.V., Mexico City, Fondo Memorias, folder "Familiengeschichte." Translation by Jürgen Buchenau.

2. John Lear, *Workers, Neighbors, and Citizens: The Revolution in Mexico City* (Lincoln: University of Nebraska Press, 2001).

3. See also the Franz Böker selection in Part IV.

4. For a study of Luise Böker and her family, see Jürgen Buchenau, *Tools of Progress: A German Merchant Family in Mexico City, 1865–Present* (Albuquerque: University of New Mexico Press, 2004).

5. Even less so at a time when many of these nations were at war with each other. The joint action of citizens whose nations fought each other in World War I illustrates the unifying force of the revolutionary violence upon foreign nationals in Mexico.

6. Based on hearsay, this statement is not true.

7. While Obregón was in the capital, Carranza operated out of Veracruz.

8. A familiar stereotype of Mexicans.

9. Böker refers to U.S. Secretary of State William J. Bryan, who advocated—and would soon award—de facto recognition of the Carranza regime.

10. See above. The Bökers were incensed that the Woodrow Wilson administration accepted Carranza as de facto ruler of Mexico.

11. These staples were not widely available in Mexico City at that time, either. The Bökers had stocked up on these items, which were full of vermin, "sometimes the only meat available." Interview with Gabriele Buchenau, Warleberg, Germany, June 6, 1992.

12. In the German original: Brötchen, the ubiquitous bread resembling Kaiser rolls that Germans particularly enjoy for breakfast.

13. World War I.

14. Böker's daughters attended the German school in Mexico City.

15. In Böker's opinion, the Germans fight the world war for a lofty cause, while the Mexican Revolution constitutes the insurrection of the rabble.

16. Obregón has left the capital, and the agrarian coalition has taken over.

16 A Revolution for the Indians?

B. Traven[1]

This excerpt from B. Traven's Land des Frühlings *(Land of Spring) gives a favorable appraisal of the work of the winners of the Revolution in the Mexican countryside, particularly as regards the indigenous population. The book is Traven's only major non-fiction work; a sojourner account that reflects his travels into the largely indigenous state of Chiapas, where the author discovered what he called the "Indian sense of community"—in his view, the panacea for Mexico's ills. It shows Traven's infatuation with the Plutarco Elías Calles administration (1924–1928), a government that promised land reform and legislation guaranteeing the rights of labor, yet ultimately fell short of the expectations of workers and peasants. Caught up in this rhetoric, Traven misinterpreted the official* indigenista *movement, which sought to redeem the "Indian" as the centerpiece of Mexican society. In his subsequent novels, this attitude yielded to harsh criticism of the continuing lack of social justice as Traven learned more about the country in which he lived, and Chiapas in particular. Not surprisingly,* Land des Frühlings *remains the only*

Traven book that has never been translated into English. It is, hence, an example of the early enthusiasm of the political pilgrims who flocked to derevolutionary Mexico, only to realize that social change was far more difficult than it initially appeared. It is also a good illustration for the endurance of Orientalist tropes such as the one of the "Indian" into a generation that reflected critically on the legacy of European colonialism and imperialism.

B. Traven is the one writer in this anthology for whom we cannot provide a country of birth. Indeed, the origins of this famous writer, whose novels memorialized the struggles of underdogs against overwhelming odds in early twentieth-century Mexico, remain shrouded in mystery. Biographers have surmised, among other theories, that he was the child of working-class parents from present-day Poland, or an illegitimate son of German Emperor William II. For his part, Traven always claimed U.S. origins, wrote in a folksy German prose appealing to a lower-middle- and working-class readership, and confused those who tried to follow him by using multiple aliases. Before assuming B. Traven as his pen name upon his arrival in Mexico, the author lived in Munich under the name Ret Marut as editor of an anarchist magazine in the chaotic days following World War I. In the 1950s, he used the alias Hal Croves and claimed that he was Traven's agent and translator. He became a Mexican citizen in 1951, married a Mexican, and lived in the capital until his death in 1969. In deference to his last wishes, his ashes were scattered over the Chiapas rainforest.²

The Mexican workers were fortunate in that the Revolution was not interrupted prematurely "in the interest of the public good.". . . They had no leaders, no public officials, and no advisers . . . with bourgeois interests to protect. And when the bloodletting had gone so far that no one would have lent the state even one dollar, or delivered a box of ammunition without prior payment in gold, the workers were on top with a forceful, radical program. They were so strong that they paved the way for the man whom they had chosen as the president of the republic. . . . They had learned a lesson that other workers have had difficulty understanding. They had found out that democracy means conducting elections in accordance with more modern rules as long as capitalism influences political elections with money rather than wisdom. Otherwise, democracy is worthless for workers. Neither former

President Obregón nor current President Calles are socialists the way the term is understood in Europe. There are few socialists in the government. Likewise, there are few socialists among the state governors—a powerful group. The people elected by the workers, however—and whom the workers do not support has little chance to be successful—are men, real men. They keep the promises they made to the workers before the elections. In many cases, and, I want to say, in most cases, they even exceed these promises once they are in office.[3]

When the last revolution broke out, the Indians knew instinctively that this revolution was for them because it was a revolution for the workers.[4] The Indians immediately fought on the side of the workers. When we speak of the Indians here, we mean those distinguished by language, habits, and occupation from the urban industrial working class, which is composed of both pure Indians and mixed blood. We thus mean the non-Europeanized Indians. The Indians were aware from the beginning that the Indian question would be resolved soon after the workers' triumph in the Revolution, because this question is intimately intertwined with the concerns of the working class. In Mexico, one cannot solve these concerns unless one simultaneously resolves the Indian question. . . .

Since the revolution, the Indian has . . . found respect as a Mexican citizen with full rights regardless of his degree of civilization. Even if he appears in rags, and even if he does not speak a word of Spanish, a Mexican will respect him at heart more than a foreigner, no matter whether that foreigner is an American,[5] a Spaniard, or whoever. Nobody in Mexico looks at the Indian with pity or even the kind of sentimentality accorded a once-proud race in the United States. For example, foreigners in Mexico who try to insult, ridicule, or scoff at an Indian (no matter how ragged or drunk this Indian may be) will at once incur the wrath of all nearby Mexicans. In addition, no one would dare to deceive an Indian who comes to town to sell some of his wares. The Mexican is an extraordinarily polite, hospitable, and helpful person, but he does not consider this issue a joking matter.

The Mexican considers the Indian his brother. When he speaks of the Mexican people or the Mexican nation, he includes the Indians of his country without even thinking about it.[6] An American or Canadian would never do that. The English hubris does not allow the acceptance of a non-white person as a brother. The white man is God and master, the Englishman is the supreme God and the supreme master, and everything else that lives or crawls on this earth are creatures, "human creatures"[7] at best. Not even the fact that many non-white peoples lived in high cultures at a time when the ancestor of the genuinely British supreme god still sipped the brain from the skulls of his slain enemies can diminish this hubris.

Although Mexicans disagree over the goals and objectives of the current government, the whole people agree to support the government in its policy of educating the Indian. Only a small stratum opposes this task for selfish reasons of a capitalist, reactionary or clerical nature. The driving motive in the desire to give the Indian more development opportunities is a reason other than kindhearted love. To the same small degree to which an American nation has emerged to this date, there is not much of a Mexican, Argentine, or Brazilian nation. These nations are now at the stage of development of Great Britain in the ninth to twelfth centuries.[8] The countries on the American continent have European languages just as the new countries under the Roman Empire had Latin. Even today, however, people in America speak English differently from those in England, and Mexican Spanish is different from that in Spain. Apart from a very small percentage, however, Indian blood suffuses the Mexican ethnic stock. The indigenous Mexican is so different from the Spaniard in both physical appearance and mannerisms that no one could ever confuse the two. The Mexican has the desire of every young people, which is to breed a purely Mexican people.[9] Particularly since the revolution . . . , he has wished [to forge] a genuine Mexican race through fusion with the indigenous inhabitants of his country. He instinctively believes that this will be a particularly good race; a race that will adapt itself in a natural way to the character of its land, its climate and its soil in such a fashion that it can become a new American[10] race that will gradually populate the entire continent. In order to integrate the Indian, however—the crucial element in this process of race formation—the Mexican needs to raise him up to a higher level of civilization. The easiest way to do that is to make the Indian's level of education more similar to his own.

There are ten million, maybe even eleven million pure-blooded Indians in Mexico.[11] Given a total population of fifteen million, these eleven million . . . are sufficient for the birth of a new race. According to the laws of biology, the blending of two opposite races always creates a new race that exceeds the two original races by at least one-third to one-half in terms of life toughness and resistance [to disease]. While the United States has witnessed only the fusion of the same basic race—the Caucasian one—race formation in Mexico occurs with two very different races. The greater success is therefore with the Mexicans. One cannot predict where the path of this new race might lead: whether it will become the new dominant race in the world, or whether it will incorporate new ideas and experiences in order to fulfill the more difficult, but noble task of creating a new culture and burying the European one. Certain basic characteristics of the Indians, and certain efforts that they undertook before Columbus found them, lead me to think that the [Indian] race will engender a new, quite un-European culture. Three different great cultures emerged on Mexican soil before Columbus.[12] None of these cultures spent itself; none of them is exhausted; none has even completed one-third of its historical trajectory. Why should the new culture not emerge from this virginal country in order to mature at last?

The difficult problem of the Mexican people is to blend the Indian in terms of culture and civilization so thoroughly with the Mexican nation that Mexican and Indian become identical terms. This problem is far more intricate than that of absorbing millions of immigrants in the United States. In my opinion, the task that the Mexican people have set themselves is the most beautiful and noble one that human beings have ever carried out. It is a quite peaceful conquest with no other than purely cultural and civilizing objectives. Only those who live in Mexico, and only those who know the country and its inhabitants are aware how difficult it will be to forge a single people out of nearly 270 different peoples with divergent languages, habits, and living conditions.[13] One has to know the educated Mexican, his racial pride, and his fine appreciation of culture. He has inherited these qualities through the blood of the brave and proud Spaniards who created a world empire in the fifteenth and sixteenth centuries, sailed through totally unknown oceans in defiance of all danger, and withstood for many centuries the Moorish assault on Europe without the help of other European peoples. One has to know this heightened racial pride of the Mexican in order to appreciate the meaning of drawing the Indian into his cultural realm. The fact that the Mexican does this despite the fact that his racial pride resists, and although the sentiments of his soul should oppose it, is a great and noble character trait the likes of which we have never seen before in all of history. All previous racial fusions and formations of nations out of different peoples occurred by armed force and with the ultimate goal of making the conquering race the dominant class of the new nation. Here the conquest is peaceful, and it involves a sacrifice considered by humans as the most difficult of all: the sacrifice of pride.

Because the European is not forced to live with colored races, he will never understand how great a sacrifice it is for a master race to give up their pride in order to embrace, kiss, and make brothers out of people they ought to consider inferior according to their education and inner feelings. The Christian Church has never done or even attempted this in the four hundred years of its limitless power. Today, the most refined and noble people in Mexico carry out this deed—the very same ones whom the Christian Church has either excommunicated or threatened with excommunication. . . .

Whoever maintains that the processes in Mexico are Bolshevik[14] or influenced by Bolshevism is entirely mistaken. Just because one cannot explain why the Mexican people have suddenly become mobile enough to cause difficulties for the capitalist structures they have hitherto welcomed, one gives the easy answer that Bolshevism must be at work. After all, no one wants to bother to look at things . . . more closely. Wherever and whenever capitalism runs into trouble, it summons the ghost of Bolshevism. Everyone understands that language and knows which side he is on, depending on the contents of his wallet. . . .

One has to point out that the Mexican Revolution, which liberated the worker, but in reality, the Indian, began in 1910. At that point, no one knew anything of Bolshevism. The spiritual leader of that Revolution, Francisco I. Madero, was neither a Socialist nor a Communist in our sense. He died—was assassinated—long before the Russian Revolution, but his ideas are enshrined in the Mexican Constitution. This constitution was approved February 5, 1917 and took effect May 1, 1917, at a time when the program of the Russian Bolsheviks was not even known in their inner circles, much less in Mexico.

What happens in Mexico today, and what will occur even more in the coming years, may look . . . like Bolshevism, but in their essence, these processes do not have anything in common with Bolshevism. At least the way it is taught in Europe, Bolshevism is as alien to the Indians as Christianity. If the men who lead the destiny of the people in Mexico were not educated in the European tradition; if they did not need to use European forms of expression in order to be at least partially understood, then one would immediately realize an important fact. The events in Mexico only find an explanation in Mexican-Indian issues rather than in similar-looking processes in Europe.

To make it short and clear: this is a rebellion of a non-European race against the European. More precisely, it is the rebellion of the awakening

Indian culture against the European civilization. This indigenous culture can only develop on an economic base pertaining to itself. What the Mexican does today is to create this economic base. . . .

I need not point out to those [convinced of the benefits of human cooperation] . . . what a fertile country such as Mexico can accomplish if a true sense of community replaces selfish individualism. . . . Therefore, no one in Europe should be surprised if Mexico increasingly becomes the focal point of world events.

One just has to be wary of misleading words. People speak of the "threat to religious freedom," of the "confiscation of foreign private property," of the "Bolshevik tendency of the government.". . . What they mean in all cases and without any exception, however, is the oil, the gold, and the silver of Mexico. . . . Today, Mexico only needs to commit an insignificant political or diplomatic error to hear a lament directed to the whole world . . . that the honorable and noble Mexican people needs to be freed from the tyranny of a brutal, tiny Bolshevik minority. . . . The whole world will fall for this lie, just as it succumbed in 1914 (Europe) and 1917 (U.S.) to a similar deception.[15] But I do hope that a few people will keep a cool head and understand that the politicians in the United States, England, and several other European countries do not care about the "freedom of conscience of the noble Mexican people" or the well-being of the Mexicans as otherwise construed. The oil [wells] and the gold and silver mines are all that is of interest to these politicians. The only reasons why the whole world hates the current Mexican government are that it is the first one to elevate Mexicans to the same level as foreign capitalists, and that it has begun to examine the ownership titles of foreign capitalists to Mexican soil and natural riches for their legal validity. The previous governments of Mexico never did that, which is why they lived in peace with foreign imperialists. In this manner, the natural wealth of a country—presumably, a blessing of its inhabitants—has become the curse of the country and the ruin of its sons.

Notes

1. B. Traven, *Land des Frühlings* (Berlin: Büchergilde Gutenberg, 1928), 18–19, 41–45, 222–23, 251–52. Translated by Jürgen Buchenau.

2. Karl S. Guthke, in *B. Traven: The Life Behind the Legend* (Chicago: Lawrence Hill Books, 1991); Heidi Zogbaum, *B. Traven: A Vision of Mexico* (Wilmington, DE: Scholarly Resources, 1992), xviii–xix.

3. In hindsight, Traven would maintain the opposite.

4. The Revolution of 1910.

5. Traven uses the term "American" meaning U.S. citizen or from the United States.

6. In theory rather than in practice.

7. Term appears in English in the original text.

8. Traven assumes the same linear historical development as nineteenth-century visitors such as Domenech and Bertie-Marriott.

9. As of the writing of Traven's book, this assertion was incorrect, as Mexican public policy continued to favor immigration.

10. Here, the reference is to North America rather than to the United States.

11. A gross exaggeration based on a racial rather than cultural definition of the "Indian" that reveals the flaws in Traven's thinking about indigenism. For Traven, "Indian" seems to be synonymous with "poor, dark-skinned Mexican."

12. Presumably, Traven means the Maya, Teotihuacán, and Aztec empires and subsumes the Toltec culture under the latter rubric.

13. In fact, sixty-three languages including Spanish.

14. The name of the majority faction in the Russian Socialist Party, the term "Bolshevik" refers to Vladimir I. Lenin's movement that triumphed in the 1917 October Revolution in Russia. Throughout the period 1917–1941, Bolshevism was synonymous with Communism in the usage common in the capitalist world.

15. Traven refers to the Allied campaign against Germany and Austria in World War I. Traven believes the Allied war aims were informed by economic motivations rather than U.S. President Woodrow Wilson's stated purpose of making the world safe for democracy.

17 Mexico for the Mexicans

Luis Araquistáin[1]

*La revolución mejicana by the Spanish
journalist Luis Araquistáin Quevedo (1886–1959), judges the Mexican Revolution
from a different vantage point than the Anglo-Saxon and German authors the
reader has thus far encountered. Spain was then one of Western Europe's least
economically developed countries. The nation remained largely rural, and more
than half of all Spaniards were illiterate; thus, Spain was far more similar to
Mexico in terms of its economic and social problems than, for example, France
or the United States. For Araquistáin, the reform program embodied in the
Constitution of 1917 inspired enthusiasm among Spanish socialists, and the
former colony appeared to have taken the lead in reform among Spanish-
speaking countries. Just as important, a common language forged a strong bond
between this observer and his host country. Like the selection by Traven, this
travel account praises the revolution, it views the future with optimism, and it
displays a tendency to accept government rhetoric as fact. The excerpt that follows gives Araquistáin's perspective on urban labor, the conservative opposition,
and anti-foreign sentiments.*

Born in Santander, Araquistáin was part of a generation of intellectuals appalled by the chronic political instability and economic underdevelopment of Spain. This generation, which included the famous writer José Ortega y Gasset, was fundamentally influenced by the carnage of World War I as well. With their country neutral in the conflict, Spanish socialists such as Araquistáin witnessed the intellectual bankruptcy of the Great Powers. The lesson for Spain, he believed, was the democratization of political life and the emancipation of the working class, but not Communism of the Soviet variety. As an editorial writer, Araquistáin traveled to Mexico in 1927 to witness a revolution that appeared to offer promising perspectives. Upon the abdication of King Alfonso XIII of Spain in 1931, he began a career in the newly democratic Spanish Republic. In various government posts, including Assistant Minister of Labor, he witnessed his country's descent into chaos. Economic crisis produced political polarization, which ultimately resulted in the revolt of the right-wing Falangist movement under Francisco Franco. Franco's accession to power forced Araquistáin into exile, where he died in 1959.[2]

The Mexican Revolution is fundamentally agrarian. The land is its principal scene, and the peasant is its protagonist. But it . . . also affects the world of large industry, perhaps the most modern of Hispanic America. In Mexico, there are almost 150 textile and garment factories, numerous mines, and industrial plants producing metal, shoes, paper, tobacco, beer, etc. This industry employs approximately 300,000 skilled workers. Apart from the peasant, the industrial worker has been the most decisive force in the . . . Mexican Revolution.

While the rural worker fought for the right to land, the urban worker fought for the right to unionize. Until 1910, this right had been virtually nonexistent in Mexico. . . . A strike was a criminal offense sanctioned in the Penal Code of 1872. The following saying was very popular in Mexico: "The wealthy only need to abide by the Civil Code, but the poor, by the Penal Code." Especially if they timidly dared to declare a strike. In 1907, Porfirio Díaz ordered the armed suppression of several strikes that broke out in Veracruz and Puebla.

The fall of the Porfirian regime encouraged the emergence of workers' associations that were tolerated by the government headed by Madero. In

1912, the Casa del Obrero Mundial was founded, a school of propagandists that brought forth the most notable leaders of the workers' movement in Mexico. In 1914, after the few men who remained in the Casa del Obrero Mundial [after the Huerta coup] had publicly accused Victoriano Huerta of Madero's assassination, [the dictator] ordered it closed. When Carranza began his uprising against Huerta, the workers organized Red Batallions to defend the Constitutionalist cause. But Carranza never favored the growth of workers' organizations, except when these organizations were helpful to him. In 1916, there was a strike to protest the unbearably high cost of basic necessities brought about by the fraudulent depreciation of the currency. Every military leader printed mountains of paper money, the value of which naturally fell to almost zero. The result was that the prices of consumer goods reached almost astronomical figures.[3] . . . Carranza shut down the trade unions and imprisoned the strike leaders. He wanted to have them shot, but the military tribunal charged with the task of trying their case absolved them two times. For Carranza, just like for don Porfirio, a strike was a crime worthy of the death penalty. . . . Finally, the Constitution of 1917 fully guaranteed the right to unionization in Article 123. . . . Among other provisions notable for their just and humanitarian character, Article 123 establishes a maximum work day of eight hours, and the obligation to submit all unresolved conflicts between capital and labor to a Council of Mediation and Arbitration.[4] . . .

Within limits, [the law] also recognizes the right to strike and picket. . . . The Constitution . . . defines as illicit those strikes in public services that are not announced ten days in advance of their effective date . . . those in which a majority of the strikers commit acts of violence against people and property, and, in case of war, those in which the strikers work in companies dependent on the government. . . . Licit strikes are those that seek an improvement in working conditions, as well as solidarity and protest strikes (as long as they are brief) against government decrees that either harm the legal status of the labor unions or provoke, for whatever reason, the opposition of the workers as professionals.

The restrictive spirit of the Mexican legislation that governs the right to strike evidently tends to moderate the influence of the more intransigent and irresponsible elements of the workers' movement in order to minimize the conflicts that can be avoided by mediation and arbitration. These conflicts can cause considerable unnecessary damage to both parties as well as indirectly to industry itself and to the nation. In addition, it is often the unions themselves that condemn a strike movement. In 1925, the CROM (Confederación Regional Obrera Mejicana),[5] the most powerful social organization of the republic, declared a strike in Puebla illicit, because [the strike leaders] had not communicated their intent to strike in time to the Central Committee, and because they had not sufficiently explained their motivation. On other occasions, it has been the Secretaría de Industria, Comercio y Trabajo that has opposed a strike. In 1926, Secretary Morones himself, the most distinguished figure of the Mexican workers' movement, declared illicit a strike by the Mexican mechanics' union, an action that led to the subsequent disappearance of that organization of railroad workers.[6]

This growing conglomerate of laws and administrative jurisprudence on the subject of strikes, which makes the question of legality an increasingly subtle affair, explains the decreasing use of this weapon. After all, everyone knows that when a strike is proclaimed illicit, its failure is preprogrammed in light of the hostility of the authorities, public opinion, and, generally, the CROM itself. On the other hand, if the strike is recognized as a licit one, its victory can be considered certain. Not only will the state give the strike its support in that case, but the two Labor Laws of December 9 and 18, 1925 also prohibit the use of strikebreakers to replace the workers who have declared the strike. . . .

In another matter, neither the state nor the Mexican workers have yet the necessary means or preparation to forcibly socialize the industry. Let us not even consider that the international conflicts touched off by a policy directed toward such a goal would probably entail great risks for the revolution and even for national independence. [Much more important], the Mexican revolutionaries, free from any theoretical dogma, are more moderate than the Russians, but their attempt [at social transformation] is no less interesting for that reason.

A Mexican strike is one of the most original spectacles of its kind. I got to witness one in Mexico City. It was not a very important one, but very much typical. The employees of a store in a downtown street had declared a strike, and in front of the closed door [of the store], the workers of both sexes held a constant vigil, day and night, flying the black flag as the strike symbol. Large placards leaning against the wall explained to the public the reasons of the [strikers'] position, which were, as one might understand, unflattering to the merchant house. The owner of the store could do nothing to avoid being discredited within his own sight, as in a picket. A couple of police officers were also present in constant guard in order to protect the workers' right to formulate their grievances and to unfurl the infamous black color of their flag. The only thing permitted [to the owner] was to defend himself against the charges of his workers by means of another placard.

A curious detail: since the strike had not been declared unanimously, the dissident minority presented on other placards—also protected by the police—the reasons why, in their opinion, the employees should go back to work. The strike had already lasted for a long time, and the public, curious about this peaceful battle of manifestos between capital and labor, weighed the pros and cons of the antagonistic positions and hoped in their inner souls for the triumph of the most just cause. A beautiful lesson in civility that shows abiding respect for the contending groups. I have never seen this lesson applied in many of the European and American countries that consider themselves very civilized and that do not tire of maintaining that all Mexicans are incorrigible savages. As everywhere, there may be savagery; but there is so much more, and much that does not exist in the rest of the world. . . .

Predictably, the Mexican Revolution encountered tremendous opposition . . . One of the most tenacious and astute adversaries has been the Catholic Church. Owing to its formidable international network, the events of 1926 . . . [when the clergy suspended religious services to protest Calles's anticlerical policies] found a journalistic resonance surpassed today only by a war among the Great Powers or a boxing match for the world championship. All of the Catholic newspapers in the world drew a somber picture of the Mexican clergy that evoked the situation of the early Christians in the catacombs of Rome . . . Even some European writers otherwise considered less than orthodox publicly advocated the "religious freedom" that they saw threatened in Mexico, and they shed some tears of ink in their sorrow about the "persecutions" committed by the Mexican revolutionaries, sons of Satan and descendants of Nero. . . .

In the course of the last century, nobody in Mexico has contributed as much as the Church to keeping the country in a state of chronic convulsion. With its immense wealth, it could at any moment buy generals to revolt against any government suspected of the most tepid liberalism.[7] The Church was able to use its spiritual dominion over the Indians, the product of three centuries of . . . [indoctrination], to incite them to follow these insurgents. The social anarchy that devoured, cancer-like, the entrails of the nation, and that signified a constant danger to its sovereignty . . . , was the work of ambitious and mercenary generals, and of a rural population desperate in its poverty and made savage by superstition. But the hand that moved these instruments—sometimes in the shadow and at other times in daylight—was the Church. The Mexican clergy has been the most anarchic element known in the history of any people. . . . Thus understood, the Constitution of 1917 restores and amplifies the Reform laws, violated during the Porfirian regime.

One of the limitations [imposed by the revolutionary Constitution] that has most hurt the clergy is . . . in Article 130: "Only Mexicans by birth may exercise the ministry of a cult in Mexico." Now the pain is clear. The majority of the Catholic priests were foreigners, Spaniards. From the days of the Viceroyalty to the present, Mexico has always served as the escape valve of the Spanish clergy. The superfluous Spaniard emigrated to that hospitable and prodigious land. But as became obvious during the U.S. and French intervention, a foreign and powerful clergy posed a threat to the nation. For the foreign Catholic clergy, Mexico was not yet a fatherland: rather, it continued being a colony to be dominated by the United States, France, or any other nation, as long as the independence and wealth of the Church remained respected. The requirement of Mexican birth for religious ministry closes the door to one of the least desirable group of immigrants . . . for a nation that has lived under constant international threats. . . .

Another conspiracy against the new Mexican state was that of the oilmen. Mexico has the fortune—and the misfortune—of having some of the world's greatest oil wealth, the precious combustible the possession of which has created conflict among the great powers. . . . Oil is the new blood of nations, the force that moves its inner life and the foundation of its international power. The prodigious development of the United States would have been inconceivable without the most splendid gift it could have received from the gods: its oil deposits. But this gift is not inexhaustible; in fact, the years of U.S. crude are numbered. . . . [The U.S. oil industry therefore] needs to make itself the owner of the reserves of neighboring peoples, those of Mexico, Venezuela, Colombia, and all of Spanish America. . . . [8]

In oil production, Mexico is presently in second place, surpassed only by the United States. . . . Naturally, as Article 27 of the Constitution shows, the Mexicans have been the first in Spanish America who have realized the good fortune and risks inherent in owning such an abundance in oil. . . . [This article] . . . returns to the nation the direct dominion over its subsoil wealth. . . . Xenophobia? No—rather, prudence learned over a century in which Mexico has been nominally independent, but in fact subjected to a foreign plutocracy. And let us not forget that the Mexican Revolution is simply a reconquest of the national territory and wealth. . . .

I have left for last an examination of a resistance force not as well organized as the Church or U.S. capitalism, but the most tenacious and, of course, the one that has elicited most hatred from the Mexican revolutionaries . . . : the Spanish colony.[9] This hatred is an old one and stems from various sources. An old Mexican proverb states bitterly: "The gringo is bad, but the *gachupín* is worse." The Mexicans call the Yankee[10] a gringo, and the Spaniard a gachupín . . . which means "young fellow."[11] . . . Gachupines were the fellows who went to Mexico to make a fortune in commerce or in agriculture. Over time, the term acquired a pejorative connotation . . . applied to all Spaniards, great or small. . . . The evolution of the term "gachupín" from a diminutive to a . . . term of hatred . . . symbolized the beginning of nationalism and class conflict.

Although a descendant of Spaniards, the creole has always resented Spanish immigration. The immigrant, no matter how worthless he was when he came, belonged to the politically dominant caste. From his disembarkation, he was a powerful man and soon became one in fact by becoming the owner of commerce, manufacturing, and agriculture. The creole seldom continued the economic ventures of his Spanish father, which in the majority of cases ended under his leadership or fell into the hands of other, recently arrived Spaniards, the new gachupines. The Caribbean saying: "The father, a merchant; the son, a gentleman; the grandson, a beggar" was also applicable to Mexico. The impoverished grandson saw the gachupín as a protected representative of a state that—from far away on another continent—maintained his land under colonial rule. At the same time, he saw in [the gachupín] someone who seized the wealth of his country. For these reasons (one political, the other economic . . .) the creole hated the gachupín. Mute and somber, and treated even worse than the creole, the Indian also participated in a silent conflict of hatreds to be resolved in the Wars of Independence. The hatred was mutual. . . .

It is human nature—albeit lamentable—that upon the outbreak of the Revolution . . . , the armed peasant masses threw themselves, in terrible vindictive pogroms,[12] upon the gachupines and their property; upon the haciendas that occupied the land the peasants desired; and upon the stores that sheltered the foodstuffs sought after by the starving troops. . . . [Typically a

Spaniard], the small merchant was the first and most hurt victim of the Mexican Revolution. I have read and heard horrible tales of brutality and heroism. No principle of natural justice can justify some of the cruel acts of vandalism. But neither can one judge these events in abstraction from the historical context in which they happened; and without taking into account the seminal resentments that the Spaniards produced in Mexico. . . .

Notes

1. Luis Araquistáin, *La revolución mejicana: sus orígenes, sus hombres, su obra* (Madrid: Editorial España, 1930), 227–29, 231–33, 263–64, 267–68, 275–76, 285–86, 289, 292, 306–8, 310–11.

2. Burnett Bolloten, *The Spanish Civil War: Revolution and Counterrevolution* (Chapel Hill: University of North Carolina Press, 1991), passim and 117–18.

3. See also, Luise Böker.

4. Consisting of an equal number of representatives from capital and labor as well as one representative named by the government, this Junta de Conciliación y Arbitraje has the authority to decree arbitration binding on both parties.

5. In English, Regional Mexican Workers' Federation, an organization allied with President Plutarco Elías Calles. Araquistáin follows Spanish linguistic conventions of spelling Mexico with a "j." For the "x" in Mexico, see Nicholson.

6. Luis N. Morones was a close ally of Calles and head of the CROM as well.

7. Defined here in its nineteenth century sense: the effort to separate church and state and to nationalize church property.

8. This assertion glosses over the fact that British and Dutch oil companies were as significant as U.S. holdings. When President Lázaro Cárdenas expropriated the largest foreign oil companies on March 18, 1938, the value of European holdings was close to sixty percent of the expropriated total.

9. This term is generally used in Mexico to describe communities of foreigners.

10. U.S. citizen.

11. In the Spanish original: muchacho.

12. This term of Russian origin ordinarily connotes anti-Semitic persecutions.

18 A Country Without Conservatives

Evelyn Waugh[1]

🔳

The following excerpt from Robbery Under Law *by the British novelist Evelyn Waugh provides a conservative, Catholic critique of 1930s Mexico generally, and the reforms of President Cárdenas specifically. Composed following a two-month vacation that took Waugh to Mexico City and southeastern tourist spots such as Cuernavaca, Oaxaca, and Taxco, this travelogue launches an all-out attack on contemporary Mexico despite the author's very cursory personal experience. In part, this predisposition against the revolution was engendered by the author's friendship with fellow Catholic writer and Mexico traveler Graham Greene, who had published his own diatribe against Mexican revolutionary anticlericalism,* Lawless Roads, *the year before. The following selection serves as an important counterpoint to those of the political pilgrims Traven and Araquistáin, unabashed supporters of the postrevolutionary order. Like the Luise Böker excerpt, it also presents a pessimistic view of Mexico and the key conservative arguments against the Mexican Revolution. Of special interest is Waugh's case against the social reforms and economic nationalism of the Cárdenas era.*

Evelyn Arthur St. John Waugh (1903–1966) grew up in London and was educated at Oxford. After years of drinking and homosexual romance, he turned his back on this former life completely after a failed suicide attempt. An artist and schoolteacher, he became one of the best-known conservative novelists of his day, the author of Decline and Fall *(1928),* Brideshead Revisited *(1945), and* Men at Arms *(1952), among others. He converted to Roman Catholicism in 1930. Five years later, he traveled to Ethiopia as a reporter to cover the Italian invasion of that country. In 1938, he and his second wife Laura embarked for their vacation that led to the writing of* Robbery Under Law.

On the first day of my visit, traffic leading to the Cathedral square was paralyzed at midday. My companion advised leaving our taxi and walking. After passing an enormous block of cars, some drivers hooting furiously, others resigned to an indefinite wait, others causing further confusion by attempting to back out in the side streets, we came upon the cause of the trouble: a huge procession of school children, of all ages, themselves halted and standing wistfully among their banners. Many of the groups wore distinguishing ribbons and uniforms; the banners seemed merely to state the localities from which they came. I asked, "Is it some football match?"

"No, it is just a demonstration of the children. They are always having them."

"What about?"

"I'll ask." My companion asked one or two spectators who shrugged indifferently, saying it was just a demonstration. Finally he obtained the information. "It is a children's strike."

"What about?"

"They do not like one of their teachers. They have come to protest to the President."

"They seem very well organized."

"Yes, the children's committees do that. The ministry of Education teaches them to organize like the C.T.M."[2]

"What will happen?"

"The teacher will be dismissed. They are always changing their teachers in that way."

Next day the newspapers had a story of a brawl between the school-boys and some chauffeurs from an omnibus garage.

Strikers are a topic of general discussion, like the weather in England, and like it, the habitual excuse for any failure of plans. The visitor may wonder why service is so bad even at the leading restaurants; if he enquires he will learn that it is practically impossible for an employer to engage temporary labour; nothing fluctuates more sharply and regularly than the tourist trade, but if a restaurateur engages a waiter for the busy months he must keep him. Under the Labour Law the least that can happen to him for discharging a man is the payment of a bonus of a quarter's wages; it is more likely that a prolonged suit will begin; he will be kept from his business day after day waiting for a hearing at the Labour Courts, paying his own lawyer and one for the man who is suing him, paying the man's wages while the case is pending, and at the end he will be obliged to reengage him permanently. So employment drops, the tourist sits hungrily at his table or rings despairingly at his bedroom bell in his hotel, the servants who are employed are worked off their feet and everyone is the worse off. The incurious visitor may merely assume that Mexicans are not very good hotelkeepers; and that also is true.[3]

Then there is the Museum. Every tourist visits it; how many bother to enquire how it is managed? Those who are told find the story incredible. These, as I learned them, are the facts: Until a short time ago the staff was divided into two groups, both directly employed by the State. There were the specialists appointed to the various departments—archaeologists, anthropologists and so on, who had mostly been trained in the United States or in Europe and knew a fair amount of their sciences; they were very poorly paid, but it was one of the few appointments open to Mexicans of education who were not active politicians; their work corresponded with that of similar officials in other museums; they were responsible for cataloguing, labelling, arranging, advising about new acquisitions and so forth. Below them were the floor cleaners, janitors and officials in peaked caps who lounged about the rooms guarding the exhibits and ordering foreign tourists to remove their hats. These had no pretensions to education, though in time they picked up a little dubious information from what they heard the guides telling the school children. These outnumbered the specialists. When the Cárdenas regime introduced the classless era, instructions were sent out that all units of workers must organize themselves into a union, which was to be a branch of the national C.T.M.—the "labour front" over which Sr. Lombardo Toledano presides. The Museum workers accordingly formed their union. Next they declared the Museum a closed shop and demanded that the specialists be made to join them. This, too, was decreed. The janitor is the boss; he enjoys meetings and calls them frequently; he has the power to fine absentees, which he uses with relish; the specialists have to come to his meetings, where all points of discipline and conditions of employment are debated and decided. It has just been decided that in future all promotions shall be by seniority alone and that all members of the union are equally eligible for all posts. Thus a floor cleaner may, and probably will, find himself in charge of the Mayan antiquities.

Tales of this kind—many of them no doubt exaggerated—form the staple conversation in Mexico. There is the story, which I believe to be perfectly true, of the woman who was ruined by her door-keeper. The door-keeper's is an important position in the Mexican family. In the old days of large households it was keenly competed for. It carried no regular wages, but board, lodging, light work and a position of confidence that could be turned to profit in many ways. In particular he got tips for being awakened after bedtime; in a patriarchal Mexican house the younger members were often anxious to conceal from their parents the hours they kept. It was a thoroughly good job. One old Indian had held this post contentedly for twenty-five years when he was caught in some unusual dishonesty and dismissed. He consulted a lawyer about the new Labour Laws and their interpretation, in the hope of getting some damages. The lawyer, learning that he had received no regular wages, filed a suit against his employer for accumulated arrears at the new rates, for compensation for their having been withheld, for fines for neglect of the labour legislation, and for overtime for having been expected to get up and open the door at night, in other words for having been on duty, at work, all night, every night of his life. The total, with legal expenses, came, I was told, to 40,000 pesos. And he won his case.[4]

It is unlikely that he profited much. It is usual in such cases for lawyers to work on a commission basis which in the case of an illiterate Indian would absorb most of the winnings, or even to purchase the rights in an action for a sum down. Litigation is universal in Mexico. "I have to see a man about an *amparo*" (stay of justice) is a normal polite excuse in refusing an invitation. European employers who find themselves constantly involved with the courts get despondent about it, but I got the impression that Mexicans, on the whole, rather enjoy it. What they do *not* like is for the game to lose the element of chance which is so dear to them. In the old days you never quite knew what decision you would get; it all depended on the pull your adversary had, on the bribe he had offered, and to whom. Now there is monotony in the judicial decisions. They go on purely ideological grounds. The proletarian is always right; between proletarians, the one who is nearest to the C.T.M. boss; between bourgeois, the one who is nearest to the governing gang. One of the present President's first reforms was to abolish the independence of the Supreme Court and make its personnel a Government Committee. Since then, no appeal has been of any efficacy where politics are concerned—and politics are concerned in every branch of Mexican life. It is no exaggeration to say that to be an employer in Mexico is to outlaw oneself. It is not surprising that business of every kind is in dissolution.[5] There are indications that Mexicans themselves are getting uneasy about their condition.

At first many of them enjoyed the spectacle of the discomfiture of the foreigners. They disliked them personally; they resented their assumption of superiority; they inherited a belief that their Government was under foreign influence, and was being conducted for foreign advantage. There was a certain tradition of misunderstanding between foreign commerce and the Mexican educated class which has had an important influence in Mexican politics. There are of course countless exceptions. There are many English and American businessmen who are popular on the golf links and even in Mexican homes. There are some Mexicans who have been educated in Europe and return more pro-British than the British themselves. But, generally speaking, there is something of the Chinese mandarin about the Mexican aristocrat in his attitude to the capitalists. In the days of prosperity, when the Jockey Club was the centre of an extravagant social life, few English or Americans obtained admission. Now the Mexicans are ruined and they attribute their ruin very largely (and I think unjustly) to the foreigners. They believe that most of the revolutionary confiscations took place with the connivance and encouragement of the United States—which backed Juárez against Maximilian, first made and then drove out Huerta, and even idealized ruffians like Villa and Zapata; which armed Calles when half the country had risen against his religious persecution; which was naturally anti-Catholic and anti-aristocratic; which took huge profits out of the country and lectured the Mexicans on their responsibilities if they went on a holiday at Biarritz; which told successive Presidents that a redivision of land would bring national salvation; which complacently watched the ruin of the Church and of the white landowning families; and which are now getting ruined themselves. They are too polite to put matters so bluntly but this is, I believe, the attitude of most of the Mexican upper class. It is only partly justified by historical facts, but that is their belief, and that the reason why, in the present crisis, the foreign businessmen found no local party to whom they could appeal.

There is a disposition, in fact, among visiting publicists to ignore them altogether or to treat them as a distressed foreign minority, like White Russian, in Paris; to accept the centuries of Spanish rule as a closed incident and to look to pre-conquest elements for the eventual salvation of the country; to speak severely of "Indo-America" in place of "Latin America." That is the official attitude of the Revolutionary Party, which finds expression in the huge and clumsy frescoes of Diego Rivera.[6] It suits the politicians and the archaeologists, but it makes nonsense of history. . . . Mexico was part of New Spain; for three centuries of undisturbed domination Spaniards lived, married and died in Mexico; they mingled their blood profusely with the various native nations; they taught the people their language, law, religion, crafts and social habits. . . . Four hundred years of history cannot be obliterated. The traditions of Spain are still deep in Mexican character, and I believe that it is only by developing them that the country can ever grow happy. I do not mean, of course, that it is possible or desirable to re-establish the vice-regal government, . . . although it was in many ways a better system than Mexico has now. I believe, in fact, that within a hundred years Mexico will form part of the United States. But I mean that for the understanding of its immediate problems fewer mistakes are made if it is remembered that the Mexicans, though they may sometimes *feel* like Aztecs or Tlaxcalans, *think* like Spaniards; their souls have been formed on the Aristotelian model.

The position of the Spanish-Mexican families has no exact parallel anywhere in the world. At the moment they exhibit many of the defects of an aristocracy that has first been deprived of power and privilege and then of livelihood. For generations, now, there has been little inducement to them to attempt to retain the leadership of their country. Under Porfirio Díaz . . . they filled the diplomatic posts and local governorships, but the national system was purely autocratic and the army a mere police force. They were precluded by their religion from joining the Freemasons who filled the bureaucracy. Moreover, they were rich. Not as rich as English or Americans or French, but comfortably provided. Díaz ensured them their incomes and left them to enjoy themselves. Díaz married into their class. It is significant that when the Revolution came it was led by a man far nearer to them than to the peon: Francisco Madero, a rich, white, landed proprietor.

Díaz has been criticized since his fall by all parties—by the patriots on the ground that he parcelled up the national resources and sold them to foreigners, by the socialists on the ground that he introduced modern capitalism and kept the peasants in degraded conditions, by humanitarians because he enslaved the Yaqui Indians, by the religious because he left the problems of the Reforms unsolved. The general feeling is that he had a unique opportunity to reconstruct the nation and that he did nothing except maintain his own authority and allow troubles to accumulate for his successors. The truth was that he set himself a simpler but no less arduous task. He should be judged as a Mustafa Kemal, not as a Mussolini.[7] He found a country which, after two generations' experiment with independence and democracy, was rapidly relapsing into savagery. For two generations the country had not known a government. . . . While everywhere else in the world the ordinary amenities of civilized life had been making prodigious advances, in Mexico they had actually receded since the Spanish occupation. In particular the United States, which at the beginning of the century was on a lower cultural level than her Spanish neighbour, was now a world power of enormous wealth. . . . In Mexico there was no law nor national unity; not only had she not kept abreast of mechanical advance; in matters of communication and personal safety she had fallen behind her colonial standard.

For thirty-five years Díaz maintained his personal government. He set an example, unique among Mexican rulers, in the integrity of his private life. He was a faithful husband. He opened up the country with roads and railways, bringing law and wealth to practically unexplored districts. Above all he kept the country's sovereignty intact—at a time when statesmen were openly claiming that the natural boundary of the United States was the Isthmus of Panama. He was only able to do this by maintaining the equilibrium of foreign investment, by getting English and French to fight his commercial war with the United States. He saved his country from absorption at the very modest price of the dividends that went to European stockholders.[8] It was a big enough achievement for one man; as time goes on perhaps the Mexicans will come to appreciate it, but as there is not yet a single memorial to Cortés[9] and his most lovely relic, the old church at Tlaxcala, has lately been ruined, perhaps this is too much to hope. (Though, come to think of it, is there anywhere in England a memorial to Julius Caesar?)[10] At the end of Díaz's reign, when his powers were weakened, he began to concern himself with the problem of a successor and for the moment toyed with the idea . . . of a constitutional opposition. Mexicans of the time had grown up under him, and knew the boredom and inevitable abuses that grow in an autocracy; [they] wished to see their country conforming still more closely to the contemporary fashion. . . . So party politics were re-introduced with pleasant expectations of candidates competing with benevolent projects and a party loyalty finding expression in coloured rosettes and rotten eggs. The result has been twenty-five years of graft, bloodshed and bankruptcy. Hardly a single prominent figure in the history of Mexico in the last generation has escaped a violent death . . . Now and then a politician gets across the border in time, either to wealthy exile like Calles or to imprisonment and death like Huerta. The constitutional opposition to which the opponents of Díaz aspired has never come into existence. There is still one political party in Mexico, now the Revolutionary Party; seats and *offices* are appointed at party headquarters as in all totalitarian states. The only difference between the Mexican system and the Fascist is that the nation has sacrificed its political liberties without getting internal security or foreign prestige in exchange. Thus it is not surprising that a political career has now few attractions for Mexicans of decent principle. It is difficult to say where the fault lies when the government of a country gets into the hands of its worst elements; there is a natural trend of all political forms in this direction. Those who have wearied of democratic forms forget that history is full of instances of legitimate royalty being ruled by corrupt courtiers; English Whigs in the Eighteenth Century enriched themselves from the public purse;[11] it is not only in France and the United States that the worst men may get to the top. What is certain, however, is that there is a Gresham's Law active in public life: bad rulers drive out good. In France and the United States it is unusual for respectable citizens to go into politics. In Mexico it is at the moment unknown.

In the United States, however, there is trade as an honourable activity and a source of power; in France there is an army. But in Mexico trade is almost all in foreign hands and the army has a very odd position. There is no recent military tradition among the Spanish Mexicans. The army forms an independent estate with a relationship to the Government and the people which is impossible for a foreigner to understand.[12]

In the ordinary way it is extremely unobtrusive. One sees far fewer soldiers about the place than in most European countries. Every town has its barracks—usually a convent appropriated "for charitable purposes;" many churches show signs of recent military occupation: bayonet cuts in the pictures, the ashes of campfires made from choir stalls, and so on—on days of national importance the streets are lined and paraded with glum, fairly smart little figures in uniform; there are guards in field uniform . . . at most Government offices; on the main roads one passes little pickets, quartered in peasant huts, employed most of the day in cooking and eating; very, very rarely a high officer appears at a night club where, if sober, he sits shyly in a corner, suffering uncertainty about his knife and fork. But one does not get the impression of a country in which the military are predominant. That, however, according to everyone who ought to know, is the case. It is in the army that revolutions start; it is from the army that rulers rise—General Cárdenas, for example. And the army is a very unusual force indeed. It is strongly anti-Catholic, pro-Freemason, anti-aristocratic, anti-foreign. Since the reforms of General Amaro it is highly disciplined—almost ascetic. One hears of local generals who maintain a feudal state . . . but for the most part they live rough. The officers are recruited from the half-caste minor bourgeoisie; they go to military schools at an early age and imbibe certain Spartan virtues and vices. The men are pure Indian, recruited in the villages, usually, I am told, by forcible methods. Once enrolled they find themselves detached from the village, the soil, the family, and the parish which have hitherto been the basis of their lives; they seem to accept the new attachment placidly enough. Their loyalty, like that of "native troops" all the world over, is to their immediate superiors. When the officers declare against the government, they march with them. They are inspired by the commander's prestige and popularity, which seem to have singularly little dependence on his qualities of justice and humanity, or even on his courage and military skill. If the general is successful they get a kind of vicarious satisfaction; if he loses they either take to the hills with him or wander home to their villages. All the fighting they have seen or heard of or are likely to see or hear of is against fellow Mexicans.

The civil service, which includes the school-teachers, is appointed purely on political grounds and reflects the opinions of the governing group in Mexico City. The personnel are subject to close scrutiny in their private lives and are liable to expulsion if, for instance, they are seen to practise their religion. Most of them are mere clerks who find it convenient to profess whatever is the current governing philosophy. Many of them are alarmed at the direction General Cárdenas's policy is taking; practically all, if they could keep their posts by so doing, would readily support an opposite policy if an opposition came into power. The whole-hearted doctrinaire communists seem mostly to be employed in the office of education, but even here there are many courageous malcontents who give secret religious instruction to their pupils.

The lawyers are an able and influential class. Apart from the endless litigation which is a feature of Mexican life, they occupy themselves prominently with political controversy in the press. There are many prominent socialists among them. Lombardo Toledano, the head of the C.T.M., the federation of trades unions which is the chief political force in the country, is a lawyer. The judges, as has been mentioned above, are now political nominees, but the bar is predominantly against the Government, largely no doubt for professional reasons; the presence of the foreign business concerns in Mexico has been a source of splendid revenue to them. The doctors are said to be highly competent, though the best of them still go abroad for their training. They have for a long time enjoyed a privileged position under the Revolution. Foreigners are forbidden to compete with them. Many of them owe their places to C.T.M. appointment. Medical service is one of the directions in which General Cárdenas promises—though up to now he has accomplished very little—unlimited expansion. Hospitals are all in Government hands. They may, therefore, be said to support the present régime as a profession, although individually many are becoming apprehensive.

The shopkeepers and small manufacturers are uniformly allied with the foreign business interests. A large number of them are themselves foreign—German and Jewish principally, but drawn from all races, even Chinese and Syrian. They have suffered most from recent events. They are, however, unorganized and, at the moment, without influence.

The priesthood . . . have been driven into the life of the catacombs. They are, of course, opposed to their persecutors but it is generally believed that their political power is completely broken.

These are, roughly, the political grouping of the elements from which a national opposition to General Cárdenas might be expected to arise. At present there is no open opposition of the kind which flourishes in a democratic country, and when one questions those who are most bitter in their complaints of the régime as to how they hope to see it altered, the answer nearly always comes back to the army. . . . Judged by recent European standards, Mexico [therefore] seems to be in the condition in which a Fascist party is due to rise and conquer.[13]

Notes

1. Evelyn Waugh, *Robbery Under Law: The Mexican Object-Lesson* (London: Chapman and Hall, 1939), 59–74.

2. The Confederación de Trabajadores Mexicanos, or Confederation of Mexican Workers; the principal labor union in Mexico.

3. A series of exaggerations.

4. A story that undoubtedly moved aristocratic Tory conservatives of Waugh's time, many of who kept butlers and house servants.

5. Yet Mexico, at the time, was emerging from the Great Depression.

6. Otherwise admired as among the finest examples of politically conscious art.

7. Kemal Atatürk was the founder of modern Turkey, who brought a Western law code and political system to the remnants of the Ottoman Empire after World War I. Mussolini was, of course, the leader of Fascist Italy (1922–1945).

8. The price was not so modest, as we have seen in the preceding section.

9. The leader of the Spanish conquest.

10. The Roman conqueror of Britain.

11. The Whigs were the liberal adversaries of the conservative Tories; advocates of free trade and the expansion of suffrage.

12. This is an important point, although Cárdenas, building on the work of Obregón and Calles, subjugated the remnants of the revolutionary army.

13. In fact, the right-wing Sinarquista movement gained strength in the Cárdenas years, fueling fears of a military coup d'état only dispelled with the peaceful transition of power to Manuel Avila Camacho in 1940.

19 Freedom for Mexican Women?

Verna C. Millán[1]

On a cold and misty April day in New York City in 1933, Verna Carleton, a young medical professional,[2] married Ignacio Millán, a physician from the state of Sinaloa, in a ceremony witnessed by the famous Mexican painters Diego Rivera and Frida Kahlo. Soon thereafter, the Milláns embarked to begin a lifetime in Mexico together. Mexico Reborn *is the fruit of six years of reflection of life as the wife of a Mexican oncologist who, during the Cárdenas years, served as director of the School of Rural Medicine and distinguished himself as an accomplished pianist and translator. Lifelong friends of Rivera, Kahlo, and other Mexican intellectuals, the couple was known for their radical political beliefs, and Ignacio was one of the founders of the Sociedad de Amigos de la URSS, or Society of Friends of the Soviet Union.* Mexico Reborn *is thus an immigrant account from the turbulent 1930s, years that included the transition from the age of Calles to the Cárdenas administration—a government that revived the promises of the Revolution for a decent living for all Mexicans.*

While Millán (unlike Waugh) sympathized with the Cardenista program, a sobering assessment of gender roles emerges from her memoir. Through her husband's work and social engagement as well as from their house in the affluent Mexico City suburb of Colonia Roma, Verna witnessed the daily lives of Mexico's new governing elite—an elite far more traditional in their social values than in their loudly proclaimed political ideas. The following excerpt provides an important perspective on the status of women in Cardenista Mexico. What makes this source so unique is that Millán writes not as an outsider, but from personal experience with Mexican attitudes toward gender. She offers interesting insights about the failure of most foreigners to acculturate to Mexico even after decades of living there. At the same time, she continues to judge Mexican society by the standards to which she had grown accustomed in the United States.

The American woman who marries into a Mexican family has a gigantic task of readjustment before her; by the mere act of crossing the border, she slips into a world that has many features of the Middle Ages. Product of an advanced civilization, her first psychological shock will take place when she realizes that in Mexico women are still considered inferior beings, unfit to manage their own lives or assume any position of responsibility. For the next few years her life will be one long, unending struggle to preserve the best of her former life and yet, at the same time, adapt herself to the demands of a new environment. This process of adaptation is so delicate, so extremely complicated and requires such flexibility of mind and character that nine out of ten women faced with this problem never really conquer it. Yet if one does not do so only two drastic paths remain; divorce, which is always a confession of failure, or suicide—a friend of mine ended her eighteen years' struggle for adjustment in Mexico with an overdose. . . . Other times the suicide is spiritual rather than physical, and then the slow, persistent disintegration of a formerly vivid personality is even worse than any death.

Mexico is full of misfit foreign women, nervous-faced and racked by inner tension, who have all the peculiar psychology of exiles. They can never return home, not because of political ideas—exiles at least have hope in this respect—but because they are bound to the country by ties of home and children. Sometimes they are beautiful homes, exquisite replicas of those they left behind in Boston, Stockholm, Geneva or Liverpool, and here they try to pretend, for brief moments, that they have not broken completely with the past. Their efforts to retain always their privileged positions as foreigners seem pathetic when viewed coldly and without emotion. The children of these unhappy marriages are brought up in foreign schools, educated always to think of their mother's tongue as really their own, with the result that Spanish becomes a secondary language. Sometimes they marry outside of Mexico and find themselves never quite accepted there because they are only half American, or English, or French, as the case may be. More often they return to the country of birth, and here they are even more out of place than their mothers before them; they feel oddly superior to the Mexicans; they never really understand anything that goes on about them. And so they live out their lives, foreigners in their own countries, and no more tragic, futile beings have ever existed.

Yet to become a part of the country is even more difficult, and in the ultimate analysis constitutes a veritable test of character. The American woman who marries a Mexican and decides to live his life without the constant barrier of race and tradition must have infinite patience and, above all, tact. She must bear constantly in mind that the Mexicans are a painfully sensitive race, smarting under centuries of foreign dominion which has bred within them a profound complex of racial inferiority.[3] They are constantly on guard against all foreigners, and sense slights and offenses which a sturdier people would never notice. She must be prepared to spend all the rest of her life assuring those around her that she really wants to understand Mexico and its problems; her criticisms, even the most constructive, will be tempered with praise, for she is in a new country and nothing is fixed or stable as yet. She will, with time, develop a prodigious memory—somewhat akin to that of the proverbial elephant—for all the people she has ever met, and learn to call them by their correct names and ask after their multitudinous children, whether they interest her or not. Perhaps in her own town she enjoyed the reputation of being somewhat Bohemian and indifferent to social niceties—but not here. Mexicans are painfully polite and given to all sorts of flowery phrases which mean nothing in cold fact but are considered indispensable requisites for well-bred people. . . .

Above all else, the woman who marries into Mexico, prepared to live out her life within its shores, must learn to hide her loneliness, because it is a terrible offense to feel lonely when one is surrounded by people who are kind and good and eager to make one feel at home. It will not be easy; moments will come over her, moments of painful unreality when the strange rhythm of a foreign language, the peculiar sounds of the street, the very color of the landscape will become jarringly merged into a wave of longing for the known and the familiar; but if she must give way to this loneliness, then let her weep alone, in the silence of her room, and face the anxious family later with serene eyes. After all, the Mexicans are not to blame for her plight. No one forced her to marry, cut off the very roots that bound her to family and friends and seek a new life thousands of miles away. Whining gets her no place, and has an appalling psychological effect upon her children. So she might as well adopt the attitude, from the very start, that every country has its interesting points, and perhaps in time she will even come to prefer living in Mexico.[4]

I prefer it now, but it took me six years to reach that point. I do not know how complete my adjustment to Mexico has been, and never will know until I go back to the United States again, but it must be fairly good; for a long while, now, Mexicans have paid me one constant compliment: they say I don't seem like a foreigner to them; and any American woman knows that they can give her no greater proof of their confidence and sympathy.

I had only been in Mexico a very short while when I became interested in the feminist movement and women's problems in general. Generalizations are perilous things, but from the start it seemed to me that Mexican women were much superior in every respect to Mexican men. The men here are momentarily brilliant and enjoy brief spells of power, but there is nothing stable behind it all, and at forty they are fatigued. The Mexicans themselves have noticed this phenomenon; "*Fulano se apagó*," they say sadly—"So-and-so is all blown out," in the same way a match is extinguished by a breath of air, for the flame of their talent is equally as fragile.

Women have given the Mexican character its most enduring qualities. The history of Mexico has been brightened many times by innumerable proofs of their stoicism and heroic patience in the face of danger. The War for Independence made the names of Leona Vicario and Josefa Ortiz de Domínguez immortal because they risked their lives to free Mexico from the grasp of the Spaniards. By the time the Revolution broke forth many women, particularly of the working class and the peasantry, were ready to take their places side by side with their men; glorious names are these, Elisa Acuña, Juana Gutiérrez de Mendoza, Dolores Jiménez y Muro, who carried the flaming message of Zapata's agrarian reform to the *campesinos*,[5] and Lucrecia Toriz, textile worker, who together with other women workers helped organize the historic strike of Río Blanco, which was a first signal for the revolt against Porfirio's corrupt dictatorship.

As for the *soldaderas*, glamorous legends have sprung up around them, these peasant women who followed their soldiers into the very camps of battle. They can still be seen today, in every *pueblito*[6] or in the fields where they work, living, breathing figures by José Clemente Orozco,[7] their striped cotton skirt brushing the dry stubble; bare feet beneath their skirts, mud-stained and bruised; long black braids, tied coronet-wise with bits of colored ribbon or string; a faded *rebozo*[8] slung across one shoulder supports the inevitable baby in its hammock-like caress. Many battles were won through the decisive aid of the soldaderas. When fighting was not intense, they would stay on the edge of the field, waiting, patiently waiting for their men to return; tiny fires were built and tortillas patted into warm, moist ovals; a pot of beans simmered over the charcoal and occasionally, very occasionally, there would be a bit of meat to roast upon the embers. When the fighting became riotous, however, babies and campfires were left to the care of the few old women while the rest plunged pell-mell into the hastily erected barricades and often grasped rifles from the still warm hands of the dead. Many fields of Mexico have seen the translucent light of dawn illuminate the quiet bodies of the *soldaderas* who fell there in battle. Many hardened soldiers tell stories of their bravery with a certain hushed reverence, for heroism that seeks no glory for itself is doubly moving. . . .

The Mexican woman of today, the woman of the towns and larger cities, has this enormous burden of race and tradition upon her shoulders; product of a mestizo culture, she is caught in the mesh of not one but two traditions, both equally repressive. The Spaniards brought to Mexico the strict Catholicism that has held women in a subjective, passive role for centuries. On the other hand, the Indian tribes since time immemorial have crushed the spirit of their women beneath ironclad taboos and repressions. Even today, these customs of the Indians remain unchanged, save here and there, in those regions where a rapidly encroaching industrialization has brought about a new concept of life and morals. . . . [9]

The Spanish Conquest was an added burden to the traditional slavery of the Mexican woman. Nowhere in the world have women been more bitterly oppressed than in Spain.[10] The early Spaniards brought their traditions with them; marriage had only one alternative, the convent. Century after century, these precepts were beaten into women's souls until they created a peculiar psychological attitude of utter passivity and abnegation which has been an overwhelming obstacle in the path of the feminist movement. Even the Revolution was not able to make a clean break with the past, and today Mexican women in general are little better off than in the time of Díaz; a great portion of this is due to the fact that they have been suppressed for so long that the mere thought of freedom bewilders them. An entire generation, perhaps two, will have to pass before a wide change becomes possible.

But when anyone takes into consideration the atmosphere that weighs upon the Mexican woman from the moment of her birth, it is a veritable miracle that any of them at all are able to escape its nerve-shattering influence. Within the home, the man reigns supreme, a heritage from the Middle Ages. The daughters are taught absolute obedience not only to their fathers but to their brothers as well. If there is little money in the family, the sons are educated at the expense of the daughters. If the family have money, they refuse to educate their daughters on the ground that they will not need a career after their marriage. Marriage is considered the supreme goal of every woman's life. The mother's marriage may have been a life-long tragedy but she can conceive of no other fate for her daughters, on the theory that any kind of marriage is better than none because at least one thus fulfills the Christian command to multiply. Never have I seen so many tragic marriages as in Mexico. . . .

The Spaniards bequeathed still another tradition to Mexico which is not precisely a guarantee for marital happiness: long engagements, coupled with the complete ignorance of sexual matters which women possess here, have caused this custom to become ever more firmly ingrained in Mexican life with the passing of years. This tradition is the Spanish one of maintaining two establishments, a large house for the legal wife and children and a little house, *casa chica*, for the mistress and whatever children result from the relationship. Most wives take this as a matter of course; my Anglo-Saxon mind has never quite been able to accept the calm excuse of many Mexican friends who say to me: "I don't care what my husband does outside of the house. He's good to my children and gives me everything I want."

I do not mean by this that all Mexican husbands support these customs. If it were so, I, as well as every other independent foreign woman married to Mexicans, would not have stayed out the first year. Indeed, I touch this subject gently because I am proud that my marriage is considered in Mexico a very successful one; but successful marriages are rare and worthy of attention precisely because these customs exist on all sides and the contrast is therefore ever greater.

A Mexican psychiatrist once expressed the opinion to me that Mexican men have a deeply rooted sexual inferiority complex, and that their incapacity for fidelity, which indicates an incapacity to maintain any consistently stable attitude, is closely related to the necessity they have for fortifying themselves with the number rather than the quality of their love affairs.

Because of all these complexes and lack of emotional adjustment, love here is a tortured, highly neurotic ailment, a perpetual conflict between the sexes that makes everything D. H. Lawrence has ever written on the subject seem very mild fare indeed. . . . [11] I never knew what jealousy could be like until I came to live in a Latin country. . . . In Mexico, jealousy takes on the finer shades of madness because the mixture of Indian and Spanish blood has produced an emotional chaos within the Mexican temperament. . . . I have Mexican women friends whose husbands are so jealous they will not let them walk on the streets alone lest some other man look at them, and so they go out accompanied always by their mothers, their sisters or friends—this in 1939, with war just around the corner. Man is the Mexican woman's worst enemy. The very politicians, I soon found out, who drip with tears when they write about motherhood have fought tenaciously, with every weapon in their power, the efforts of organized women to secure the vote and thereby obtain really effective laws to protect maternity, which the country does not possess at present; the very revolutionaries who praise with tremulous emotion the glorious lives of Rosa Luxemburg, Krupskaia and other heroines of the revolutionary movement[12] refuse to let their own wives attend the meetings they address.

"My husband is afraid I'll become infected with his ideas," one woman said to me dryly when I asked her why she had never heard her husband speak in public.

"Mexican husbands are feudal Marxists," another explained, "Marxists outside and feudalists within their homes.". . .

But, people then ask me, if Mexican marriages are so one-sided and unfair, why isn't divorce more prevalent? It is not easy, however, to break with centuries of tradition. The Mexican Revolution, it is true, brought legal divorce as a boon to women, but very few have had the courage to take advantage of it. The Catholic tradition is still strong within the family, and the woman who divorces her husband knows that she must do so in the face of opposition from all her relatives. The man may be an out-and-out scoundrel, diseased and morally corrupt, but her mother would rather see her dead than divorced, as one mother said in my presence. Then, the Mexican laws are delightfully flexible as far as foreigners are concerned, but the Mexican woman is up against a barrier more solid than steel. Divorce for Mexicans must be the result of mutual consent. If the husband decides to fight the divorce the woman is generally lost, unless her political connections are better than his. . . .

In spite of family opposition and social taboos, women are breaking away from their traditional lives, and when they do they become the most passionate defenders of the feminist movement. I like to tell the story of my friend Carolina as an illustration of what Mexican women can accomplish with courage and faith in themselves. Carolina is the dark-eyed, sensitive daughter of one of Mexico's most outstanding leaders, a man whose name remains in history as one of the most integral talents that the Revolution brought to the fore. Like most Mexican revolutionaries, however, he brought up his daughters in the convent and married them off as soon as they were able to think for themselves. Carolina, at twenty-two, found herself the bride of a man she scarcely knew, because like all *noviazgos*[13] her friendship with him had taken place beneath the watchful eyes of the entire family, and never had she been alone with him a minute. For the next twelve years Carolina scarcely left the house. She lived the traditional life of the Mexican woman, babies and babies and more babies—eight in all and of these three died. Her husband was intent upon his career; a lawyer of considerable prestige, he became a well-known figure in the revolutionary movement and had little time to spend at home. So Carolina, with time on her hands and a keen, actively intelligent mind . . . spent most of her difficult pregnancies with a book. In the course of twelve years she acquired a very solid education by the mere process of reading her husband's entire library devoted to sociology, science, history and literature. One crucial evening she decided to hear her husband lecture, and without warning him she took a seat in the auditorium. In one hour she learned two important facts: her husband whom she had looked up to as a paragon of wisdom was a terrific fake; having actually read the books that he was supposed to have read, she saw with horrible clarity all the flaws and errors of his reasoning; also she learned that the dark-haired little school teacher who hung so attentively on his words was his current mistress and the mother of a baby by him. The next day she moved out of the house and has never been back since.

Now, at thirty-six, Carolina is a social worker and very active in the organization of women. She supports her five children by her own efforts because her husband will neither consent to a divorce nor contribute to the upkeep of the children, a dog-in-the-manger attitude which is, unfortunately, very prevalent. But Carolina, in spite of everything, feels that she is independent at last. This year she began to speak at political meetings, and I shall never forget the radiance in her eyes when she told me that she realized, at last, how much life held for her.

It is due to the bravery of women like Carolina, and others who have suffered the same fate, that a strong feminist movement has sprung up in Mexico in recent years, despite fanatical opposition. The difficulties that these women are up against surpass anything that ever existed in the United States, even a century ago.

Notes

1. Verna C. Millán, *Mexico Reborn* (Boston: Houghton Mifflin, 1939), 148–52, 154, 157–58, 160–64.
2. Ibid., 3–6. The exact circumstances of Verna Millán's life are unknown, and we only know what she relates in her memoir. She later served as associate editor of a volume on mental health edited by her brother-in-law. *Proceedings of the Fourth International Congress of Mental Health, Mexico City, December 11th to 19th, 1951* (Mexico City: Prensa Médica Mexicana, 1951).
3. At this very time, Mexican intellectuals such as Samuel Ramos and Octavio Paz had begun to reflect on this inferiority complex.
4. Millán stereotypes foreign women here, rather than Mexicans.
5. Peasants.
6. Little village.
7. Together with the aforementioned Rivera and David Alfaro Siqueiros, one of Mexico's three foremost mural painters of the postrevolutionary era. These painters sought to create a shared political consciousness in Mexico by creating gigantic didactic paintings on the walls of government buildings that displayed their view of the country's history.
8. Traditional Mexican shawl used also as a carrying device.
9. A stereotype, as gender roles varied widely throughout indigenous Mexico.

10. An exaggerated statement.

11. Lawrence not only wrote the two famous novels *Sons and Lovers* and *Lady Chatterley's Lover*—both dealing with the subject of gender relations—but also *Mornings in Mexico,* a travelogue based on a trip to Mexico.

12. Women who headed Marxist movements in Germany and Russia, respectively.

13. Period of courtship and/or engagement.

PART IV

The "Mexican Miracle" and Its Collapse

Beginning in the 1940s, U.S. dollars and tourists poured into Mexico to an unprecedented degree. At the same time, the Mexican government invested heavily in import-substitution industrialization, an effort directed at lessening the country's dependence on imported manufactured goods. During the following decades, the years of the so-called Mexican miracle, this model contributed to high economic growth. Increasingly tied to the United States though nominally nonaligned during the Cold War, Mexico appeared on the brink of joining the exclusive club of the world's most economically developed nations. In turn, economic growth contributed to political stability and the emergence of a consensus among the Mexican elite and middle classes. Every six years, the ruling PRI (Institutional Revolutionary Party), the successor of the party established by former President Calles, racked up impressive numbers in presidential elections. While most of Latin America chafed under repressive military regimes and left-wing guerrilla movements, Mexico appeared to be moving forward into the future, leaving its problems behind.

Ultimately, however, the Mexican miracle proved as hollow as the notion that the PRI could control Mexico forever. On October 2, 1968, the government's massacre of hundreds of student protesters on the eve of the

Olympic Games in Mexico City revealed the authoritarian nature of the PRI state. Even though economic growth continued into the early 1980s, government corruption and mounting public debt soon took their toll. Mexico's much-touted agrarian reform from the Cárdenas days also ended in failure, as the PRI's neglect of the agricultural sector forced millions of peasants and their families into the growing shantytowns of the capital and other major cities, if they did not leave for the United States.

In 1982, the Mexican economy collapsed after the government announced it could no longer meet payments on its foreign debt. In the next two decades—years known today as the "lost decades" in recent Mexican history—gross national product slumped, the middle class lost half of its earning power, and crime skyrocketed to unprecedented levels. As a result, the tourism that had helped finance the miracle declined, except in specially designed "tourist paradises" such as Cancún and Cabo San Lucas. The Mexican government reacted by ending its experiment in import substitution and moving the country into the North American Free Trade Agreement (NAFTA), a trade compact with Canada and the United States that has thus far failed to jumpstart the Mexican economy. Ultimately, even the iron horse of Mexican politics, the PRI, ran out of steam. In 2000, it lost power to opposition candidate and current President Vicente Fox Quesada.

The foreigners who witnessed the rise and decline of the PRI state and the import-substitution model held widely divergent views on the processes they were observing. In the age of the airplane (discussed below), most of the foreign visitors were tourists rather than investors, journalists, scholars, or other individuals interested in a long-term engagement with the country. These tourists only gained a superficial understanding of Mexican society, and they commented favorably on the material progress the country seemed to be making. However, during the years of the so-called miracle, these tourists were not alone in singing the praises of modern Mexico, as scholars, journalists, and politicians alike predicted a great future as well. With few exceptions, this new generation of observers bought into the PRI myth of a golden future for Mexico. It was not until after the 1968 massacre and the economic crisis of 1982 that the optimism of foreign observers gradually turned to gloomy analyses of the reasons for what had turned out to be the ultimate failure of the Mexican miracle.

After World War II, yet another revolution in transportation—travel by airplane—changed the modes of travel of these observers. Gone were the days when European travelers spent weeks at sea before reaching a port in the United States, from where they slowly made their way south toward Veracruz. Even long-distance travel by automobile, bus, or train became a rarity in the era of air and hotel package tours. Today, travelers make the nonstop trip from London to Mexico City in just eleven hours, and their first impression is the thick, yellow layer of smog over the capital rather than the majestic landscape of the Gulf Coast. Here today, gone tomorrow—air travel amounts to an impressionistic stroke rather than a painted canvas; a snapshot rather than a movie; a single note rather than a symphony. Of course, not all visitors came by airplane, and many stayed for years, or made repeated visits to Mexico. In any case, air travel has widened the chasm between the occasional traveler and the immigrant, making the analytical distinction among the various types of foreign observer accounts even more important.

The six readings in this section view the road from the "Mexican miracle" to the crisis of the 1980s and 1990s. The first three selections comment on the "Mexican miracle." Franz Böker's "Ueber die Lage—1958—in Mexiko" ("On the situation in Mexico in 1958") gives a German entrepreneur's pessimistic assessment of industrialization and one-party rule. Irene Nicholson's *The X in Mexico* is a British journalist's enthusiastic endorsement of the industrial development project. Taken from Mexico's Archivo General de la Nación, the assorted letters of several "ordinary" U.S. citizens shared their view of Mexico with President Gustavo Díaz Ordaz. The second three selections analyze the recent crisis in Mexico. The selection from Judith Hellman's *Mexican Lives* is the result of the interview of a North American sociologist with a poor Mexico City housewife and mother. Isabella Tree's *Sliced Iguana* shows a British journalist on the trail of the Zapatista rebels in Chiapas. Finally, the selection from Sam Quinones' *True Tales from Another Mexico* is a U.S. writer's interpretation of violent crime against women in the border town of Ciudad Juárez.

20 The Downside of the Miracle

Franz Böker[1]

◩

Mailed to the German shareholders of a hardware import firm in Mexico City, the following unpublished report by German merchant Franz Böker (1877–1965) provides an insider's view of the Mexican miracle. Apart from its interpretation of the causes for Mexico's new-found political stability, the report is most interesting for its views about the future of the import-substitution industrialization (ISI) project. While his contemporaries lauded annual economic growth rates averaging eight percent, Böker, whose company depended on selling the very foreign-made goods that industrialization sought to displace, expressed deep skepticism about ISI. Whether driven by self-interest or sound economic analysis, his predictions (though laced with deprecating and prejudiced remarks) would prove essentially correct.

These reflections grew out of a residence of almost six decades in Mexico. Böker hailed from the industrial town of Remscheid in western Germany. He came from a family of merchants and industrialists, producers of cutlery and other steel objects that gained world renown under the "Arbolito" trademark. His father, Robert Böker, had spent eight years in Mexico City building up a retail and wholesale business that soon grew into one of the city's most important hardware stores. In 1899, Franz traveled to Mexico in order to assume a position in this business and eventually serve as director, upon which, he hoped, he would return to Germany. However, the Revolution and World War I intervened, keeping him rooted in Mexico, where the "Casa Boker" remains in operation under the direction of two of his grandsons. He was my great-grandfather and the husband of Luise Böker, whose letters are introduced earlier in this volume.[2]

A diehard Porfirista who, along with other foreigners, had enjoyed favored status in fin de siècle Mexico, Böker abhorred both the Revolution and, to a lesser extent, the PRI. As an octogenarian immigrant with a great personal stake in his host country, he had long left the traveler and sojourner stages behind. His writings reflect six decades of experience as a conservative, anti-Communist entrepreneur, conscious of his precarious position as a foreign businessman.

❖

For the last thirty-five years, we have had a state of peace in Mexico, without monarchy or apparent one-man rule. In the past two decades, we have also enjoyed a visible, even screaming prosperity. How did that happen? Certainly not because the people have embraced a clearer concept of and more honest participation in democracy, an attitude that would have rendered them satisfied with the authorities they have elected. Whoever knows Latin America can only scoff at such notions.

But the improvement is there, and its causes . . . lie in a multitude of processes, some of them internal and some of them external. I will first relate the latter. It is a platitude that the complications in the white world have helped the colored peoples (among whom one must number the Mexicans today) in political terms.[3] The fact that the world wars have greatly benefited the coloreds economically is equally true, but much less commonly known. One only has to recall the prices that products [from Latin American countries] fetched during the war, as well as the money of tax evaders from the United States . . . and the millions realized by the seizure of German and Italian property that have flowed into the Latin American economies. Above all, though, the Americans pump billions of dollars into the Latin American economies each year with the officially stated purpose of helping these countries escape their underdevelopment. The beneficiaries, however, interpret this process very differently, *i.e.*, as a new form of Dollar Diplomacy, an ongoing bribery with the . . . purpose of rendering the Latin American peoples deaf to the siren song of the Russians.[4] . . . These funds contribute significantly to the . . . pacification of Mexico. Among these external factors, . . . one has to mention the steep increase in tourism in Mexico. . . . Today, all the world talks about Mexico, because . . . scientific publications . . . and the accounts of traveling journalists, sold in the hundreds of thousands, have . . . advertised Mexico as a tourist destination. These authors . . . from outside Mexico have introduced this country to the realm of desires and thus done much good . . . by diverting money [to Mexico]. Through the resultant road construction, they have indirectly elevated internal security.

I will now comment on the internal developments that have increased peace in this country. Most immediately . . . a significant deterrent [to future violence] remains in the collective memory: the horrible conditions in Mexico during the past revolutionary period. . . . Even Mexicans who have grown accustomed to the "Mexican miracle" will always recall—or be reminded—that toward the end of this period of terror, all haciendas and railway stations in the interior had been burned; all but one restaurant in the capital had been closed; sales of import businesses had decreased to 1 percent of their 1910 level; endless series of paper money were imposed at gun point, only to disappear; the market women no longer came to sell their tomatoes, which they had eaten . . . or bartered for other necessities; to make firewood for tortillas, trees had been felled in the parks and rolled through the streets; corpses doused with petroleum smoldered in the streets and were carted off without a coffin; and human life was as worthless as paper money. As Europeans still suffering from the memories of two world wars, we cannot be surprised that such misery will eventually produce political calm.

A second internal process . . . is the sudden industrialization . . . the most significant process affecting the Latin American economies in general and the Mexican economy in particular. One might wonder in amazement why the transition from agriculture and mining to industry had a politically soothing effect, when the European experience appears to indicate the opposite.[5] Well of course, as a European who does not believe in miracles, I can only express my greatest concern about the future problems that the [emphasis on industrialization will] place on the non-industrial sector. Our topic, however, only concerns the immediate results of the process of industrialization. During a time of worldwide economic boom, this process had a soothing effect by providing a population that multiplies like rabbits . . . with [what the ancient Romans would have called] *panem et circenses*:[6] tortillas and the movies.

I cannot leave the topic of industrialization . . . alone without mentioning the down side of this process . . . Everywhere in Latin America, the idea of industrialization has been linked with the hopes of attaining a greater degree of independence from foreign countries and saving hard currency. But . . . in Mexico, neither goal will probably ever be realized. For now, the expensive machinery and technological innovations [necessary for industrialization] threaten Mexico's foreign currency holdings no less than the previous imports of manufactured goods. And it is not obvious how the government intends to limit an increase in dependence on foreign countries—not to mention a decrease.

Furthermore, since it was clear from the beginning that domestic products could only compete with imported ones by pulling a net of high tariffs over the country, [the government][7] has needed to raise these tariffs to . . . almost 100 percent of trade value. Politically, this unfair situation is not dangerous because the newspapers have sent the Mexican masses in such a nationalist frenzy that they cannot recognize it. In addition, even if they did recognize [the unfairness], they would be too indolent to do something about it. But the [high tariffs] are dangerous for the industry itself, because the virtual elimination of foreign competition has also eliminated the necessity of . . . fighting [for market share] and perfecting their products.

The exaggerated privileging of the working class has borne even worse results than this . . . coddling of domestic industrial producers. Of course, [the government] wanted and needed to keep wages low . . . in order to compensate for a much lower level of productivity. . . . Instead, it . . . froze all wages below 300 pesos per month[8] . . . and imported staples such as corn that the country should be able to produce itself. We should not forget that the land reform of President Cárdenas dealt a fatal blow to the provision of the urban working class with basic foodstuffs by . . . emphasizing subsistence production. Since it is impossible to change these agrarian laws that have led to a *reconquista de la tierra*[9] by the Indians, and because we cannot count on the possibility that the Indians will endeavor to modernize their production of corn, the economic leadership of Mexico has resolved to procure the . . .

foreign currency necessary for these agricultural imports by... prohibiting foreign imports.... Thus far, all these dangerous consequences of industrialization: greater rather than decreased dependence on foreign countries; lowered rather than increased reserves in foreign currency; the monopolization of industry and the privileging of workers; prohibitive import tariffs; ... and neglect of agriculture have remained in a latent state of tension without hampering the progress of industrialization—but only thus far.

By themselves, however, the economic impulses I have mentioned would not have sufficed to lead the country into a peaceful direction had they not been accompanied by a political transition.... In late 1946, with the departure of General [Manuel] Avila Camacho and the accession to power of Lic. [Miguel] Alemán, power passed from a revolutionary-military clique to a civilian one,[10]... organized in the "Partido Revolucionario Mexicano" that has led Mexico's destiny until today.[11]

"Partido Revolucionario Mexicano"—a strange denomination of a prospective ruling party. The term is intentionally misleading. Because when revolutionaries found a party to assert their rule and in order to... throw others out of power, they will certainly not call their new party "revolutionary." That will be what their opponents will call them, the ones who have just lost power. The revolutionaries will usually insert terms such as "order," "restoration," "legality," and others into the name of their party. They will not forget the word "freedom" in one of its many variations, but they will never portray themselves as revolutionaries. A truly revolutionary movement can therefore not hide behind this name.

Quite the contrary: the Partido Revolucionario Mexicano is a creation of firmly entrenched ex-revolutionaries. Its program: realization of the ideals... of the great revolution of 1910–1917. Its true goal, however, is to keep its members in power, and to accept or reject new aspirants to membership. It is thus not a party at all, but a club with restricted membership to whom all higher officials of federal and state governments belong as well as [most] members of the Senate and Congress.[12] The Mexican Revolutionary Party is therefore neither a party nor revolutionary, and the only title that it bears with justification is "Mexican." And a few years ago, even that word has been deleted in favor of the adjective "Institucional," which has greatly accentuated the deafening effect of the absurd name.

"Here we are, the old worthy revolutionaries, at the center of the government, and therefore we have claimed (institutionally!) the ultimate goal of our glorious Revolution of 1910–17. At the same time, we have precluded any further necessity or opportunities for revolutionary movements, whether out on the streets or in the countryside. But why would you toil on the streets? Come inside and join us! Here, you will find everything that you (maybe) can attain outside with much effort and danger!"

One cannot dispute the . . . genial nature of this appeal ensconced within the name of the party. But we also cannot deny that this appeal has worked, and that the club of *caciques*[13]—a club that operates behind a virtually impenetrable curtain—has managed for many years to govern the country in dictatorial fashion by keeping a semblance of democratic forms. It has done so by either co-opting or eliminating outsiders who challenged the system; by nominating a slate of candidates for Senate, Congress, state governors, and President; by manipulating the polling process; by giving newspapers paper as long as they complied and left the truth alone; and—above all, and here we have the flip side of an otherwise tolerable situation—by making sure that each one of their hungry members had a bone to chew on.

El Hueso! The bone![14] Politicians depend on the bone and want to get to it. That does not cause any difficulties in the case of all the bone seekers who get a post in the administration or the judiciary. A Minister, a judge, a state governor has always found the table set for him upon his nomination. But what do we do with the equally needy . . . Senators and members of Congress, who could . . . never afford a glamorous house, one or several women decked in pearls, the indispensable Cadillac, and solid bank accounts in foreign countries? If left to their own destitution, these politicians would topple the whole edifice. Well, if there are no bones available, they have to be created. And they are created, of course, by instituting some kind of control . . . or state enterprise at the expense of the free economy, and, therefore, the public. . . . It is possible to elicit streams of money out of the state management of corn, milk and eggs; out of state control over transportation and the insurance sector; out of the granting . . . of import licenses; out of the . . . steady conflict between capital and labor; out of traffic accidents and other incidents involving the police; out of the nationalized oil industry and the equally nationalized, *i.e.*, failing, railroad system. These streams of money amount to hundreds of millions . . . at the expense of the public, or, to put it precisely, at the expense of the neediest part of the population. And . . . this system, once established, cannot be either abolished or even contained, but instead continues to affect new areas each and every day. . . .

What will the future hold? In any event, I do not count on the possibility that economic development will proceed as rapidly and yet as quietly as before, even if the global crisis does not reach Mexico. I have no worries regarding the political aspect as long as the *caciques* are happy, *i.e.*, as long as their bones do not get smaller as a result of an economic crisis. The masses will not rebel; because of their Mexican indolence, they can be compressed to zero. Politically dangerous situations can therefore only occur via the detour of economic difficulties. These economic difficulties, however, are very likely, because Mexico has bet on the wrong horse in economic terms— a course of action that will lead to complete bankruptcy... There are only two ways out: a fast but dangerous one—the one led by oil; and a very slow, but healthy one—the one via agriculture.[15]

Notes

1. Franz Böker, "Ueber die Lage—1958—in Mexiko," Archivo Boker, S.A. de C.V., Mexico City, Fondo Memorias, folder "Familiengeschichte." Translated by Jürgen Buchenau.

2. For a study of the Bökers, see Buchenau, *Tools of Progress.*

3. Böker refers to the fact that the end of World War II ushered in the era of decolonization in Africa and Asia.

4. The author refers to Soviet propaganda in Latin America during the 1950s. This statement is a stark exaggeration—in fact, until the Cuban Revolution, the U.S. government provided only minimal funds toward Latin American economic development.

5. The author refers to the causal connection between industrialization and revolutionary upheaval in nineteenth-century Europe, and especially in his native Germany.

6. Bread and games.

7. Böker was concerned enough about censorship of the mail that he rarely mentioned the government directly. Instead, he often wrote in the passive voice. For reasons of style, this translation gives the implied rather than the literal meaning.

8. US $24.

9. Reconquest of land.

10. This transition at the presidential level is still regarded an important turning point in postrevolutionary history.

11. In fact, Alemán had renamed the party twelve years before this report. Since 1946, the party has been known as Partido Revolucionario Institucional, or PRI.

12. Böker means the Chamber of Deputies, which, together with the Senate, forms the Mexican Congress.

13. Nahua word for local bosses used to describe minor political leaders with an independent power base.

14. The reward for corruption.

15. This reference to the potential of agriculture shows von Humboldt's influence on Böker.

21 The Best of Tradition and Modernity

Irene Nicholson[1]

The following selection from Irene Nicholson's The X in Mexico *distills the impressions of a British bookseller and journalist gathered during eighteen years in Mexico. In contrast to Böker's brief report, it is an optimistic appraisal of the 1950s and 1960s. Accustomed to explaining Mexico to British listeners and readers, Nicholson praises the PRI government for helping Mexicans acquire a shared sense of national pride based on the nation's diverse cultural riches. Written in the early 1960s, this excerpt reflects the heyday of the PRI, a time when the party ruled virtually unchallenged over a politically stable country. This period coincided with the single longest period of uninterrupted economic growth in twentieth-century Mexico. Infected by the giddiness of the government officials with whom she worked, Nicholson believes in a bright future. She asserts that Mexicans have begun to resolve successfully their country's many contradictions: modernity and tradition, nation and region, rich and poor. In contrast to Millán, she even prognosticates significant improvements in the position of women. Despite her understanding of the legacy of the past in the*

Mexico of her time, Nicholson reinforces the propaganda of the ruling party and broadcasts its official image of Mexico to the rest of the world.

Nicholson was born in 1911 in Valdivia, Chile, as the daughter of an English banker and merchant. She received her formal education in London and New York City and began work as a writer for several specialized journals in the medical field. She founded the Librería Británica (British Bookstore) in Mexico City, where Nicholson served as manager from 1949 to 1954. The store was highly successful, doubling its sales every year under her direction. In 1955, she moved to London as editor of the popular science magazine Discovery. *Two years later, Nicholson returned to Mexico as correspondent of the* Times. *She also served as radio reporter for the BBC, as well as several other media. She dedicated herself to the study of Mexican symbolism and Náhuatl poetry, and published three books on these subjects.* The X in Mexico *appeared in 1965, when illness forced her to return to London, where she died three years later.[2]*

Myth and Mexico: they blend imperceptibly. For Mexico is a land in which men have survived against heavy odds, like a cactus in the desert or a golden dome built far from civilization. It is a country that seems to have been created to show man where he stands in the cosmic scheme. A godmother has bestowed talents generously, but there are ogres, too, macabre transformations of flowers into skulls, queer shapes like those thorny organ cacti that can be explained only as one of nature's jokes or as a symbol of life's resilience in the midst of drought.

The abrupt contours of mountain and canyon, the dry maize, the misty yet spiky cacti, the great wheel hats above oriental faces: the very harshness of the material shapes leads the mind on to metaphysical speculation. Every opposite is true in a land that is arrogant and poor; delicate and tough; cynical and tender; hot and cold; high and low; garrulous and silent; passionate and indifferent; courteous and crude; hospitable and introspective; kind and stern. If we look at the outer skin alone we can make nothing of it. Mexico is more hidden, more oriental, than any other country in the western hemisphere, and yet it is a leader in the Spanish-speaking West. It was the first country in Latin America to achieve a modern social revolution and a take-off into industrialization. But it is not a forward-looking country. It is forever turning back to its past, to its myths.[3]

Irene Nicholson

At each crossroads in history it has reaffirmed a principle enunciated long before. Even the Aztecs, arriving late on the high plateau, adopted the gods and the speech of their predecessors. The Spanish friars studied the ancient religions (even while they were destroying them in fear) in order to base their new Christian faith firmly in the minds of a tradition-loving people. The seventeenth-century nun, Sor Juana Inés de la Cruz, linked Christianity with the symbolism of blood sacrifice.

The 1910 revolution returned a second time to the same principles. Revolution has never meant for this country a blind jump into the future but literally re-volution—return to the best of its past in an attempt to correct the errors of each historical cycle. We see the name Mexico on a printed page and the X jumps to the eye because it is an anachronism. It ought not to be there. Modern Spanish would turn it into a J. But paradoxically it is this old-fashioned spelling that has come to stand for modern Mexican liberalism. The outmoded X has become a symbol of revolt—revolt against Spain, against corruption in the Mexican hierarchies, back to Indianness and national identity. . . . Modern Mexico [is] compounded of the Spanish, the French, the Irish, the American, and a good bit else besides the indigenous Indian. But in order to understand this amalgam [one needs] to look back to the remote past that has stamped on Mexico that typographically assertive X; and also to the long struggle between the forces of die-hard reaction and the liberal idealism that has in a defiant gesture kept the X intact.

Latin America stands at a crossroads. Either it must overcome the niggling, petty jealousies of centuries, or go under. . . . Because of political unrest, military coups, and economic depressions in many countries, Mexico has almost involuntarily jumped into the lead. Ever since independence . . . Mexican idealists have upheld policies of self-determination and non-intervention. They have resented any attempt by foreigners to order them about. They have included in their condemnation the Church in Rome and the international financiers. Their stubborn (some people would say intransigent) Mexicanism is one of the first things the foreigner notices when he comes new to the country. These idealists have been both heroic and quixotic. Their ends have been achieved sometimes at such cost that the clock has been put back half a century. All the same, without them Mexico would long ago have become a hopeless dictatorship and a toady to the richer countries of the world.

Ever since the conquest the idealists have been opposed by a totally different type of Mexican—thugs who have seemed to believe that laws were made for their own convenience, to be wriggled out of whenever too great a respect for justice might obstruct the amassing of fortunes. Yet there is no sharp line—such as the left would like to draw—between exploiter and exploited. Out of the ranks of the die-hard right have come men with a sense of responsibility toward their professions, and these have built the solid basis of Mexico. They have taken a generous slice of material reward, but have felt justified in doing so.[4]

The people, with their gentleness and artistic talents; . . . with their apparent disregard for life; and with their ability in whatever circumstances to extract fun from trivial things: these have for the most part shrugged their shoulders and continued to till the soil with the inadequate means at their disposal. Now and then they have weighed in on one side or the other according to their special notions of what life is about. Their day-to-day common sense has restrained the idealists, but when their patience with the exploiters has become exhausted, there has been bloody revolution. Their sense of humour—macabre at times but unembittered by rancour—has allowed them to bear a good many things that might have become intolerable, including their meagre staple diet of beans and maize pancakes. They are long-suffering, but not for ever.

Their *tierra*, the little, circumscribed world of their village or ranchland, has been in the past the extent of their horizon. Today the government is trying to extend their vision. . . .

On the forty-first floor of a skyscraper you may dine off lobster and white wine. From here you look over the lights in the valley, the lights climbing the far hills, marking the presence of nearly five million city dwellers. From a building across the way a sky-sign, brazen and cocksure, announces, "There's a Ford in your Future."

It is an effort to remember the saddle-sore donkeys; the peasant families living on maize, beans, and chocolate gruel; the remote Indians such as the Huicholes[5] with their traditional *peyote*[6] ceremonies and their coolie-like dress; Indians to whom a city Mexican is as odd a bird as any foreigner.

The names of Mexican wines and rum, Mexican petrol, Mexican office furniture flash off and on in neon signs. If it is Christmas, wire-and-bulb Magi will be prancing in the wind among the treetops. Little Mexicans in silver-buttoned trousers will sweep their *sombreros* in jerky, neon salutations.

The twang of American tourist voices sounds in the restaurant, the feline tread of waiters in the discreet half dark of this expensive observatory high in the sky. Outside a motto keeps vying with the stars: "There's a Ford in your Future."

You are at the hub of a vast republic whose essence is contrast, in the Latin-American Tower at the centre of [Mexico City]. . . . Mexico. So much of its palpable materiality ready at any moment to vanish in cloud or sunlight. . . .

Mexicans are agile and quick, not beautiful and graceful. Those who can see no charm in the ancient clay figurines will find them, probably, frankly ugly. The men have a predilection for absurd hats and loud ties, the women for frizzing their hair till it conceals the sharp outlines of Indian bones. But it is quite untrue, of course, to suggest (as a lecturer on a foreign television station did) that they normally dress in *fiesta* frills and flounces, that they never go out, have no intellectual life, but just mind the babies and cook.[7]

This kind of generalization affronts Mexican women who crowd the universities, who write and paint, practise medicine, and study nuclear engineering. Even those who, intractably feminine, are absorbed in the eternal problems of servants, shopping, and dress, must choose their wardrobe so that it stands up to the wear and tear of modern city life.

Sidesaddle, in a snowy tumult of flounced petticoat, the young girls can ride as swift and as strictly aligned as cavalry officers when they perform in the colourful Mexican rodeo called *charrería*. Changing petticoats for frilly panties, they win applause on the world's tennis courts. Mexican women range from bureaucrats high in the administration to servile Indians who are beasts of burden at the men's command. Peasants deftly turn ceramics with one hand while the other is steadying the inverted plate used as a potter's wheel. They arrange flowers, not perhaps with the sophistication of the Japanese, but with as much colour sense and feeling for growth. The matriarchal Tehuanas,[8] whose erect carriage is accentuated by flowing skirts and a traditional red and orange bodice, have a reputation for dominating the men. No wonder that if you ask Mexican women about their position in the world you will get contradictory replies. In the Ministry of Labour, Señora María Cristina Salmorán de Tamayo has been president of the Committee for Conciliation and Arbitration: a long-winded title but it gives her weight to deal with serious labour disputes such as crop up in the unions. There is not much doubt that she has earned the respect of the toughest workers.

As in England, some Mexican families have a tradition of intellectual activity and public service. One of Mexico's leading sociologists is Professor Catalina Sierra, a descendant of Justo Sierra. In a busy office of the department of the Federal District, a tiny woman, Angela Alessio Robles—daughter of a Mexican statesman—looks after all public works in Mexico City, which is a mighty task indeed. Another administrator, Señora Amalia de Castillo Ledón, was appointed under-secretary for a newly created sub-secretariat to the Ministry of Education dealing with cultural affairs. When questioned about prejudice against women in public offices she retaliated: "Isn't it a matter of ability?"

There are those who disagree: the aggressive feminists who chill by being so unfeminine in their methods of demanding feminine rights. Thanks, perhaps, to Britain's suffragette movement, aggression is hardly necessary in modern Mexico, and in 1958 women voted for the first time in presidential elections. Though cartoonists parodied them—"Do we wear our new sack line at the polls?"—their presence helped to create the calmest elections ever recorded. Nevertheless, there are still societies, universities, and magazines exclusively for women. Most have a jaded, outmoded look.

A balanced view on the position of women today was given by Señora Carolina de Fournier, who runs a medical publishing house and who described how ideas have changed in her own working life. Girls from the best families will serve today behind the counters of department stores. But Señora de Fournier added, "I think Mexican husbands still need educating!"

Cultured and landed families are no longer always rich, and their womenfolk are glad to have a profession and an income. Only on a lower social level, where fear of losing a precarious social hold is a stronger urge than money, do anomalies still exist. A self-styled "good-family girl" says she cannot work because it would degrade the standards by which she has been brought up. Among the rising middle classes—readers of glossy magazines, watchers of the telly[9]—there are husbands who carry on even their social lives so apart from their wives that it seems to be a "top secret" whether they are married or not. Such men marry intellectually beneath them and soon demote their wives to the position of cook-nannie, while they carry on their home and office lives in separate compartments. The fault is not altogether the men's. The wife of a well-known writer is capable of hiding behind the refrigerator to escape her husband's bookish guests. In a provincial town there is a local girl who serves her husband's meals as if she were the hired servant. If a guest offers her a chair, she takes fright, retreats to the kitchen, and does not emerge until the moment of farewell.

Women in the skilled and semi-skilled labouring classes have in some ways more social freedom than those clinging to the outer edges of the professions. In the proletarian suburbs it seems to matter less what the neighbors are gossiping, and an easy companionship between boy and girl comes naturally—as it does now, too, among university students. Indeed, many trends toward a completer life for women will show results in another ten years as higher education for them becomes more general. In a country where the customs of Spain, with its Arab-influenced cloistering of women, mingled after the conquest with those of the ancient Indians who had also a severe code of feminine behaviour, old conventions cannot be broken down overnight. . . .

Nevertheless, the eternal mystery of love and of the seduction of a woman's charms is present in myth and in the figures of strange and terrifying goddesses. Ixtaccíhuatl, so legend goes, was a lovely princess wooed by Popocatépetl. When he failed to win her, he turned her to stone and then himself, too, so that he might contemplate her forever. Ixtaccíhuatl presides over the valley of Mexico, her formidable mass of lava rock etherealized under snow and wispy clouds.

Coatlicue, the goddess, is another story: colossal, powerful, and uncompromising. With her petticoat of serpents, her bifurcated reptile head, and the skulls adorning her, she is a paradox representing all the contradictions of an immense cosmic process and perhaps of modern women too.

Ixtaccíhuatl and Coatlicue, Malinche, the brown Virgin of Guadalupe, and the poet-nun Sor Juana: these are the prototypes of Mexican woman. If it seems fanciful to think they bear any resemblance to their modern sisters, one need only look at the sturdy little girls on their way to school in their starched and frilly pinafores, at the sculptural firmness of their heads, the hair pulled starkly back into pigtails; at the contradictory mischievousness which recalls all the elusive variety of mountain and goddess, lover-interpreter, gentle Virgin, and intellectual nun.

Mexican women would scarcely trouble to think of these prototypes as they pursue their daily tasks. Nevertheless, in a history-ridden country, it is not altogether fanciful to think that they still preside. Even while some women are overcoming obstacles to recognition in the professions, millions still suffer fate blindly. Like the Indian women of Yalalag, in the Oaxaca hills, they wend their tragic way each night of All Souls to commune with their dead. One poor burdened villager graphically described their fate: "We are always being used up so we wear out soon like mops." Then her wrinkles broke into laughter to prove her humble life had not embittered her. She could scarcely imagine another. . . .

From being traditionally a country dependent on agricultural and mineral raw materials, Mexico is advancing toward full industrialization at a speed that makes foreign observers dizzy. Youthfulness, readiness to experiment, vitality, unorthodoxy, and above all, impatience to get through the transition stage: these are the characteristics that make Mexico a fascinating study and also—or so newspapers in France said on the eve of a state visit there by President López Mateos[10]—"the most promising risk in the world today." Timid collaborators are out, together with all those who fear government participation in industry, nationalization, and Mexicanization. . . .

Can we rightly regard 1960 as approximately the beginning of the industrial revolution? And, if so, where is that revolution to lead? Thoughtful Mexicans may be forgiven for asking whether the nationalism that accompanies the drive toward material progress is only self-deception. Every year Mexico becomes clogged with more and more international technological bric-à-brac, transistor sets and all. Some think it is not unlikely that the Communist murals and the radio jingles, only apparently at opposite poles, will some day find a common meeting ground; and that the essential oneness of their materialist points of view will be evident. If such a culmination to Mexican endeavour is accepted and welcomed, it will be the end of the way of life that inspired the ancient Nahua[11] poets, the builders of baroque, the modern architects with their churches and their efforts to create housing estates in which flowers and theatres and old symbols are as prominent as the supermarkets. It will be the end of the principles of Morelos and the reforms of Juárez. On the whole, though, the prognosis . . . is bright. . . .

Not with bloodshed as in some Latin-American countries still, but calmly in July 1964 the country elected a new President: the former Minister of the Interior Gustavo Díaz Ordaz. . . . Señor Díaz Ordaz was disliked at first by the extreme left and was an easy butt for cartoonists because of his protruding upper teeth and his horn-rimmed spectacles. (He is not photogenic but face to face has a charm of manner that does not appear in his poster image. He took jibes against his person in good part, however, and told foreign correspondents he had invented many himself.) . . .

Today the X in Mexico, with its archaic appearance, represents more importantly than ever the re-volution which seems to have taken place at all critical moments in the country's history. Mexicans have tried to assimilate the material benefits of modern industry while re-inquiring into the old beliefs. There are skeptics today who like to suggest that Mexico is advancing and prospering merely because she happens to be next-door neighbour of the United States. This is a great deal less than fair and discounts many qualities of dignity and seriousness from which other countries—not excluding the U.S.A.—could profit. Mexico's problems are the problems of a region that has had its ideals and its heroes, but has been frustrated at every turn by selfishness and villainy from certain sections of the community. In a sense they are the problems of a country that has set its sights too high.

The future must depend upon whether the whole Latin-American area can devise means to curb its predatory citizens so that the idealists can at last establish the basis for welfare states that take into account the whole man. In this task, Mexico must be among the leaders . . .

Notes

1. Irene Nicholson, *The X in Mexico: Growth Within Tradition* (London: Faber and Faber, 1965), 15–19, 115–18, 148–49, 290, 296. Reprinted by permission of Faber and Faber.
2. Diadiuk, *Viajeras anglosajonas*, 119–21.
3. This is an excellent example of an Orientalist dichotomy. Like Gooch before her, Nicholson divides the world into a progressive, or "Western," and a traditional, or "Oriental" sphere. This view conflates the enormous cultural differences among and within non-European societies. Nicholson also repeats the trope about Mexico as a country of irreconcilable opposites.
4. Nicholson would have come to a different verdict twenty years later, when the corruption of the PRI state reached record dimensions in the 1970s and early 1980s.
5. Indigenous people in the western state of Nayarit. See also, Lumholtz.
6. The *peyote* is a hallucinogenic cactus at the center of a major indigenous cult.
7. A half-hearted retrenchment from a series of stereotypes.
8. Indigenous people from the southeastern state of Oaxaca.
9. Television.
10. Governed 1958–1964.
11. The pre-conquest inhabitants of the Valley of Mexico and surrounding areas.

22 Tourism, Bullfights, and Bullets

Letters to President Gustavo Díaz Ordaz[1]

The papers of Mexican President Gustavo Díaz Ordaz in the Archivo General de la Nación include several boxes of letters written to the president by private citizens from the United States and a variety of other countries. These letters cover the period of his time in office (1964–1970). About eighty per cent were written by men, and over ninety per cent by inhabitants of the United States. These unpublished writings offer a fascinating view of what "ordinary people" thought about Mexico. Many of the letter writers were tourists who had just returned from Mexico, but some of them were relatives of U.S. residents in Mexico, or television viewers and/or newspaper readers who followed world affairs from the safety of their armchairs. A selection is included here to show the diversity of foreign views during a time in which mass media and tourism reshaped foreign images of Mexico. Taking advantage of the new media, the PRI government advertised the country to tourists as a land of eternal spring, of boundless natural beauty, and cultural wealth. In turn, the resultant influx of tourists allowed the PRI to improve infrastructure and strengthen

its hold over Mexico. Despite these changes, old stereotypes and attitudes re-mained, and they emerge clearly in these letters.

Just as Böker's unpublished report, the letters that follow are unembell-ished responses to what their authors saw, heard, and read about Mexico. Some offer heartfelt congratulations, others contain pleas for change; some are permeated by racist assumptions, yet others seek empathy. In general, however, most admire Mexico's material progress and cultural traditions from a roman-ticized, idealized point of view. Many of the letter writers from the United States visit Mexico in a quest for authenticity, which they consider diminished in their own country, yet assert the need for U.S. political, economic, and cul-tural guardianship over Mexico.[2]

Written by travelers and—at least in one case—people who knew Mexico only by watching television, the following letters address the tourist experience, opposition to the bullfights, and the government massacre of student protest-ers in Tlatelolco, Mexico City. The latter event proved a turning point by unmasking the hollowness of the PRI's claims to political inclusiveness and openness to dialogue. The death of more than four hundred students on a sin-gle day, at a time when student groups in France, Germany, and the United States staged massive demonstrations in opposition to the Vietnam War, out-raged many around the world. Yet, as the reader will find out, many conserva-tive U.S. citizens wished their own government had acted just as ruthlessly as that of Díaz Ordaz, sweeping the senseless slaughter under the rug in order to justify brutal action against supposed Communists.

Danville, CA, July 26, 1967
Dear Sir,
I am a teenager of the U.S.A. I was in Mexico City during Easter vacation. What a wonderful, beautiful place!! We (my father and I) came in by plane at night and before us sprawled M.C. It was just breathtaking, glowing with lights, bright and waiting for us.

The hospitality of your country [is] wonderful. The people are so warm, friendly and sincere. I loved everyone I met. A family opened their arms wide for us, we ate dinner with them, talked and laughed together. I could feel the bond between North and South America become closer in our own hearts. I cried when I had to say goodbye.

The people are *so real*, while with my countrymen, they try to hide themselves and feelings deep within them. The hatred and cruelty between the Negroes and the whites is something I am ashamed of and I apologize. . . .

Please never let vanity, hatred or unhappiness enter the beautiful haven of Mexico. I just wish my country could be just as proud as yours deserves to be. I promised myself I would return, and I shall, once more.

May God bless you and your people.

Sincerely,

Debbie Miller

Independence, MO, [no date]

Dear Mr. President:

Recently we had a very wonderful trip to your exotic country. The people, the flowers, the climate were all wonderful. However, we would like to urge you to consider the proper legislation to rectify the unsanitary water. You cannot imagine how good it felt to re-cross the border and get pure water—everywhere, in the U.S.A.

We know many people who will never go back to Mexico because of your famed "turista"[3] sickness. Mexico is so up and coming in so many ways, it is a shame that the inhabitants and the visitors must be subjected to these poor health conditions.

You have no idea what it would mean to your tourist business if you would be able to advertise "Mexican water is pure." It would really put Mexico up to par.

I realize that such programs take time and money but the pay off would begin to return immediately.

Very truly,

Mrs. C. M. Zerr

Elkins Park, PA, September 26, 1967

Dear Dr. Ordaz:

Regretfully, last Saturday I had an opportunity to see on television, a show called "Corridas de Toros"[4] directly from Mexico. I am deeply sorry and disgusted by the fact that until today, in a country like Mexico, such a barbarous and dreadful sport takes place. I saw how those illiterate men killed the poor animals, little by little, stabbing them many times to see their blood flow down to the ground. What a poor taste for sport! What kind of human being are those that perform such a horrible deed and what a sadistic spirit of those that go there to enjoy the killing of the animals! I am sure that the Mexicans would have much more fun if instead of subjecting those somewhat defenseless animals to such a tremendous cruelty, by having to fight with five or six men at the same time, why not put two men in the "arena" armed with two two-edged sharp knives and have them perform a fair sport by killing each other? This I believe would be correct because I know the Mexicans seem to have a special taste for cruel sports. Maybe, by seeing their own blood running down to the ground they would realize how horrible the sport is. It is not fair to have an animal fight with another kind of more savage animal (man) who has a much more well-developed brain. Besides, the bull does not fight with one man alone, it fights with half a dozen at the same time, and this is totally distasteful and incriminating.

To my point of view and to the point of view of those many million Brazilians as I am one, this is the most stupid and brutal kind of sport that could ever happen on earth. I beg you to do something to stop this murdering of defenseless animals. Mexico considers itself the "Latin America" of the world, why should Mexico be so dreadful?[5] We are living in a civilized world nowadays and this kind of murder should be definitely abolished. . . .

Hope you understand why I wrote to you directly about this matter, because undoubtedly only you can stop it for ever.

Respectfully,

Leny Santana

Mexico City [no date]

Your Honor, Mr. President:

We the undersigned are taking the privilege of writing this letter to you concerning the bullfights. We are vacationing here in your country for 18 days, and we are delighted with what we saw, and found the people very nice, polite and courteous.

But the bullfights, we were disgusted and we think are the most inhuman, gruesome and cruelest act on this earth. It is very cruel to take any animal into the arena, and have at least six human beings with spears, spearing and doing such barbarous treatments to the poor innocent bull, who never did any harm to those people in the arena, or anyone else.

We understand that cockfights are illegal all over the world, no cockfights are not near as inhuman and cruel as bullfights; also prize fights are not so popular, but prize fights people are not forced into fighting like the poor innocent bulls are. They go into it of their own free will. We understand the only large countries in the world who have bullfights are Mexico, Spain, and Portugal. So we hope Mr. President you will take our letter into consideration and help to erase this inhuman sport from your country. So Your Honor we will be waiting and hoping that you will answer our letter, and give us your opinion on this subject. We understand that it is part of the Spanish custom, and we hope you would abolish this custom in your country

Sincerely

Josephine Zaratsky, Victoria Wallace, and Frances Ingram

New Orleans, LA, September 23, 1968

Dear Sir:

With reference to the continual riots at the University of Mexico, which could possibly—and probably would—hurt Mexico's image at the Olympic Games next month . . . we respectfully suggest that you should appeal directly to the patriotic, pro-Mexican students at the University of Mexico, and tell them that you will personally support them, if they will rough up the 3% red students in their University.

There is nothing a Red fears more than a good licking from someone his own size.

Just a few days ago, some conservative students in France bodily ejected a bunch of Reds who were occupying their dormitory building, pretending to be students. It so developed that a majority of these agitators were not students at all.

We further suggest that you jail the leading agitators and keep them in jail until the Olympic Games have been concluded.

I just recently spent a vacation in Mexico City, Cuernavaca, Taxco, and Acapulco, and I "fell in love" with Mexico and its people. I am now telling everybody I know to take their next vacation in Mexico! During our visit to Mexico, we had the best of treatment; the best meat we had ever eaten; the bread was fresh and crispy at all times; and we were AMAZED at the wide streets, the cleanliness, and the hospitality.

MEXICO, SI—CASTRO, NO !!!

Very sincerely,

Paul Revere Assoc. Yeomen, Inc. (P.R.A.Y.)

H. S. Riecke, Jr.

P.S. Why not use Mace chemical on these anti-Mexico agitators, as well as police dogs. Give them the same treatment that Mayor Daley of Chicago did, multiplied many times.[6]

New York, October 15, 1968

Sir:

You have recently made a move against the rebellious, lawbreaking anarchists and extremists that would destroy Mexico. Those are the same people that have taken the processes of peaceful living and proper law out of the hands of the police and the judiciary into the streets. I say that you have done a great service to the people of Mexico just as my fellow countryman Mayor Daley of Chicago has, and George Wallace will.[7]

My heart springs forth in joy. May it run with the blooded men that have gathered for the games in your Federal City! Long live Mexico!

Very respectfully,

George R. Bullard

Beckville, TX [no date]

Dear Hon. Sir:

I read in our paper this week that your country had prohibited the hippies of this country from coming into your country, and I am prompted to write you a letter of congratulation.

I wish our government had the backbone to take a stand against such un-Godly, trashy mess as you have. But it seems that here such takes the spotlight, the radicals etc. They riot, loot, burn and defy the law and get up and speak advocating and threatening the overthrow of our form of government and go scot free.

I want to say again that I admire you for what you did. I believe we could put a stop to riots here as you did, when they tried to prevent the Olympics from being held in Mexico. . . .

Sincerely,

James C. Belew

Brooklyn, N.Y., May 11, 1970

Mr. President:

It has always been that at the inception, the revolution represented the hopes and aspirations of the people. It is also true that with the consolidation of power, the revolutionary movement changed its clothes. Those who made the revolution, or their descendants, are the conservatives who attempt to avoid signs of discontent. They may lose sight of the fact that they live—as a government—only for the people. When a government fears the people and must imprison those who ask for changes, it is no longer progressive, it is reactionary.

There are many in the United States who have spoken out against the inhumane actions of its elected representatives. Now, I appeal to the righteousness of the Mexican government. There are hundreds of students residing in your jails. These people dared to speak out against the established authority because they felt the need for change. If this was wrong then the revolution in Mexico was wrong since it too was a case of men speaking out, demanding that ills be cured.

Perhaps one day we shall recognize that we need not fear students. They are filled with a beautiful quest that for older men has begun to recede into the shadows and is replaced by what we like to think of as necessity and realism.

Mr. President, I ask you, not as a citizen of the United States but as a human being, to free these political prisoners. The people of the world await your brave act. Free the students.

Respectfully yours,

Bernard M. Smith

Notes

1. From Archivo General de la Nación, Mexico City, Archivo Gustavo Díaz Ordaz, uncataloged boxes 422–25.

2. Eric Zolov, "Discovering a Land 'Mysterious and Obvious:' The Renarrativizing of Postrevolutionary Mexico," in *Fragments of a Golden Age: The Politics of Culture in Mexico Since 1940*, eds. Gilbert M. Joseph, Anne Rubenstein, and Eric Zolov (Durham, NC: Duke University Press, 2001), 249–52.

3. Term for a variety of water- and food-borne intestinal infections that affect many visitors during their first week in Mexico.

4. Bullfight.

5. The writer refers to the fact that Brazilians, unlike Mexicans, seldom refer to themselves as "Latin Americans." Whereas Mexicans share a long border with the United States and construct their identity in part in reference to Anglo-Americans, Brazilian identity is shaped by being the only Portuguese-speaking country in the western hemisphere.

6. On October 2, 1968, nine days after the writing of this letter, security forces killed hundreds of peaceful student protesters in the "Plaza de las Tres Culturas" in Tlatelolco, Mexico City.

7. Governor of Alabama who ran for U.S. President on a platform of continuing racial segregation.

23 Survival in the Shantytown

Judith Adler Hellman[1]

By way of individual sketches of a variety of Mexicans from a diversity of backgrounds, Judith Adler Hellman's Mexican Lives *portrays the deep economic and social crisis of the* décadas perdidas, *the lost decades since the debt crisis of 1982. Under President Carlos Salinas de Gortari, whose government (1988–1994) produced gaudy economic numbers in large part by selling off state-owned enterprises, Mexico once again embraced export-led modernization, this time by way of the North American Free Trade Agreement, which took effect January 1, 1994. But free trade with Canada and the United States did not prove to be a panacea. It helped least of all the inhabitants of Mexico's shantytowns, who continue to eke out a living on a few dollars per day. This excerpt written by a social scientist provides a view of the life of a woman from Mexico City, Lupe González, and especially her efforts to use some money she has saved to help herself or other members of her family escape poverty. Crafted by a scholar trained in analyzing oral testimony, it offers an intimate glimpse of survival strategies employed by the urban poor.*

It also reveals some of the methodologies used by anthropologists and sociologists to elicit someone else's perspective without superimposing—at least as far as possible—one's own.

Born in Manhattan, Hellman (1945–) was an undergraduate at Cornell in 1965 when the U.S. invasion of the Dominican Republic gave rise to a campus protest movement and, later, to the founding of the North American Congress on Latin America (NACLA). She became deeply involved in both political commitments. Hellman first traveled to Mexico as a research assistant on a sociology project on land reform and peasant unions to interview ejidatarios, *the peasant holders of a land grant from the government. As a graduate student at the London School of Economics, she became convinced that the dominant scholarly literature, which conceived the Mexican political system as a "one-party democracy," required the kind of critique that only a bottom-up study could provide. Hellman soon found that history was about to provide its own critique of this system when she participated in the student movement of 1968 and survived the Tlatelolco massacre. She turned her experiences into the book* Mexico in Crisis, *first published in 1978. Now a Canadian, she has taught at York University in Toronto since 1972 and is editor of the* Canadian Journal of Latin American and Caribbean Studies.[2]

On Thursday, Lupe González's turn to draw water came at 3 A.M. Eighteen families in eighteen single-room dwellings share a single water tap in the courtyard of the *vecindad*[3] in San Miguel Iztacalco, where Lupe lives with her second husband and six of their children. The tap runs nonstop, and each household has an assigned hour during which it is entitled to fill the oil drums from which to draw water for drinking, bathing, cooking, and household cleaning.

Her family's laundry is something that Lupe looks after on Mondays, when she washes and irons for two *señoras* who live in the Polanco neighborhood on the other side of Mexico City. These ladies pay less than the going rate for washing, which is five pesos (about US$1.75) for a dozen articles of clothing. But the *señoras* let Lupe use their water and hang out her family's clothing with their own in the fenced and padlocked area on the roof of their apartment building meant for this purpose. This is an arrangement that Lupe prizes because it guarantees not only the continuous and ample supply of water she needs for her laundry but also the security of a clothesline less open to theft than in her own courtyard.

This morning Lupe's efforts were rewarded. Often, during the dry season, for no reason that the landlord or the local politicians seem ready to explain, there is no water for days at a time in the *vecindad* or, indeed, in the whole *barrio*.[4] But this time water trickled from the tap slowly, but in a steady stream and Lupe managed to fill three drums and move them across the courtyard to her door on a small cart before her neighbor appeared to take her turn at four o'clock.

Bleary-eyed, Lupe returned to the bed she shares with her eldest daughter. She looked around the room to where the others lay sleeping: her husband with the two boys, and the other three girls in another bed. But Lupe never fell back to sleep. As she would later tell me in careful detail, going around and around in her mind were a series of problems she was trying to sort out.

For starters there is the matter of the *tanda*. When I ask her how it works, she explains that it is a kind of lottery. But in fact the *tanda* is more like a "forced savings club" than a game of chance. A group of people undertake to contribute a fixed sum to a common fund every week. In the case of Lupe's *tanda*, the weekly contribution is one hundred pesos (roughly US$36). On a pre-established schedule, each participant is entitled to collect the total pot. The *tanda* in which Lupe is involved has twelve participants, so she can expect to collect the jackpot once every three months. Although Lupe thinks of it as "winning a lottery," in reality, the only element of uncertainty the *tanda* holds is whether all twelve people committed to putting their pesos into the kitty will continue to do so after their turn to collect the twelve hundred peso jackpot has passed.

Lupe can only remember one occasion in which a participant in the *tanda* either absconded with the common fund or refused to contribute after receiving her share. She laughs at me but also looks a little hurt when I ask how she could be so certain: is it not self-evident that only a certain kind of person, a person who inspires confidence in others, would be invited to participate in a venture of this kind?

Lupe is now preoccupied with the *tanda* for two reasons. To begin with, she faces another three weeks in which she is obliged to contribute her hundred peso share. But in this same period, as she tells me, she anticipates some special expenses. She has to find money for books and school uniforms for the younger girls and meet the tuition fees for her eldest daughter's secretarial course.

In addition she is concerned about the fourth week in which she is slated to be the person who collects the jackpot. Lupe explains that she finds herself, in one fashion or another, committed to use this windfall in three different ways,

The first involves a scheme Lupe has worked out with her sister, Marta. The plan calls for Marta to take the twelve hundred peso payoff, hop a bus for Laredo, Texas, and return with an industrial sewing machine that a cousin purchased from her former boss, the owner of a sweatshop who is moving his operation to Taiwan. With this machine Lupe and Marta plan to position themselves to profit from the coming free trade agreement with the United States.

There are, however, a lot of intangibles and uncertainties in this plan. Do I know, Lupe inquires, if they are paying too much for the machine? I don't. After she discounts the cost of the bus fare, her sister's expenses, the packing and cartage of the machine, and the bribes to the border guards and customs officials, she reckons they will have US$200 to pay for the machine and related equipment. I say that seems reasonable to me. But what kinds of clothing, she wonders, should she make for North American women? Will I send her a fashion magazine when I return, as she puts it, *al otro lado*, "to the other side"? I say I will.

Lupe has not begun to work through the problem of marketing the clothing she intends to produce with the new sewing machine. This will be Marta's department. Marta has been to the other side. She knows how to move around Laredo and the border region. But her experience was limited to a short and unhappy stint as a domestic servant. Lupe says she wishes that her sister knew more about the flow of goods over the border, about the appropriate amounts to pay in bribes, about wholesale and retail markets in Laredo, about a host of details that their *comadres* who have dealt for years in contraband used clothing would know. She wishes that I knew and could tell her more about what the treaty would mean for someone like herself living in a *ciudad perdida*, a "lost city" on the outskirts of the capital. However, for now, Lupe is focused on the production end of the plan, and so she is thinking about the *tanda* and the machine that the money could buy.

But it wasn't the sewing machine and all the unanswered questions associated with that scheme that kept Lupe from returning to sleep on Thursday morning. The problem was that there are at least two, perhaps three other ways in which she feels she may need to use the money she expects to receive in four weeks' time.

Lupe's oldest son, age twenty-one, left with a friend for the other side more than a month before. As far as Lupe knows, Jorge is working in Los Angeles and making good money. At least that was the plan. Lupe herself underwrote this trip, matching the four hundred pesos that Jorge had saved with eight hundred that she had put aside. A thousand pesos was earmarked to pay the *coyote*[5] who would sneak Jorge across the border, she wasn't sure how. The rest was meant to support Jorge while he was laying low and looking for work.

The problem is that Lupe has received no word, let alone money, from Jorge since he crossed the border weeks earlier. Now her next two sons, José Luis and Ricardo, are preparing to join their brother in Los Angeles, but the plan is on hold. Lupe has promised them the funds they would need, a sum they calculate would be lower than Jorge's expenses because they count on their brother to look after them and find them work once they make their way across. They also plan to save on *coyote* fees by crossing on their own. José Luis favors the strategy by which a large group of Mexicans mass on the Tijuana side of the border and dash for the U.S. side running helter-skelter along Interstate 5, as cars speed by and the U.S. Immigration and Naturalization Service agents, the *migra*, pursue the slowest in the pack while the rest escape.

Ricardo is indifferent to the method they use, be it climbing the guard fence at night, burrowing under it, or running up I-5, he is ready to try any of the high-risk/low-cost techniques he and his brother have learned about from friends. Ricardo is optimistic: he assumes that if for each time they are caught by the *migra* and returned to the Mexican side they try again, they will eventually make it across. But a long stay in Tijuana worries him, because the border zone has the highest prices of any region in Mexico.

Lupe is waiting to hear from Jorge, but is not yet worried. She has no phone and a letter could take more than a month to reach her in a *vecindad* in San Miguel Iztacalco. What she is hoping now is that José Luis and Ricardo will postpone their journey and she can meet her commitment to fund them later on. For now, she is thinking about the sewing machine—and about the down payment on the new house.

The question of the deposit on the house is by far the most complicated of all Lupe's financial concerns. Two years earlier Lupe's sister-in-law, Elena, persuaded her to attend a demonstration organized by the Asamblea de Barrios, a popular urban movement that grew out of the mobilization following the earthquake that struck Mexico City in 1985. Initially formed by those left homeless in the disaster, the Asamblea outlived the emergency, expanded its membership, and is now dedicated to organizing slum dwellers around a broad series of issues and demands. By the late 1980s the Asamblea boasted a "Women's Commission" concerned with the widest conceivable range of women's problems, and it became involved as well in electoral politics, backing Cuauhtémoc Cárdenas, the opposition candidate for the presidency in the elections of 1988. But while it ranged beyond the housing issue, the Asamblea's efforts continued to focus on the demand for affordable houses for slum dwellers in the center city, and for the extension of urban services—potable water, sewer lines, electricity, schools, clinics, and bus lines—to poor people living in makeshift dwellings in the *ciudades perdidas* of the periphery.

Lupe attended her first demonstration, a march on the ministry of housing, in June 1989. From that point on she gave every bit of time she could spare to the movement. At first, she explained, her motives were uncomplicated and frankly self-interested. Elena had convinced her that the most militant activists are the ones who move to the head of the lists that the Asamblea presents to the authorities when demanding new houses. So Lupe made sure to be conspicuously present at every meeting, demonstration, march, and sit-in.

But in the course of this calculated participation, Lupe was, by her own account, transformed. "I started to work in the Women's Commission," she explained. "We composed a pamphlet on AIDS, we organized a convention for peasants, we worked on human rights violations. I learned about politics. I even learned how to talk about sex without embarrassment. I learned so many things I never knew before. Most important, I learned how to deal with people, to talk to people. And now I know how to get more information out of the people who really know what's going on. I learned that only when we unite do we achieve anything."

Even as Lupe's participation intensified and her consciousness rose, her family's name moved higher and higher on the list of those waiting for the chance to buy into a new government housing project on the southeastern edge of Mexico City's vast sprawl, about two hours by public transport from the city center. As the day approached Lupe knew she would have to come up with three thousand pesos as an *enganche*, or down payment, on the four-room house and prepare to meet mortgage payments of two hundred pesos a month.

When she first enrolled the family on the Asamblea's list, her plan was to ask each of her four grown sons to contribute five hundred pesos, to borrow a thousand from a *compadre*, and to sell some personal possessions—she never told me which—to make up the difference. But as the months rolled by, she realized that none of the four sons, except perhaps Jorge, if he were to find work in Southern California, would soon be in a position to contribute even this modest amount (then about US$180).

Just as the financial crunch was about to come for Lupe and her family, in the very month that their request reached the top of the list, they learned that all work had halted on the housing project because the contractor had absconded with the funds. He is now in prison, but for the time being the construction project is on hold. Thus Lupe is wondering if it doesn't make sense to channel whatever money she has raised for the down payment into one of the other projects. Finally, there is one last financial demand that weighs on Lupe, and this she speaks about only with difficulty and embarrassment. It would be easy, she tells me, to get the wrong impression.

In July of the previous year, Lupe's younger brother, Alfredo, was leaving a late-night fiesta when he was set upon by three youths—glue sniffers and drugheads, by Lupe's account. They demanded that he hand over the leather jacket he was sporting that night. When Alfredo resisted, they tore the jacket from his back, threw him to the ground, kicked him in the ribs and stomach and, for good measure, sliced up his face with a knife.

Now Alfredo is badly scarred and cannot get work. During the period he was recovering from his broken ribs, he lost his job plucking and eviscerating chickens in a huge industrial *pollera*. And now, no one will hire him. As Lupe explains, potential employers take one look at Alfredo's scars and say no. They have him figured for some kind of bandit, *mariguano*,[6] or pimp. Alfredo's only hope is the plastic surgery that the doctors at the Social Security hospital suggested could repair his face. But he is required to come up with more than two thousand pesos, because the operation falls under the category of "special surgery" and the IMSS, the Social Security Institute, will cover only half.

Lupe herself is unclear about whether the IMSS would pay the full amount had the injury been officially recorded by the police when it occurred. But, in any event, an official report was never an option that the family considered: they feared reprisals from Alfredo's three attackers who were members of a powerful and large *banda,* or youth gang.

So now Lupe is wondering if Alfredo still means to go ahead with the operation, or if perhaps it is too late to treat his face. It is hard to know, because Alfredo is depressed and won't address the issue with her. But if he wants to borrow the money, Lupe feels bound to give him what she can.

Her current situation, she tells me, reminds her of a time, a few years earlier, when she had a particularly good run of luck in the herb market where she works when she isn't washing laundry or busy at the Asamblea de Barrios. Lupe had done particularly well selling what she refers to as "Christmas spices" and she had just collected the jackpot in a *tanda*—and she was hoping to use these windfalls to pay for a technical course for Jorge. But Jorge had the bad luck of riding with a friend in a pickup truck that the *policía de tránsito*[7] decided to pull over and ticket, alleging, as they do, some sort of traffic violation. When Jorge's friend could not come up with the money to pay the *mordida*[8] that the police demanded, both men were clapped into jail and Lupe's nest egg went to pay the bribes to gain Jorge's release a week later. As Lupe explains, the transit police tend to prey on those traveling in beat-up pickup trucks, because they fall into a category that perfectly suits the police's pattern of extortion: these drivers aren't rich and powerful—if they were, they'd be tooling around in a fancy car, not a beat-up truck—but they can be assumed to have some money, otherwise they'd be hanging off the side of second-class bus rather than driving their own vehicle, however humble.

Lupe can't help but feel that however she spends the money from the *tanda*, it is important to act quickly, before her plans can be overtaken by some unforeseen misfortune. But she is uneasy with the idea of disappointing Marta, or of letting Jose Luis and Ricardo down, or of failing to aid Alfredo if he decides to go ahead with the operation. On balance, she thinks there is still plenty of time to put together the money for the down payment on the house, and it makes more sense to worry about that when the time comes. She figures the boys are not yet ready to leave for the United States, and for the time being Alfredo has said nothing more about a loan. It was 5 A.M., Lupe tells me, before she rolled over for what was, at best, another half hour of sleep before she had to rise to prepare the children's breakfast.

Notes

1. Judith Adler Hellman, *Mexican Lives* (New York: The New Press, 1994), 15–23. Reprinted by permission of The New Press.
2. Author's email exchanges with Hellman, June 3–9, 2003.
3. Complex of single-room dwellings.
4. Neighborhood.
5. Person paid to help an undocumented worker cross the U.S. border.
6. "Pothead," or marijuana user.
7. Traffic police.
8. "Bite," literally, a bribe.

24 Travels Among the Zapatistas in Chiapas

Isabella Tree[1]

The following selection from Isabella Tree's book Sliced Iguana *retells the author's encounter with the Zapatista rebellion in Chiapas. For almost five centuries, as B. Traven has shown us, the predominantly indigenous population of that state has chafed under hacendados who have appropriated most of the region's best land, and in few areas of Mexico is the disparity of wealth between rich and poor as pronounced as in Chiapas. Not surprisingly, Salinas's neoliberal recipe for modernization, a model that emphasized private property and the free play of market forces, encountered stiff opposition. On January 1, 1994—the same day when the North American Free Trade Agreement went into effect—Maya peasants under the leadership of the mysterious "Subcomandante Marcos" rose up in a rebellion dedicated to the memory of Zapata. Like Traven, Tree visited Chiapas as a political pilgrim interested in witnessing a process of social transformation. Unlike her predecessor, however, she is a New Age political pilgrim who travels in a quest to reconnect to nature. This endeavor results in a search for cultural authenticity, a search that reflects the*

author's disenchantment with modern industrial life. The subtitle of her book,
Travels in Unknown Mexico, *invites comparisons to Lumholtz's account of the*
early twentieth century.[2] This perspective occasionally leads Tree to romanticize
rural life in Mexico from her standpoint as a member of a technologically
advanced society and thus bring her own cultural context into the story.

    Tree was born in London in 1964 and raised in Dorset in southwestern
England. She studied Classics at the University of London and developed a
passion for travel writing early on. Her writings are suffused with a progres-
sive, New Age credo that upholds the intrinsic value of indigenous societies in
the face of globalization. Not surprisingly, Tree has written about areas of the
world where she could witness firsthand the encounter of globalizing moder-
nity and local tradition. From 1993 to 1995, Tree served as senior travel corre-
spondent at the Evening Standard, *and she has also written articles for the*
Sunday Times *and the* Observer, *among other publications. Two recent books,*
Islands in the Clouds: Travels in the Highlands of New Guinea *(1996) and*
Sliced Iguana: Travels in Unknown Mexico *(2001) established her as a well-*
known travel writer. She is currently working on a novel set in Kathmandu,
Nepal, and she lives in West Sussex, England.[3]

When I arrived in Chiapas . . . the situation was still nowhere near resolution
though things had started well. Peace talks between the Zapatistas and the
PRI government had been instigated only six weeks after the storming of San
Cristóbal and as a gesture of good will the Zapatistas had released their
hostage, the former governor, condemning him "to live to the end days with
the pain and shame of having received the pardon and the good will of those
he had killed, robbed, kidnapped, and plundered." Two weeks later, thirty-
two tentative accords had been announced covering broad-ranging issues of
political, economic and social reform. It looked like the Zapatistas had done
in two months and with fewer than five hundred deaths what had taken the
Salvadoran guerrillas a decade of brutal fighting.

    But the Zapatistas soon became victims of their own success. The
uprising had thrown the whole of Mexico into crisis. Since the rebellion of
Juchitán,[4] cracks had begun to appear in the PRI's defences. But the subsequent Chiapas insurrection, highly publicized thanks to [Subcomandante]
Marcos's expertise, proved a body-blow to the old political dinosaur. It had

attracted international scrutiny and thrown the old bogies of corruption, government fraud and dereliction of duty into the public arena where they were being torn to shreds.

The government, fearful that it was setting a dangerous precedent for the rest of the country, began to stall on delivery of the peace agreement; and the Zapatistas, tired of waiting and being toyed with, eventually withdrew their support for it, too, insisting on the withdrawal of the army from Chiapas before entering into talks with the government again.

Then, on 22 December 1997, forty-five defenceless villagers—twenty-one women, fifteen children and nine men—were gunned down in the village of Acteal in Chiapas by government-trained paramilitaries. The dead were all members of Las Abejas, "The Bees," a citizens' organization sponsored by the diocese of San Cristóbal and known to be sympathetic to the Zapatistas. They had been praying at a local shrine when they were attacked. . . .

If anything, the situation in Chiapas, as I wandered the dreamy streets of San Cristóbal on a crisp, sunny morning in 1998, was more polarized and more entrenched than ever before. Marcos was, after a couple of years of low morale (there'd been rumours that he'd been murdered or paid off, or simply given up of his own accord), back in the headlines with a vengeance. In 1995 he'd been unmasked by President Zedillo whose exhaustive research had revealed the Subcomandante to be Rafael Sebastián Guillén, the son of a fur-niture salesman from Tampico, a former university professor, and veteran socialist activist. But subsequent attempts to smear the Subcomandante with allegations of corruption and power-grabbing at the expense of the Indian poor failed to stick. Marcos had continued to wear his disguise as a point of principle. The Zapatista command would remain symbolically anonymous, he insisted, because they represented people who were, as far as the world was concerned, invisible. This was not a publicity stunt, the Zapatistas claimed, but poetic justice. "Below in the cities, the Mayans of Chiapas did not exist. Our lives were worth less than those of machines or animals. We were like stones, like weeds in the road. We were silenced. We were faceless." By masking themselves the Zapatistas were forcing the world to stop ignor-ing their plight. "We are the voice that arms itself to be heard," they explained, "the face that hides itself to be seen."

Marcos himself, waging what the US military had begun to describe as a "netwar," had carried the analogy of "non-self" even further. "My mask is a mirror," he declared to the world at large. "We are you. Marcos is gay in San

Francisco, black in South Africa, an Asian in Europe, a Chicano in San Ysidro, an anarchist in Spain, a Palestinian in Israel, a Maya Indian in the streets of San Cristóbal, a Jew in Germany, a Gypsy in Poland, a Mohawk in Quebec, a pacifist in Bosnia, a single woman on the Metro at 10 P.M., a peasant without land, a gang member in the slums, an unemployed worker, an unhappy student and, of course, a Zapatista in the mountains."

Marcos's message was resonating across the world. In an age of cynicism, he was daring to appeal to something beyond the intellect, to the sense of wonder and intuition that he'd found in the mountains of Chiapas. And he'd become an international new-age hero in the process. He'd been filmed by MTV; even the film director Oliver Stone had come to the jungle to sit at his feet. Benetton had asked him to pose for a corporate advert, but he'd declined. His principles, remarkably, had held firm. And in Mexico, among the indigenous poor, Marcos was now an icon of mythic, almost magical, proportions. The Zapatista propaganda stall I'd noticed outside the Cathedral in the central Zócalo in Mexico City had become a permanent fixture. Copycat rebel groups kept popping up over the country. Meanwhile, 5,000 Zapatistas were still holding out in the Lacandón jungle, just a few hours away from San Cristóbal, hosting highly secretive conferences, continuing their unignorable racket about the plight of the Mayan Indian.

It was not long before I witnessed the groundswell of support for the Zapatistas myself. It was Saturday—market day—and the uncharacteristic hush around the sacks of multicoloured beans and spices, coffee and herbs and raw chocolate, the pyramids of vegetables and fruit, the buckets of flowers, was unmistakable. There was only the bare minimum of stall owners holding the fort. The mestizo shops and cafes were doing business as usual; tourists wandered the streets with their fingers in the pages of guidebooks, and queued at the automatic cashpoints; students chatted over cappuccinos. But there was, unusually, no traffic. Then, like the cry of distant birds, I heard the drifting rise and fall of people chanting.

Gradually sounds burst into shape—words like "liberty," "land," "solidarity," "Indian," "water," "electricity," "hunger," "Zapata." Curiosity amassed a pack of *ladinos*,[5] mestizos and gringos on the pavements as the first ribbon of *indios* threaded their way into the town square. They marched with fathomless determination as if this was a rhythm that could propel them through mountains.

They came in blocks. Four abreast. Village by village. There were men marching in the red and white striped tunics and flat, ribboned palm hats of Zinacantán; there were villagers from Comitán; women from San Andrés Larrainzar wearing highland-style *huipiles*[6] with a distinctive design I later learnt represented the ancient Mayan concept of the cube shape of the universe. There were banks of black skirts and red sashes; solid blocks of white wool tunics and long white *pantalones*;[7] followed by rows and rows of white shawls with red pom-poms; then red shawls picked out with white. Dotted throughout the procession like human safety matches were men wearing Marcos's black wool balaclava; while others, too hot from marching in suffocating ski-masks, pulled cotton neckerchiefs up over their noses like *bandidos.*

Their slogans called for food, clean water, medicine, transport, roads, electricity, for an end to racism and repression, for human dignity for all. "To be brown is to be forgotten," read a banner painted the breadth of three people, "[t]o be Indian in Mexico is to be lost." The sentiments blazed with emotion but the demonstrators themselves looked as collected and non-confrontational as a congregation on its way to church. Only the front-liners seemed to be chanting.

The hundreds became thousands filing past the onlookers crushed together on the pavements—pavements that, only thirty years ago, were out of bounds for Indians. If the protesters were nervous their faces—those that weren't covered—betrayed nothing but solemn purposefulness. The army kept their distance though there were conspicuously more soldiers in town than the day before. On they threaded, still chanting, to the big open Plaza in front of the cathedral where they jostled to find spaces and then lapsed into an expectant silence.

One of the organizers stood up to address the crowd from a rostrum, in front of an amateur dramatic backdrop painted with masked gunmen. A TV crew whirled into action. Journalists and excited tourists raised their cameras. "Today we are happy for people to take our photographs," the speaker announced, attempting to reassure the camera-shy, "the media is our friend. The world outside must see our faces."

There followed a number of interminable speeches from local trade union leaders through which the Indians stood as patiently as if they were waiting for a bus. Then copies of a letter from "Subcomandante Insurgente Marcos" were circulated through the crowd. It was dated the previous month and addressed to the "Workers' Trade Union and the Municipality of San Cristóbal de las Casas, Chiapas." This was characteristically more stirring:

Brothers and sisters,

With interest and indignation we have read your letter describing the atrocities and humiliations which have been dealt you by the municipal authorities in San Cristóbal de las Casas, headed by the dissembler Rolando Villafuerte. We have also read, this time with admiration and respect, about your struggles and your commendable resistance against the injustices of government. It is well known that the present state and municipal authorities are not in control of the land of Chiapas, that the work of government is in the hands of the military, and that the civil authorities are only concerned with appearing to govern in the press and during festivals. This irresponsibility is reflected in the increasing public insecurity, the deterioration in the standard of living of the people of Chiapas (not only the indigenous people), the total absence of any social works that don't serve some strategic, tactical or military purpose, and the violation of the civil rights of everyone who has raised the name of Chiapas out of the mire in which the present government leaders have plunged it.

Your struggle is just and, for this reason alone, merits success . . . Farewell. Good wishes and may the dignity of the workers be like a flag that gives shelter to everyone.

From the mountains of south-east Mexico,
(signed) Subct. Marcos, December 1996

The letter fluttered in hands the length and breadth of the Plaza but few heads bent to study it. Unable to decipher the words the crowds waited for the speaker to read it aloud. There was a tiny, polite clatter of applause when he finished and then, finally, as if suddenly succumbing to the old, familiar world weariness once again, the assembly drifted apart, back to the buses and *colectivos* (collective taxis) that had brought them from their villages. A few dozing protesters in balaclavas were left stranded on benches, exhausted by the pre-dawn start to get here. . . .

Marcos's Zapatista rebellion has epoch-making resonances and is carried on a tide of local and international optimism. Though emphatically secular as an organization, the movement itself is swathed in divine and mythical portent. In March 1994, just over two months after the Zapatistas'

New Year uprising, shamans representing the five Maya groups—Tzotzil, Tzeltal, Tololabal, Chol, and Main—convened at the Temple of the Inscriptions in Palenque, site of the tomb of Lord Pakal and the Maya Tree of Life, to conduct an important ceremony of worship. Climbing the precipitous steps to the top of the Temple, in which Lord Pakal had been entombed in AD 683, they set up a sacred shrine with multi-coloured candles, wild plants and copal incense burning in a large censer, symbolizing "the heart of heaven and the heart of earth." There they announced the end of the era of the Fifth Sun, the time of hunger and disease, and the dawning of the era of the Sixth Sun—a time of hope and unity for indigenous peoples everywhere.

In December that same year, as if fulfilling the shamans' prediction of the collapse of the old world order, three weeks after a new President, Ernesto Zedillo, took over from the discredited Salinas, the country suffered its severest economic crash in modern times: the peso lost half its worth, US$10 billion of capital fled the country in panic and the stock market, once the best performer in the world, became the worst. And, true to form, that national Geiger counter, the mighty Popocatépetl volcano, blew its top. The whole country, it seemed, was reacting in sympathy with the uprising of the Maya.

My *pensión* in San Cristóbal is a right-on, PC, ethnic jewelry and hairy jumpers, big bear-hugs and back-rubs kind of place. It's called "Na Bolom," which is Mayan for "House of the Jaguar" and was once the home of the Danish archaeologist Frans Blom and his Swiss wife Trudy Duby Blom, the conservationist and photographer. . . .

Trudy Duby Blom died in December 1993, less than a month before the Zapatista uprising, and though then in her nineties is said to have entertained Marcos and other key insurgents in the run-up to the rebellion. Certainly their strategy would have appealed to her notoriously fiery temperament and communist leanings. Ever since she arrived in Chiapas in the 1950s Trudy Duby had championed the cause of the Mayan Indian, focusing in particular on the pathetic plight of the Lacandóns—a distinctive tribe from the Lacandón rainforest who were down to barely a couple of hundred in number when she discovered them. Their elder, Chan-kin, became Trudy's closest friend—her soulmate the Indians believed—so no one was surprised when the two died exactly a month apart.

Trudy's photographs of Chan-kin and his family, dressed in their traditional white *shikurs*—a kind of coarse, long shirt looking unfortunately like something from a lunatic asylum—cover the walls around the courtyard of

Na Bolom. They are frozen in time, these Lacandóns with their straight, long hair, paddling dug-outs across misty lakes, hunting with arrows, leaping over tree trunks, playing with wooden toys around their huts deep in the rainforest. On the pin-board in reception, leaflets invite you to visit the last families still living in the forest. This is part of Trudy's legacy, a desperate attempt to provide the last of the Lacandón people with medical support and an alternative income to logging and cattle farming—the means to provide some kind of bulwark against the outside world.

Of all the Mayan peoples the Lacandón have had the sorriest time in terms of numbers surviving to the present day. Resorting to a primitive existence deep in the rainforest sometime after the collapse of the last Maya strongholds in the seventeenth century, they retained the purest relationship of all to their forebears. Unlike the Highland Maya who were enslaved by the Spanish, the Lacandón cut themselves off from the mainstream populations in the region and avoided the diluting effects of intermarriage and cultural exchange. Farming tiny gardens, familiar with more edible and medicinal species of plant than most modern botanists could name, they continued to worship the ancient gods, traipsing through the jungle to light copal in the temples of their ancestors at Palenque, Bonampak and Yaxchilán. Hidden away in their jungle villages they avoided direct confrontation with the Spanish, only to be decimated by proxy when the European diseases finally caught up with them. They were brought to the verge of extinction, it is said, without ever setting eyes on a white man. And there they remained, isolated in the forest, their culture intact, their numbers dwindling beyond the point of no return, until the arrival of rubber-tappers, roads, ranchers, loggers, oil prospectors, archaeologists and the photographic lens of Trudy Blom brought them into the limelight.

It is difficult to believe, looking at these fading pictures, that the three hundred or so remaining Lacandón—those who have not already become converted *evangélicos*[8] or thrown in their lot with the rancheros—could survive the onslaughts of the twenty-first century, galloping deforestation and the inexorable process of *mestizaje*[9] of intermarriage and cultural dilution, particularly now Trudy and Chan-kin, the twin pillars of their tiny culture, are gone. Traditional Lacandón say the reign of the God of Creation is over: the supreme god is now the Lord of Foreigners and Commerce.

Notes

1. Isabella Tree, *Sliced Iguana: Travels in Unknown Mexico* (London: Hamish Hamilton, 2001), 177–86. Reprinted by permission of Gillon, Aitken Assoc. and Penguin, Ltd.

2. See selection 10.

3. Author's email exchanges with Isabella Tree, June 3–5, 2003.

4. Popular revolt in the Isthmus of Tehuantepec (eastern Oaxaca) against the corrupt PRI local and state government.

5. This word has many different meanings throughout the Maya world. Tree uses it here in the usage of Guatemalan activist and Nobel Peace Prize winner Rigoberta Menchú, meaning a person of indigenous descent who has assimilated into the dominant, Spanish-language culture.

6. Traditional Maya embroidered dress.

7. Pants.

8. Evangelical Protestants.

9. Mixture of Spaniards and indigenous people.

25 The Dead Women of Juárez

Sam Quinones[1]

The following excerpt from U.S. journalist Sam Quinones's True Tales from Another Mexico *relates the rapid rise of crime against women in the border city of Ciudad Juárez, across the Rio Grande from El Paso, Texas. This rise of crime has occurred against the backdrop of industrialization led by the* maquiladora, *or partial assembly plant—perhaps the most visible byproduct of the globalization of the Mexican economy and society in recent decades. The* maquiladoras *have funneled single women from throughout the republic into a border zone in which transient lives and mass migration have created urban sprawl without community, and economic growth without development.*

The crimes against the lonely and defenseless victims identified in this story reveal the gendered nature of work, life, and crime in the border area. Like the selections by Hellman and Tree—authors similarly sympathetic to the plight of Mexico's poor majority—Quinones's description is a grim testimony of the effects of globalization in Mexico, written in large part to increase awareness of the downside of NAFTA in the United States and Europe. But its setting, the U.S.-Mexican border, is very different from Mexico City and Chiapas. As a result, Quinones emphasizes individualism and the absence of community in Ciudad Juárez; whereas the other two contemporary writers, as we have seen, focus on the ways in which the working poor of Mexico City's ciudades perdidas *and the highlands of Chiapas forge strategic and ethnic alliances in their quest for survival.*

The son of U.S. academics, Quinones was born in 1958 in Munich, Germany. He grew up in Claremont, California, and he received bachelor's degrees in economics and history from the University of California at Berkeley. He started out his career as a journalist at various newspapers on the West Coast. He came to Mexico in 1994 to work for Mexico Insight Magazine. *Following the failure of that publication in the wake of the peso devaluation crisis of 1994, he became a freelance writer based in Chicago and Mexico City. He has been interviewed on National Public Radio, and his stories have appeared in the* Los Angeles Times, Baltimore Sun, *and* Houston Chronicle, *among many others. In 1998, Quinones was awarded the Alicia Patterson Fellowship, one of the most prestigious awards in U.S. print journalism.[2]*

Seven men were already in jail in Ciudad Juárez, charged in the serial murder of seventeen young women—the case apparently solved—when Sandra Juárez's body turned up on the banks of the Rio Grande.

One Saturday in July 1996, Sandra, seventeen, walked into Ciudad Juárez from Lagunillas, a village of forty adobe houses, thirty miles from the nearest telephone, in a parched region of the state of Zacatecas. She was no match for the city. On Monday she went looking for work in the *maquiladoras*—the assembly plants—that dominate the Juárez economy. A few days later they found her blouse on the Mexican side of the river. She lay strangled to death on the U.S. side. Her case has not been solved. No one knows where she went, or with whom, that Monday.

For the people of Ciudad Juárez, Sandra's case, and others that turned up that summer, played havoc with some accepted beliefs. Until then, for example, they had believed that the city's first serial-murder case, which had attracted news media from across Mexico and the United States, had been put behind them. They believed that a foreigner and a group of U.S.-style gang bangers were responsible. Given the town's border location, Juarenses are used to blaming things on people from somewhere else; 80 percent of the town's prison population is from somewhere else, is an oft-quoted statistic.

But about the time Sandra Juárez died, people in town finally had to start listening to Esther Chávez. Chávez is a thin, almost frail retired accountant who lives in a middle-class neighborhood of Juárez and wouldn't seem the type to get involved in a serial murder case. Nor did Chávez have much history of feminist involvement when she organized a women's group known as Grupo 8 de Marzo. But from newspaper clippings, Chávez had been keeping an informal list of cases involving dead young women ever since she noted the rape and murder of thirteen-year-old Esperanza Leyva on November 15, 1993. By that time the list was already thirteen cases long. "We had gone to talk to the mayor," Chávez says. "He promised to get higher authorities involved. He was my very good friend, but he never did anything for us. What we were trying to get people to see was a general climate of violence against women."

The cases were notable in that the identifiable victims were usually young and working-class. A good number had worked in the *maquiladoras*. These were not murders of passion, taking place in a bar or bedroom. Some of the women had been raped, many had been mutilated, and a good many more had been dumped like the worn-out parts to some machine in isolated spots in the deserts surrounding the city. Their killer or killers didn't even take the trouble to cover them with dirt, believing, with good reason, that the sun and the desert's scavengers would quickly wipe their corpses from the face of the earth. By the summer of 1996 Chávez had counted eighty-six of these cases, dating back to Esperanza Leyva in 1993. Actually, that turned out not to be a whole lot in the larger scheme of things; Juárez tallies more than 250 homicides a year, of which a good number are drug-related executions and well more than eighty-six are gang killings. But Juárez is also a place where, according to the assistant attorney general based in the city, those who aren't gang members or drug smugglers can live free of the fear of murder. So the women's deaths, finally, were notable in their number as well. By the time Sandra Juárez's body appeared on the banks of the Rio Grande, people in town had to listen to Esther Chávez and consider the possibility that behind the dying women of Juárez was something even more disturbing than a lone serial murderer, something that had to do with what the town had become.

Ciudad Juárez spreads low, bleak, and treeless across the valley floor south of El Paso and the Rio Grande. The smell of fetid sewers is a constant companion through town, a nagging reminder that the desert is no place for a major industrial center.

Years ago Juárez thrived because it understood that beneath America's puritan rhetoric, a buck was always waiting to be made. During Prohibition Juárez produced whiskey and beer and ran it across the border. Bars emerged along Avenida Juárez, the main drag leading to the bridge into El Paso, and have never left. "Divorce planes" brought American couples in to quickly end their marriages. To women looking for work, Juárez offered prostitution. Until the mid-1960s Juárez was a bustling city of sin.

Then the *maquiladoras* arrived. Over the next three decades the assembly plants turned dusty border outposts into major stops in the global economy, assembling televisions, telephones, appliances, clothes, calculators, car parts—all for export to the world's wealthiest market across the border. In Juárez several *maquiladoras* even count America's coupons.[3]

Mexico began allowing *maquiladoras* on the border in 1964. The idea was to sop up migrant workers returning after the United States ended the so-called *bracero* treaty, a twenty-two-year-old agreement that allowed Mexicans to work seasonally and legally in America's fields. The *maquilas* began as an afterthought. But beginning in the late 1970s, the country lurched through recession after recession, and the peso steadily lost value. Many U.S. and foreign firms saw a payroll paid in a currency that always lost value as a nifty proposition. As Mexico staggered, the *maquila* sector along the border became an increasingly important job provider. Today some 970,000 people—mostly unskilled and low paid—work in more than 3,800 *maquiladoras*, completing in twenty-five years one of the most remarkable industrial transformations anywhere in the latter half of the twentieth century. Virtually all the plants are owned by foreign companies: General Motors, Ford, Hughes, Phillips, RCA, Sony, Toshiba, Daewoo, and on down to minor candy and clothing manufacturers.

Juárez saw the twenty-first century in the *maquiladora*. The city always had more *maquila* jobs than any other city—178,000 today. As the *maquila* grew, so grew Juárez. The city went from 407,000 inhabitants in 1970 to what townspeople can only estimate is about 1.5 million people today, with several thousand more wandering through in any given month.

But since in Mexico, border towns barely qualify as Mexican, Juárez was always last on the list when the central government in far-off Mexico City doled out the resources. The city couldn't provide basic municipal services for everyone the *maquiladoras* pulled from the interior. Urban planning was an impossibility. And on a *maquiladora* salary, no worker could afford much rent. So shantytowns leaped into the desert. They were without drinking water, sewers, parks, lighting, or paved streets. An apocalyptic folk craft— shack building—developed, using plastic tarp and barrels, wood pallets, cardboard, wire cord—anything that was *maquiladora* detritus. Bottle caps were used for bolts. Nor was moneyed development controlled. A lot of people got rich selling the desert to foreign *maquilas*. Meanwhile a collection of cheesy strip malls hunkered down around town as developers mimicked what they saw across the border.

Juárez grew rootless and cold under the desert sun, a place to make money but not a place to love or know or drink from a faucet. Here five hundred street gangs fought a war of attrition among themselves; walking among the cars at intersections were Indians in plastic sandals hawking gum and Mennonites[4] in overalls selling cheese; narcos in gold chains and snakeskin boots, driving Chevy Suburbans and carrying assault rifles, winked again at El Norte's puritan rhetoric and used Juárez as the mainline into the American vein. Coming off the border is a gaudy collection of neon nightclubs, advertising profiles of buxom, naked women, and cheesy curio shops that sell tequila and serapes to day visitors from El Paso.

As Juárez grew, an anonymity that characterizes many large U.S. cities settled on it. Police make a lot of the fact that so many of the dead women— more than half on Chávez's list—are unidentified. Nor do they have missing person reports matching their descriptions. No one claims these bodies. Their families in some isolated part of Mexico may believe they live somewhere in the United States or simply don't care where they are. This, police say, is what they're up against. . . . It's hard to imagine a city with more bars over it, windows and doors than Ciudad Juárez. Even in the shantytowns, where people have little to steal, some shacks of cardboard and plywood have barred windows. Everywhere, too, is the incessant babble of gang graffiti marking Juárez as a border town—too close to the gringo is what the rest of Mexico would say.

But Juárez offered jobs, and that makes it like America in the most important way. Like the United States, Juárez attracted Mexicans from the interior who were restless and willing to risk a lot to change their lives. People from rural states of Durango, Zacatecas, and Coahuila continue to trudge into Juárez in huge numbers, figuring anything is better than the brutish life of the bankrupt Mexican *campo*.[5] But unlike the United States, which attracts mainly men, Juárez became a magnet for women, especially young women. The *maquila* did not, as Mexican planners hoped, employ many men returning from the United States. Instead the plants pulled young women to the border from deep in Mexico's countryside. In Juárez for many years, more than 80 percent of all *maquila* workers were women. Even today, with *maquila* work heavier, two-thirds of the *maquila* workforce is female. These were women with few of the skills that the industrial economy would reward. They were interchangeable and they moved frequently between jobs, which were generally similar in their monotony. Juárez thirsted for them, and the *maquilas* put up help-wanted banners that fly almost all year round.

One of the women that Juárez attracted was Elizabeth Castro, a seventeen-year-old who had come from the state of Zacatecas. On August 10, 1995, Castro's decomposing body appeared along a highway. At the time no one thought much of it. . . . Then, through August and September, the bodies of more young women began showing up, several of them in Lote Bravo, a magnificent sprawl of caramel-colored desert south of the airport. . . . Pressure mounted and headlines grew shrill. Juárez had seen a lot, but never this. . . .

It takes a lot to shock Juárez, but the continuing discovery of bodies did the trick. Civil patrols were now organized to protect children getting out of school and young women as they returned home from their *maquila* jobs. The shantytowns of Anapra and Lomas de Poleo formed squads to comb the desert areas for more corpses. The newspapers were filled with the latest news, clues, and conjecture about the case. Police competence was routinely questioned. . . .

[T]hen came the summer of 1996. More dumped bodies showed up. They continue to be found. So while evidence points to a serial murderer in some of the cases, what now seemed clear was that Juárez had something much larger on its hands.

Indeed, since . . . early 1996, the bodies of almost fifty women have turned up. Rocío Miranda, a bar owner, was raped by seventeen young men, then dumped in a vat of acid. The only parts of Miranda that remained when she was found were her hands, feet, and the silicon implants that police used to identify her. Silvia Rivera, twenty-one, was stabbed to death by her husband and buried out near the prison; she was first identified and buried as one Elizabeth Ontiveros, who'd been reported missing, until Ontiveros showed up, having run off with her boyfriend. Soledad Beltrán, a stripper known as Yesenia, turned up in a drainage ditch, stabbed to death, her killers unknown. Sonia Yvette Ramírez, thirteen, was raped and killed and left a block from police headquarters. Her father spent two months tracking down her boyfriend, who had fled south to Chihuahua City. There he cornered him in an auto-repair shop, thrashed him, and turned him over to police, who charged him with Sonia's murder. Brenda Nájera, fifteen, and Susana Flores, thirteen, were both raped, tortured, and shot in the head. An autopsy showed Susana had had four heart attacks before dying. And there were more women who turned up whose identity still is unknown, leaving behind only the grimy detritus of a dime-store novel: a tattoo on the wrist, black jeans, fingernails painted dark red, green socks, white panties, a black bra, and often the signs of rape. One woman was found with two brassieres lying by her side. Two others were found on a motorcycle racetrack in the desert, wearing slippers and bathrobes.

There was no one thing—or one person or group—to pin the bodies on anymore. If a serial murderer was at large, there was a lot of horrible other stuff going on as well. It came to seem as if Juárez was awash in dead women merely because it was Juárez.

Among the corpses that summer was Sandra Juárez's. A lot about Sandra was typical of the young country women whose labor forms the backbone of Ciudad Juárez. Like many of these women, Sandra's last little piece of the world was a concrete-block house on the outskirts of town in a neighborhood with neither pavement nor a sewer system. Her street—Capulín Street—got electricity only five years ago. This is where her aunts and cousins live. . . .

In coming here, Sandra followed a new tradition for women in her family, indeed in most of her village. "There's no work there," says her cousin Joel Juárez, who left Lagunillas twelve years ago. "The men work part of the year in the fields. For women there's nothing. Life's hard. About twenty years ago the first family left [for Ciudad Juárez]. They came back and told us about it, and we came running."

Behind her relatives' concrete-block house are signs of the limbo world between rural and postmodernity that Sandra's family occupies: a traditional adobe bread oven, a chicken coop, and a one-room shack made of pallets, cardboard, and plastic tarp discarded by *maquiladoras* where family members have worked. Their house stands as a symbol of the wrenching social changes that Ciudad Juárez is as unprepared to address as its residents' demand for paved streets.

People here surmise that these changes are one reason why women are murdered and tossed away. On display in Juárez is the quick and brutal mashing of a rural people into an industrial workforce. Thousands of women like Sandra come here, hoping to be part of it. The *maquiladora* yanked these women from the farm with the offer of their first paycheck; they became Mexico's "Rosie the Riveter." In a matter of a few years the *maquiladora* turned time-honored sex roles upside down: women became the family providers. *Maquiladoras*, for all the nastiness associated with them, created a new Mexican woman. *Maquila* workers often came to see the world, and their place in it, differently. But this same process did not create a new man.

The case of Marcela Macías, a thirty-five-year-old mother of four, is instructive in that regard. On June 19 Macías's decomposing body was found buried under some tires near a highway leading out of town. Two days later police arrested her husband, Ramón Ochoa, forty-nine. Ochoa told police that his wife had become more independent since taking a job at a *maquiladora* and had been talking back to him. He believed she had a lover. He said he would spy on her at work and see her eating lunch with other men. She told him she was going to sit with whomever she pleased. "My sister was very independent," says Macias's half sister, Silvia. "He was afraid of that and felt she was unfaithful." In the year since she took the job, the couple fought constantly. Ochoa said he strangled her during one such fight, buried her, and reported her missing.

"This is so symptomatic of the way men respond when women begin to leave home and to their not being dependent on them," says Maria Antonieta Esparza. Community pressure surrounding the deaths of the women prompted officials to set up an office to handle reports of sex crimes and domestic violence, staffed entirely by women. Esparza, an attorney, is its director. She says men from rural areas are used to controlling women down to how they dress and speak. Women, once they get to the *maquila*, often aren't as disposed to take it as when they were down on the farm. No one knows how many of the cases of murdered women have to do with domestic violence or a general male resentment toward uppity women. But the reports Esparza's office handles have risen steadily every month in the year since it opened and show no sign of tapering off. Says Esparza: "We don't stop being part of a culture. In some sense, men may feel unprotected in not having a woman to cook and clean for them, like a mother. This vision of women's work is what makes them feel, when the woman does work, like they're losing control."

Esparza believes the crude and quick modernization of country women going on now in Juárez has another role to play in the killings. Nothing about Mexican country life prepares a young woman for Juárez. In their villages they're prohibited from even being out after dark; the first boy they sleep with they marry. But in Juárez all the chains come off. . . .

Juárez today is part Dodge City, part Dickens's London, nestled at the dawn of the twenty-first century. The growing stack of unsolved cases of murdered women is in some twisted sense a measure of the city's growth, of the distance it's putting between itself and the Third World. . . . Perhaps that is part of what's behind these killings: that growth does not necessarily equal development or sanity, and Juárez's expansion was too quick, tore too many bonds that gave life balance. Juárez has married itself to the *maquiladora* for thirty years and, without an accompanying social development, those eighty-six women are the downside. Perhaps, too, it's that Mexico's rural young women have changed Juárez, responded to what it asked of them, and now are resented for it.

Notes

1. Sam Quinones, *True Tales from Another Mexico: The Lynch Mob, the Popsicle King, Chalino, and the Bronx* (Albuquerque: University of New Mexico Press, 2001), 137–45, 151. Reprinted by permission of The University of New Mexico Press.
2. "About the Author," *www.samquinones.com/aboutauthor.html* (accessed June 3, 2003); author's telephone conversation with Sam Quinones, June 3, 2003.
3. The coupons turned in for redemption at supermarkets and stores.
4. German-speaking religious group of which 20,000 settled in the state of Chihuahua in the early 1920s.
5. For an example of the situation in rural Mexico, see Tree.

Conclusions

From Alexander Humboldt's *Political Essay* to Isabella Tree and Sam Quinones's reflections on the impact of NAFTA, the writings of foreign observers have helped intertwine the history of Mexico with that of the rest of the world. Indeed, it is impossible to see either Mexico or the foreigners who have described it in isolation from one another. The enduring symbiosis of foreign observers with the Mexican intellectual elite, a symbiosis that existed as much in the era of scientific racism of the nineteenth century as it does in the current era of postmodern skepticism, forces the historically minded reader to seek models of interpretation that transcend traditional dichotomies of "insiders" and "outsiders," and "observer" and "observed." This anthology is not a monograph, and its primary objective has been didactic rather than theoretical. But if a collection of foreign observer accounts that spans two hundred years and eight countries has any value as an analytical tool, it lies in the fact that a comparative interpretation reveals the value of these sources for the study of Mexican cultural and social history *as well as* European and U.S. intellectual history.

As the examples in this volume show, an uncritical reading of foreign observer accounts as fact misses the mark. Foreign visitors arrived in Mexico with preconceived notions, viewed and ordered the world around them according to these notions, and often directly or indirectly served larger objectives of imperial dominance, economic penetration, and/or cultural hegemony. In doing so, the most influential of these observers, such as von

Humboldt and Calderón de la Barca, also transformed the terms in which the Mexican elite saw itself and its country, and hence affected rather than merely reflected historical reality. Thus, a naïve interpretation of foreign observer accounts as "true" or "factual" sources not only misleads readers as to historical processes in Mexico, but also robs them of an opportunity to ponder the intellectual and social worlds of affluent travelers and immigrants as well as the nature of historical evidence.

On the other hand, the over-skeptical paradigms of recent literary criticism go too far in discounting foreign observer accounts as historical sources.[1] In particular, the application of Mary Louise Pratt's "imperial eyes" paradigm raises the question of objectivity in general. For example, if we dismiss John K. Turner's portrayal of labor conditions in Yucatán as the product of a Western mind, are we then to put more trust in the writings of a Yucatecan hacendado just because the writer happens to be a Mexican rather than a foreigner? And is Subcomandante Marcos, an intellectual from the northeastern state of Tamaulipas, not as much of an "outsider" in Chiapas as the anthropologists Frans and Trudy Blom, not to mention Isabella Tree who follows their trails? Subjectivity pervades all sources, and the biases of foreign observer accounts do not detract from their usefulness any more so than those of other documents do.

Dismissing foreign observer accounts as mere agents of imperialism also constructs western capitalism as a monolithic Leviathan that has the entire world in its grasp. The notion that foreign observers slavishly parrot an ideology serving the existing world system—and that their discourse wields hegemonic power among subaltern populations hence unable to throw off the shackles of capitalist domination—overestimates the power of foreigners to affect the culture of Mexico or any other Latin American society. Moreover, this paradigm discounts the process of adaptation and acculturation in longtime residents (as occurred with Sartorius, King, Böker, and others in this collection) that blurs the boundaries between "foreigner" and "Mexican." Finally, foreign observers engaged in a complicated give-and-take with the host society, a reciprocal interaction that changed both of them in the process. Whether in the United States or Mexico, foreigners such as Alexis de Tocqueville or Baron von Humboldt helped shape political debate in the countries they had visited. Yet their writings also reflected what they had heard and seen in those countries, and hence often the agenda of at least a significant subset of the governing and/or intellectual elite.

Read with care and in their proper context, then, foreign observer accounts constitute an important source on Mexican history. In describing what is unfamiliar to them, observers provide rich detail about Mexican culture, society, and daily life. Whether Calderón's account of the taking of the veil of a Mexican nun; Kollonitz's portrayal about the crème of society on the Paseo de Bucareli; Bertie-Marriott's view of three days of fiesta in the capital; Gooch's difficulties with housekeeping in Saltillo; Reed's encounter with Pancho Villa; Luise Böker's everyday experiences with the revolution; Millán's frustrations with the persistence of machismo; a U.S. tourist's unpleasant surprise on seeing a bullfight; or Hellman's expedition into a Mexican *ciudad perdida*—these and all the other vignettes described by foreign observers add much to our knowledge of the Mexican cultural and social kaleidoscope.

A look at the sources in this volume also reveals the significance of chronology in an analysis of foreign observer accounts. While some basic patterns remained the same across two centuries, many others changed over time. The notion that Mexico is a land of irreconcilable opposites, of "unlimited impossibilities"—persisted throughout modern history, as did the principal patterns of analysis for the origins of these opposites in terms of wealth and ethnicity. With few exceptions, including Humboldt himself, Sartorius, Traven, and Nicholson, we also find a pessimistic outlook in most foreign observer accounts. Indeed, optimism was reserved for propaganda pieces and the occasional halcyon periods in Mexican history, in which the country appeared to escape its state of economic underdevelopment, only to fall back when the next crisis hit. Finally, we find throughout time a fascination with what is different about Mexico from the vantage point of a European or U.S. citizen: the exotic, the tropical, and, in particular, the indigenous Mexican.

Attitudes and political views, however, changed over time, and travel became faster and more comfortable. The scientific racism of the stagecoach era gave way to a desire to explain Mexico to expanding capitalist societies in the train era. Then, as the Mexican Revolution shook the world at the beginning of the automobile era, many foreign observers discovered a social conscience that led them to embrace rather than reject Mexico's indigenous cultures; and to welcome rather than to oppose efforts at self-sustaining development and limited foreign influence. Finally, in the airplane era, cosmopolitan travelers judged the processes of industrialization and globalization, following the ups and downs of the Mexican economy and the waxing and waning of the PRI state.

It is not clear whether contemporary observers understand Mexico better than Humboldt or even Poinsett did. What is obvious, however, is that the foreigners' way of seeing Mexico (and hence, the preconceived notions observers bring with them) has changed profoundly over the last two hundred years. In the case of the United States, whose nationals form the largest foreign-born contingent in Mexico, only time will tell if the onset of yet another era—that of the Internet and the mass movement of Mexicans to the United States—will at last improve our understanding of the neighbors "south of the border."

⣏⣹

Notes

1. As examples, see Pratt, *Imperial Eyes*; and Cooper, *Aztec Palimpsest*.

Glossary and Abbreviations

aguador: Water carrier

alcabala: Internal tariff levied by provinces, states, and/or cities in colonial and early national Mexico.

alcalde: Mayor

cacique: Local boss

cargador: Porter

charrería: Mexican version of bull tailing steer wrestling; considered the national sport in the nineteenth century.

ciudad perdida: Literally, "lost city;" slum.

comadre: Denotes the sharing of ties among women, whereby one woman serves as godmother of another woman's boy or girl, or vice versa. The forging of these ties was and still is an important strategy in establishing patron-client relationships in Mexican politics.

compadre: Denotes the sharing of ties among men, whereby one man serves as godfather of another man's boy or girl, or vice versa. See also *comadre.*

coyote: Person who helps migrants cross the U.S. border for a fee.

creoles: Descendants of Spanish conquistadors and immigrants.

CROM: Confederación Regional Obrera Mexicana (Mexican Regional Workers' Confederation). Leading labor union in the 1920s.

federales: Government troops in the Porfiriato and Mexican Revolution who were loyal to Presidents Porfirio Díaz, Francisco I. Madero, and Victoriano Huerta, in succession. They disbanded after Huerta's exile in July 1914.

frijoles: Pinto or black beans; a staple of the Mexican diet.

gachupines: Derogatory term for native Spaniards who live in Mexico

gente decente: Literally, "decent people;" people of education and money. Frequently used to denote whites.

jefe político: Local official; often with sweeping powers.

léperos: Literally, "lepers;" term applied to urban proletariats, beggars, and street urchins in the nineteenth century.

madrina: Godmother

mañana: Literally, "tomorrow;" also what outsiders often portray as the Mexican habit of putting things off.

mantilla: A variant of the veil, this lace garment in dark colors covered a woman's head and shoulders.

maquiladora: Partial assembly plant established by a multinational corporation, usually in the border region.

mestizos: Mexicans of mixed ethnic origin; usually of European and indigenous descent.

migra: Mexican term for U.S. immigration officials.

mordida: Bribe

mozo: Man-servant

NAFTA: North American Free Trade Agreement

novio/novia: Fiancé/fiancée; also used for boyfriend/girlfriend.

PRI: Partido Revolucionario Institucional. Ruling party of Mexico, 1929–2000.

pronunciamiento: Declaration that begins a coup d'état; often used to describe the coup itself.

pulque: Fermented sap of agave plant; until the mid-twentieth century, the most important alcoholic beverage in Mexico.

pulquería: Establishment where pulque is served.

ranchero: Rural outfit considered by foreigners to be a typically Mexican way of dressing. Also used to denote middle-class farmers as well as a type of Mexican country music.

rebozo: Handwoven shawl

rurales: Mounted rural police force established under the Restored
Republic (1867–1876) and greatly expanded under dictator Porfirio
Díaz, composed in part of former bandits.

sarape: Handwoven blanket

soldadera: Female fighter in the Mexican Revolution.

tanda: Savings club in which each participant is required to contribute
a set amount per month, in order to take turns claiming the
entire amount.

tierra caliente: Literally, "hot country;" tropical regions of Mexico close
to sea level.

tierra fría: Literally, "cold country;" region above approximately
6,000 feet.

tierra templada: Literally, "temperate country;" subtropical regions
at approximately 3,500–6,000 feet elevation.

tortilla: Flattened cake made of ground maize (in center and south)
or flour (in north); a staple of the Mexican diet.

vecindad: Neighborhood; also refers to the dwellings in a lower-class
apartment building.

Zócalo: Originally, only the main square of Mexico City, the largest such
square in the Western hemisphere, bordered by Cathedral, National
Palace, and Mexico City government. A term later applied to many
central squares in state capitals and provincial towns.

Suggestions for Further Reading

(English language only)

Ballentine, George. *Autobiography of an English Soldier in the United States Army*. London: Hurst and Blackett, 1953.

Beals, Carleton. *Mexican Maze*. Philadelphia: Lippincott, 1931.

Berger, Bruce. *Almost an Island: Travels in Baja California*. Tucson: University of Arizona Press, 1998.

Blake, Mary E., and Margaret Sullivan. *Mexico: Picturesque, Political, Progressive*. Boston: Lee and Shepard, 1888.

Brehme, Hugo. *Picturesque Mexico: The Country, the People, and the Architecture*. New York: Brentano's, 1925.

Brenner, Anita, and George R. Leighton. *The Wind that Swept Mexico*. New York: Harper, 1943.

Bullock, William. *Six Months Residence and Travels in Mexico Containing Remarks on the Present State of New Spain, Its Natural Productions, State of Society, Manufactures, Trade, Agriculture, and Antiquities, &c.* London: Murray, 1824.

Cerwin, Herbert. *These are the Mexicans*. New York: Reynal and Hitchcock, 1947.

Clark, Sydney A. *All the Best in Mexico*. New York: Dodd, Mead, 1956.

Dana, Richard Henry, Jr. *Two Years Before the Mast: A Personal Narrative of Life at Sea*. Boston: Houghton Mifflin, 1911.

Daniels, Josephus. *Shirt-Sleeve Diplomat*. Chapel Hill: University of North Carolina Press, 1947.

Gage, Thomas. *The English-American: A New Survey of the West Indies, 1648*. London: Routledge, 1928.

Greene, Graham. *The Lawless Roads*. 3rd ed. London: Heinemann, 1950.

Griffin, Solomon B. *Mexico of To-Day*. New York: Harper and Brothers, 1886.

Lawrence, D. H. *Mornings in Mexico*. New York: Knopf, 1927.

Oster, Patrick. *The Mexicans: A Personal Portrait of a People*. New York: Morrow, 1989.

Riding, Alan. *Distant Neighbors: A Portrait of the Mexicans*. New York: Knopf, 1985.

Robinson, William Davis. *Memoirs of the Mexican Revolution*. Philadelphia: Lippincott, 1820.

Ruhl, Arthur. *The Central Americans: Adventures and Impressions Between Mexico and Panama*. New York: Charles Scribner's Sons, 1928.

Salm-Salm, Agnes Prinzessin zu. *Ten Years of My Life*. New York: Worthington, 1877.

Sanborn, Helen J. *A Winter in Central America and Mexico*. Boston: Lee and Shepard, 1886.

Spratling, William. *A Small Mexican World*. 2nd ed. Boston: Little, Brown, 1964.

Stephens, John L. *Incidents of Travel in Central America, Chiapas, and Yucatan*. 2 vols. New York: Dover, 1969.

———. *Incidents of Travel in Yucatán*. 2 vols. New York: Dover, 1963.

Tannenbaum, Alfred. *Mexico: The Struggle for Peace and Bread*. New York: Knopf, 1950.

Toor, Frances. *A Treasury of Mexican Folkways*. New York: Crown, 1947.

T'serstevens, Albert. *Mexico: Three-Storeyed Land*. Trans. Alan Houghton Brodrick. Indianapolis, IN: Bobbs-Merrill, 1962.

Works Cited

ARCHIVES AND PRIVATE COLLECTIONS
Archivo General de la Nación, Mexico City.
    Fondo Presidentes.
    Gustavo Díaz Ordaz.
Boker, S. A. de C. V., Mexico City. Archivo Histórico.

PUBLISHED ACCOUNTS
Araquistáin, Luis. *La revolución mejicana: sus orígenes, sus hombres, su obra.* Madrid: Editorial España, 1930.

Bertie-Marriott, Clément. *Un Parisien au Mexique.* Paris: E. Dentu, 1886.

Calderón de la Barca, Fanny. *Life in Mexico during a Residence of Two Years in that Country.* London: Chapman and Hall, 1843.

Domenech, Emmanuel. *Le Mexique tel qu'il est: la verité sur son climat, ses habitants et son gouvernement.* Paris: E. Dentu, 1867.

Flandrau, Charles M. *Viva Mexico!* New York: D. Appleton & Co., 1908.

Gooch [Iglehart], Fanny Chambers. *Face to Face with the Mexicans: The Domestic Life, Educational, Social, and Business Ways, Statesmanship and Literature, Legendary and General History of the Mexican People as Seen and Studied by an American Woman During Seven Years of Intercourse with Them.* New York: Fords, Howard, & Hulbert, 1887.

Hellman, Judith Adler. *Mexican Lives*. New York: The New Press, 1994.

Henry, William S. *Campaign Sketches of the War with Mexico*. New York: Harper and Brothers, 1847.

King, Rosa. *Tempest Over Mexico*. Boston: Little, Brown & Co., 1935.

Lumholtz, Carl. *Unknown Mexico: A Record of Five Years' Exploration Among the Tribes of the Western Sierra Madre; in the Tierra Caliente of Tepic and Jalisco; and Among the Tarascos of Michoacán*. 2 vols. London: MacMillan and Co., 1903.

Millán, Verna C. *Mexico Reborn*. Boston: Houghton Mifflin, 1939.

Nicholson, Irene. *The X in Mexico: Growth Within Tradition*. London: Faber and Faber, 1965.

Poinsett, Joel R. *Notes on Mexico Made in the Autumn of 1822 Accompanied by an Historical Sketch of the Revolution and Translations of Official Reports on the Present State of That Country*. Philadelphia: H. C. Carey and Lea, 1824.

Reed, John S. *Insurgent Mexico*. New York: D. Appleton & Co., 1914.

Quinones, Sam. *True Tales from Another Mexico: The Lynch Mob, the Popsicle King, Chalino, and the Bronx*. Albuquerque: University of New Mexico Press, 2001.

Sartorius, Carl C. *Mexico: Landscape and Popular Sketches*. Darmstadt, London, and New York, 1858.

Traven, B. *Land des Frühlings*. Berlin: Büchergilde Gutenberg, 1928.

Tree, Isabella. *Sliced Iguana: Travels in Unknown Mexico*. London: Hamish Hamilton, 2001.

Turner, John Kenneth. *Barbarous Mexico*. New York: Cassell, 1912.

von Humboldt, Alexander. *Political Essay on the Kingdom of New Spain*. Trans. John Black. 5 vols. London, 1811.

von Kollonitz, Paula. *The Court of Mexico*. Trans. J. E. Ollivant. 2nd ed. London: Saunders, Otley, and Co, 1868.

Secondary Literature

Bazant, Jan. "From Independence to the Liberal Republic, 1821–1867." *Cambridge History of Latin America*, ed. Leslie Bethell. Cambridge: Cambridge University Press, 1985.

Beezley, William H. *Judas at the Jockey Club and Other Episodes of Porfirian Mexico*. Lincoln: University of Nebraska Press, 1987.

Bernecker, Walther L. "Reiseberichte als historische Quellengattung im 19. Jahrhundert." In *Die Wiederentdeckung Lateinamerikas: Die Erfahrung des Subkontinents in Reiseberichten des 19. Jahrhunderts*. Eds. Walther L. Bernecker and Gertrut Krömer. Frankfurt: Vervuert, 1997.

Bolloten, Burnett. *The Spanish Civil War: Revolution and Counterrevolution*. Chapel Hill: University of North Carolina Press, 1991.

Bourke, Eoin. "'Der zweite Kolumbus?' Überlegungen zu Alexander von Humboldts Eurozentrismusvorwurf." In *Reisen im Diskurs: Modelle der literarischen Fremderfahrung von den Pilgerberichten bis zur Postmoderne*. Eds. Anne Fuchs and Theo Harden. Heidelberg: Universitätsverlag C. Winter, 1995.

Buchenau, Jürgen. *Tools of Progress: A German Merchant Family in Mexico City, 1865–present.* Albuquerque: University of New Mexico Press, 2004.

———. "Small Numbers, Great Impact: Mexico and Its Immigrants." *Journal of American Ethnic History* 20.3 (2001): 23–49.

Cooper Alarcón, Daniel. *The Aztec Palimpsest: Mexico in the Modern Imagination*. Tucson: University of Arizona Press, 1997.

Covarrubias, Enrique. *Visión extranjera de México, 1840–1867: el estudio de las costumbres y de la situación social*. Mexico City: Universidad Nacional Autónoma de México, 1998.

Delpar, Helen. *The Enormous Vogue of Things Mexican*. Tuscaloosa: University of Alabama Press, 1992.

Diadiuk, Alicia. *Viajeras anglosajonas en México*. Mexico City: SepSetentas, 1973.

Fisher, Howard T., and Marion Hall Fisher. "Introduction." In Fanny Calderón de la Barca. *Life in Mexico*. Eds. Howard T. Fisher and Marion Hall Fisher. Garden City, NY: Doubleday & Co., 1966, xxi–xxix.

Fuentes Mares, José. *Poinsett: historia de una gran intriga*. Mexico City: Editorial Jus, 1951.

Gardiner, Harvey C. "Foreign Travelers' Accounts of Mexico, 1810–1910." *The Americas* 8.3 (Jan. 1952): 321–51.

———. "Introduction." In Charles M. Flandrau, *Viva Mexico!* Ed. C. Harvey Gardiner. Urbana: University of Illinois Press, 1964, xi–xxv.

———. "Introduction." In Fanny Chambers Gooch, *Face to Face with the Mexicans*. Ed. Harvey C. Gardiner. Carbondale: Southern Illinois University Press, 1966, vii–xx.

Gunn, Drewey W. *American and British Writers in Mexico, 1556–1973*. Austin: University of Texas Press, 1974.

Guthke, Karl S. *B. Traven: The Life Behind the Legend*. Chicago: Lawrence Hill Books, 1991.

Hahner, June. *Women in Women's Eyes: Latin American Women in Nineteenth-Century Travel Accounts*. Wilmington, DE: Scholarly Resources, 1998.

Harding, Bertita. *Phantom Crown: The Story of Maximilian and Carlota of Mexico*. Mexico City: Ediciones Tolteca, 1960.

Lear, John. *Workers, Neighbors, and Citizens: The Revolution in Mexico City*. Lincoln: University of Nebraska Press, 2001.

Lehman, Daniel W. *John Reed and the Writing of Revolution*. Athens: Ohio University Press, 2002.

Lowe, Lisa. *Critical Terrains: French and British Orientalisms*. Ithaca, NY: Cornell University Press, 1991.

Meyer, Jean. "Les Français au Mexique au XIXème siècle." *Cahiers des Ameriques Latines* 9–10 (1974): 43–86.

Mills, Sara. *Discourses of Difference: An Analysis of Women's Travel Writing and Colonialism*. London: Routledge, 1991.

Mostkoff Linares, Aida. "Foreign Visions and Images of Mexico: One Hundred Years of International Tourism, 1821–1921." Ph.D. dissertation, University of California, Los Angeles, 1999.

Naggar, Carole, and Fred Ritchin. *México Through Foreign Eyes, 1850–1900: visto por ojos extranjeros*. New York: Norton, 1996.

Ortega y Medina, Juan Antonio. *México en la conciencia anglosajona*. Mexico City: Gráfica Panamericana, 1955.

Parton, Dorothy Martha. *The Diplomatic Career of Joel Roberts Poinsett*. Washington: Catholic University of America, 1934.

Pferdekamp, Wilhelm. *Auf Humboldts Spuren: Deutsche im jungen Mexiko*. Munich: Max Hueber, 1958.

Pratt, Mary Louise. *Imperial Eyes: Travel Writing and Transculturation*. London: Routledge, 1992.

Rippy, J. Fred. *Joel Poinsett, Versatile American*. Durham, NC: Duke University Press, 1935.

Said, Edward. *Orientalism*. New York: Random House, 1979.

Sánchez, Héctor, ed. *Mexico nueve veces contado*. Mexico City: Secretaría de Educación Pública, 1974.

Saragoza, Alex. "The Selling of Mexico: Tourism and the State." In *Fragments of a Golden Age: The Politics of Culture in Mexico Since 1940*, eds. Gilbert Joseph, Anne Rubenstein, and Eric Zolov. Durham, NC: Duke University Press, 2001, 91–115.

Siemens, Alfred H. *Between the Summit and the Sea: Central Veracruz in the Nineteenth Century*. Vancouver: University of British Columbia Press, 1990.

Tenenbaum, Barbara. *The Politics of Penury: Debts and Taxes in Mexico, 1821–1856*. Albuquerque: University of New Mexico Press, 1986.

Tenorio Trillo, Mauricio. *Mexico at the World's Fairs: Crafting a Modern Nation*. Berkeley: University of California Press, 1996.

Traven, B. *Land des Frühlings*. Berlin: Büchergilde Gutenberg, 1928.

Vogt, Evon Z. "Introduction." In Carl Lumholtz. *Unknown Mexico: A Record of Five Years' Exploration Among the Tribes of the Western Sierra Madre; in the Tierra Caliente of Tepic and Jalisco; and Among the Tarascos of Michoacán*. Repr. New York: AMS Press, 1973, vii–x.

Walker, Ronald G. *Infernal Paradise: Mexico and the Modern English Novel*. Berkeley: University of California Press, 1978.

Zantop, Susanne. *Colonial Fantasies: Conquest, Family, and Nation in Precolonial Germany, 1770–1870*. Durham, NC: Duke University Press, 1997.

Zogbaum, Heidi. *B. Traven: A Vision of Mexico*. Wilmington, DE: Scholarly Resources, 1992.

Zolov, Eric. "Discovering a Land 'Mysterious and Obvious:' The Renarrativizing of Postrevolutionary Mexico." In *Fragments of a Golden Age: The Politics of Culture in Mexico Since 1940*, eds. Gilbert Joseph, Anne Rubenstein, and Eric Zolov. Durham, NC: Duke University Press, 2001, 234–72.

Sources on the World Wide Web

Lozano, Ann. "Domenech, Emmanuel Henri Dieudonné." *Handbook of Texas Online. http://www.tsha.utexas.edu/handbook/online/articles /view/DD/fdo9.html* [accessed June 14, 2003].

Munnerlyn, Thomas O. "Henry, William Seaton." *Handbook of Texas Online. http://www.tsha.utexas.edu/handbook/online/articles/view/HH/fhe39.html* [accessed June 12, 2003].

Also Available from UNM Press